BUILDING THINKING SKILLS®
PRIMARY

SERIES TITLES
BUILDING THINKING SKILLS®
BEGINNING
PRIMARY
LEVEL 1
LEVEL 2
LEVEL 3 FIGURAL
LEVEL 3 VERBAL

WRITTEN BY
SANDRA PARKS
HOWARD BLACK

GRAPHIC DESIGN BY
DANIELLE WEST
BRAD GATES
ANNA ALLSHOUSE

EDITED BY
PATRICIA GRAY

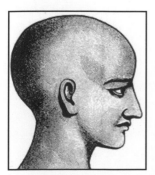
© 2008
THE CRITICAL THINKING CO.™
(BRIGHT MINDS™)
Phone: 800-458-4849 Fax: 831-393-3277
www.CriticalThinking.com
P.O. Box 1610 • Seaside • CA 93955-1610
ISBN 978-0-89455-887-0
This book is non-reproducible.
Printed in China

Table of Contents

Aria R
12-8-22

Chapter One
Describing Shapes

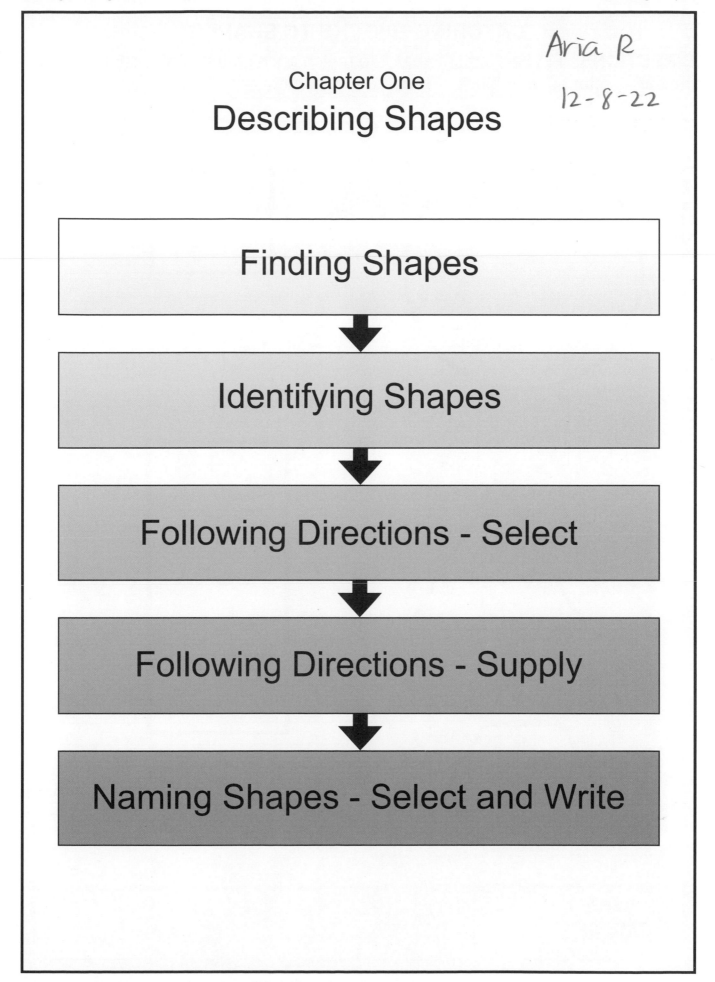

Finding Shapes

Identifying Shapes

Following Directions - Select

Following Directions - Supply

Naming Shapes - Select and Write

MATCHING BLOCKS TO SHAPES

DIRECTIONS: Find an attribute block to match each shape. Color each picture the same color as your block. Then trace its name.

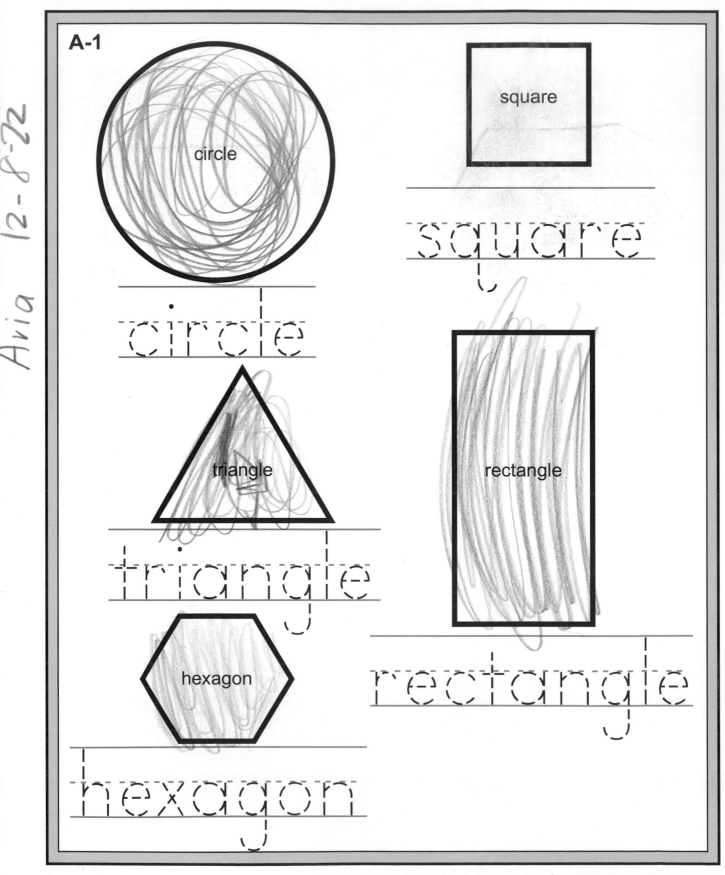

A-1

circle

circle

square

square

triangle

triangle

hexagon

hexagon

rectangle

rectangle

Aria 12-8-22

MATCHING BLOCKS TO SHAPES

DIRECTIONS: Find an attribute block to match each shape. Color each picture the same color as your block. Then trace its name.

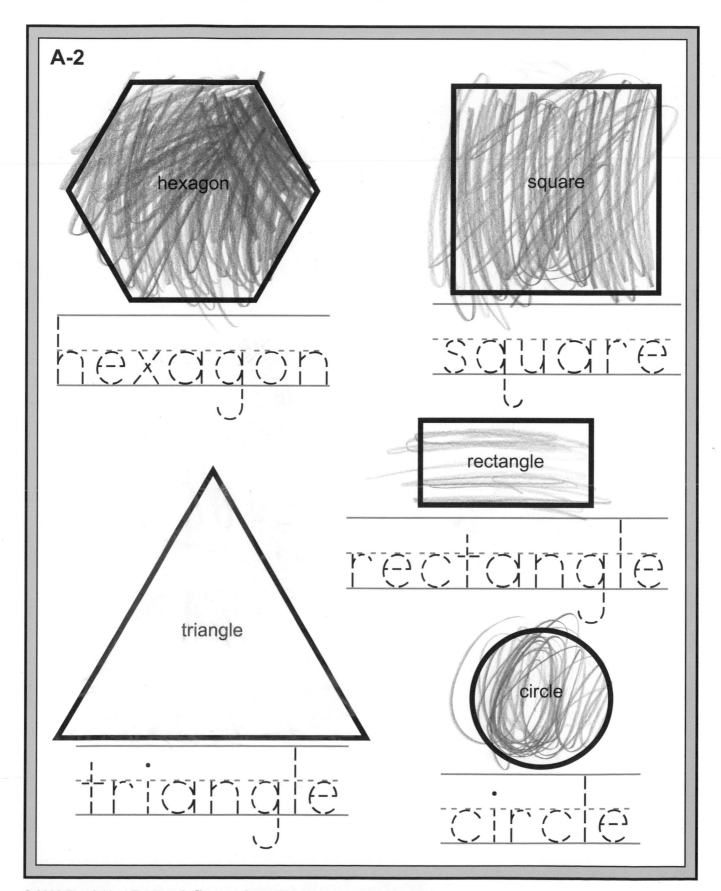

A-2

hexagon

square

hexagon

square

rectangle

triangle

rectangle

triangle

circle

circle

FINDING SHAPES

DIRECTIONS: Find an attribute block that is named in each box. Put the block in the box and trace around it. Then color your picture the same color as your block.

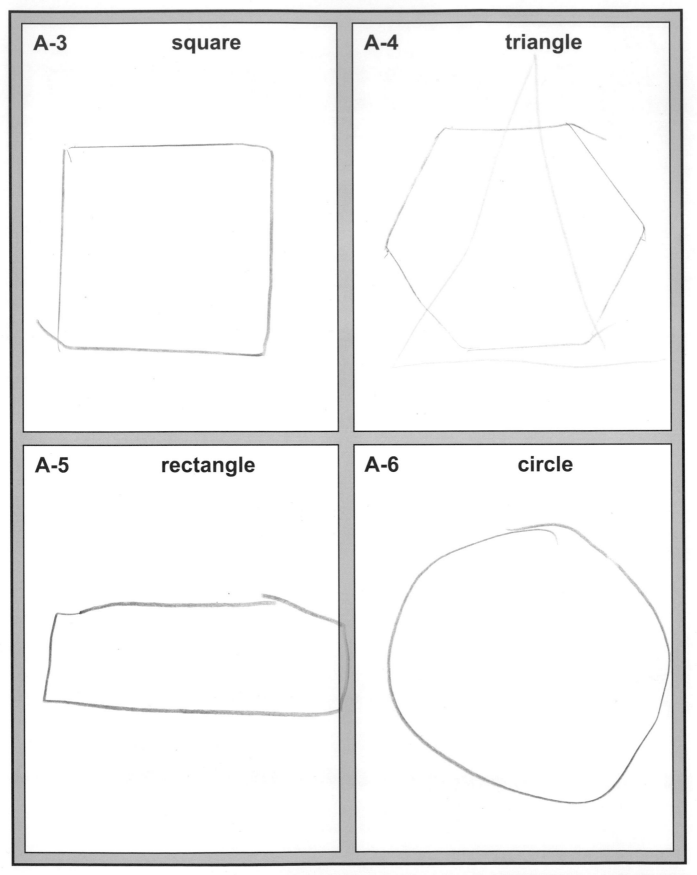

A-3   square

A-4   triangle

A-5   rectangle

A-6   circle

Aria 12-8-22

DESCRIBING SHAPES—SELECT

DIRECTIONS: Find an attribute block like the one shown. Feel and count the sides and corners of the block. Then circle the number that shows how many sides and corners this shape has.

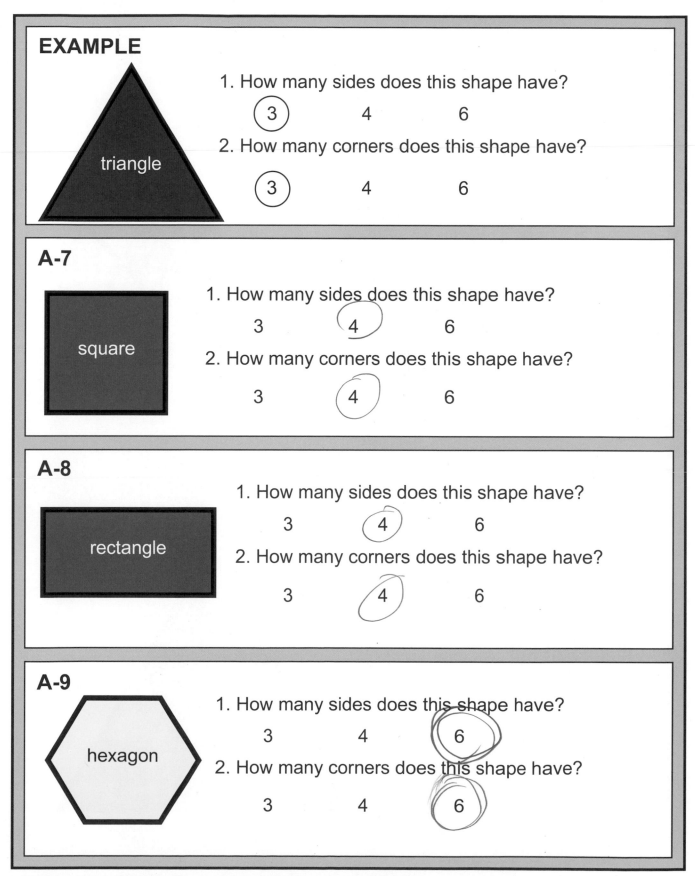

EXAMPLE

triangle

1. How many sides does this shape have?

　(3)　　　4　　　6

2. How many corners does this shape have?

　(3)　　　4　　　6

A-7

square

1. How many sides does this shape have?

　3　　　(4)　　　6

2. How many corners does this shape have?

　3　　　(4)　　　6

A-8

rectangle

1. How many sides does this shape have?

　3　　　(4)　　　6

2. How many corners does this shape have?

　3　　　(4)　　　6

A-9

hexagon

1. How many sides does this shape have?

　3　　　4　　　(6)

2. How many corners does this shape have?

　3　　　4　　　(6)

DESCRIBING SHAPES—SELECT

DIRECTIONS: Draw a circle around the shapes that are large. Then cross out the shapes that are small.

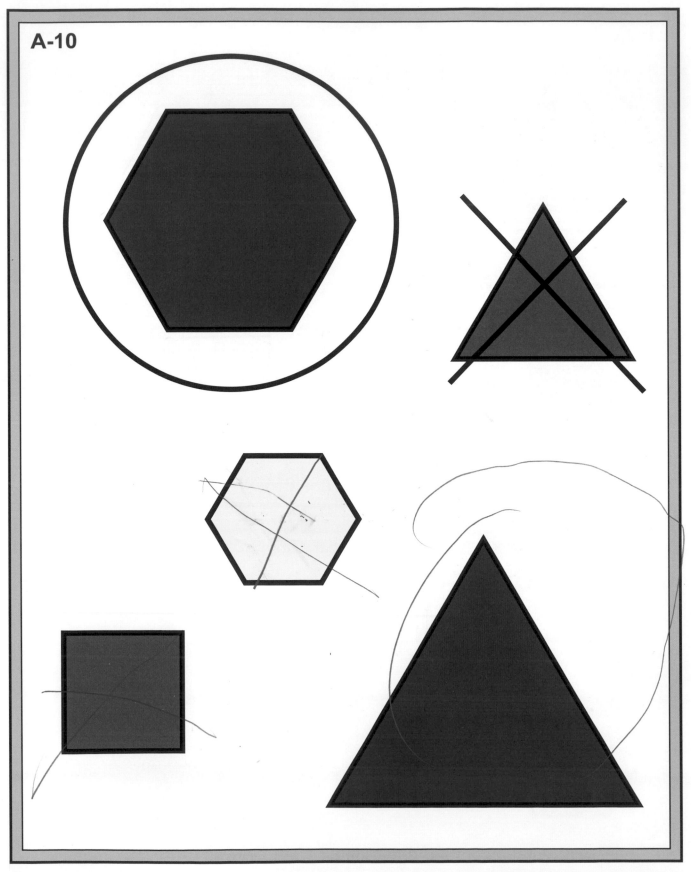

A-10

DESCRIBING SHAPES—SELECT

DIRECTIONS: Draw a circle around the shapes that are small. Then cross out the shapes that are large.

A-11

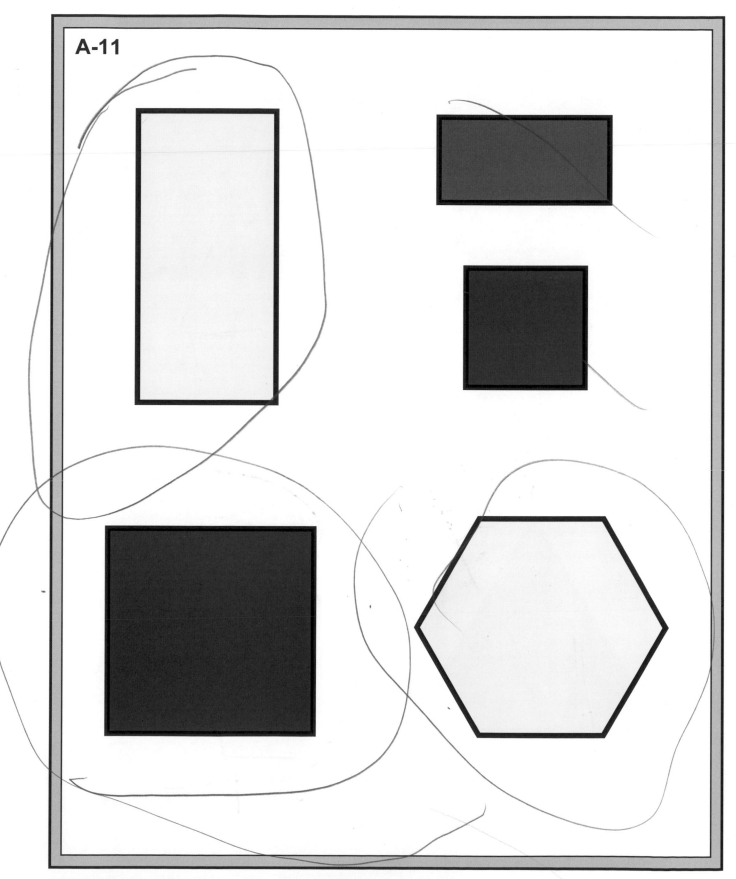

DESCRIBING SHAPES—SELECT

DIRECTIONS: Trace the words on the lines. Then draw a line from each shape to the word that describes it.

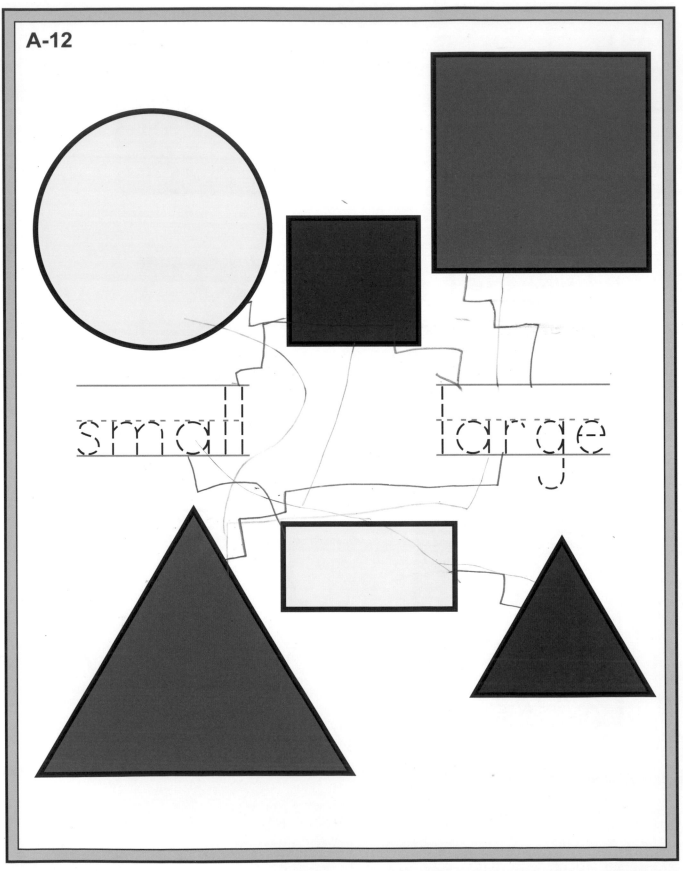

A-12

small   large

© 2008 The Critical Thinking Co™ • www.CriticalThinking.com • 800-458-4849

FINDING SHAPES BY SIZE

DIRECTIONS: Find an attribute block that is named in each box. Put the block in the box and trace around it. Then color your picture the same color as your block.

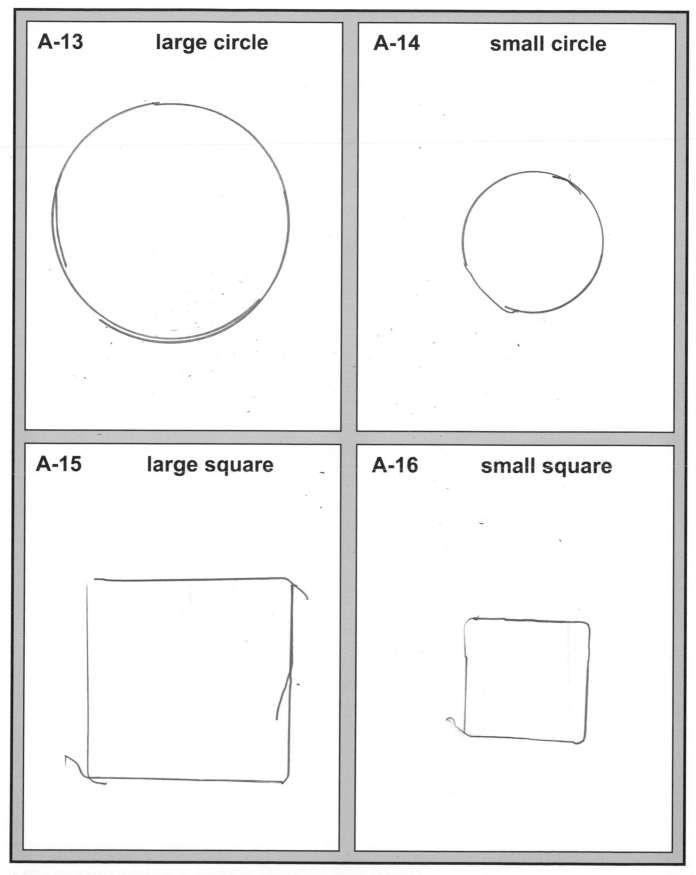

A-13	large circle
A-14	small circle
A-15	large square
A-16	small square

FINDING SHAPES BY SIZE

DIRECTIONS: Find an attribute block that is named in each box. Put the block in the box and trace around it. Then color your picture the same color as your block.

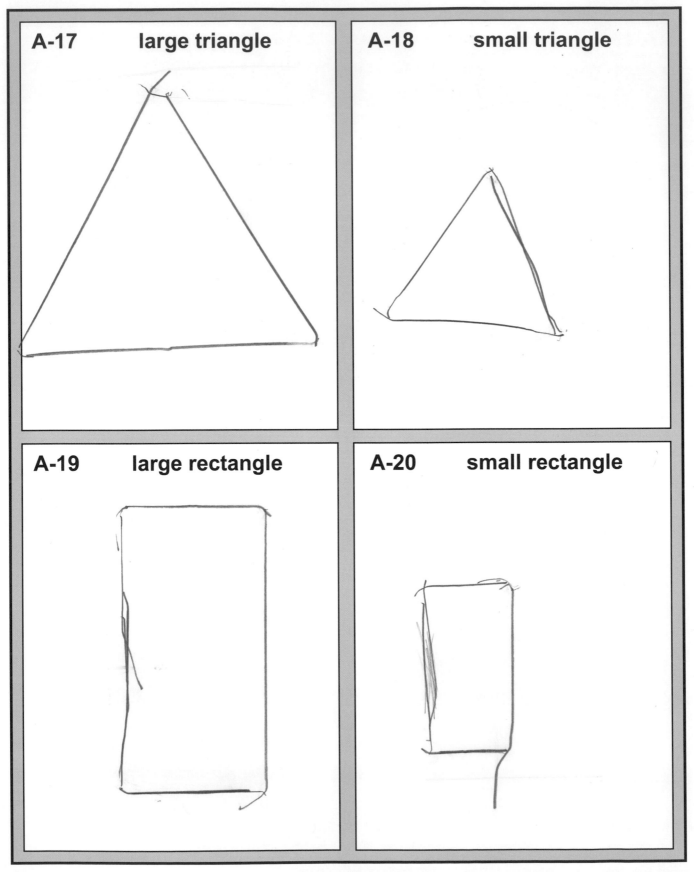

| A-17 | large triangle | A-18 | small triangle |
| A-19 | large rectangle | A-20 | small rectangle |

DESCRIBING SHAPES—SELECT BY COLOR

DIRECTIONS: Trace the word for each color. Then draw a line from each shape to its color.

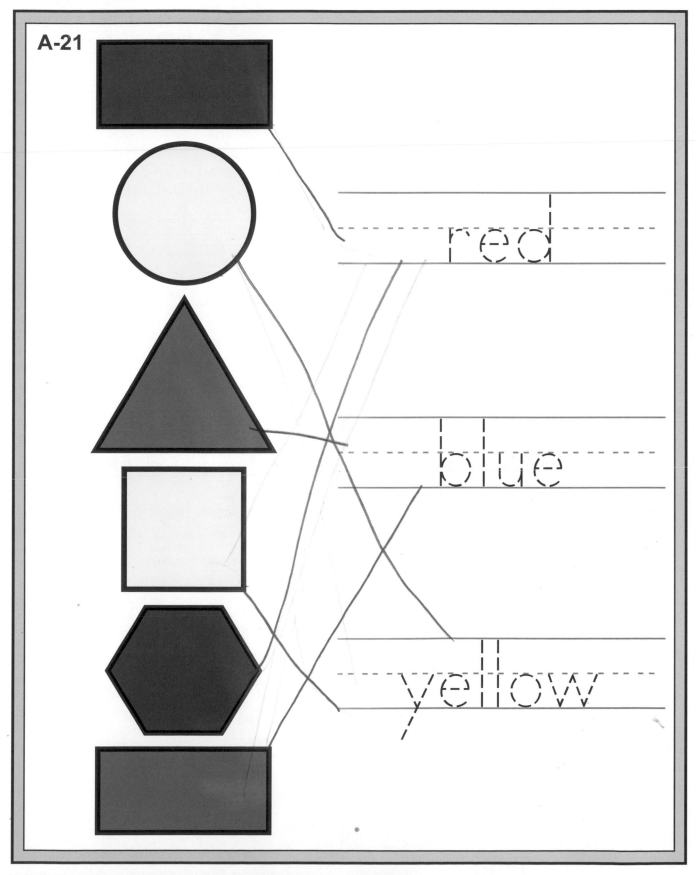

A-21

red

blue

yellow

FINDING SHAPES BY SIZE AND COLOR

DIRECTIONS: Find an attribute block that is named in each box. Put the block in the box and trace around it. Then color your picture the same color as your block.

A-22 large red square	A-23 small blue circle
A-24 large yellow hexagon	A-25 small red triangle

FOLLOWING DIRECTIONS—SELECT FIRST TO LAST

DIRECTIONS: Follow the directions to color the shapes.

Aria 12-12-22

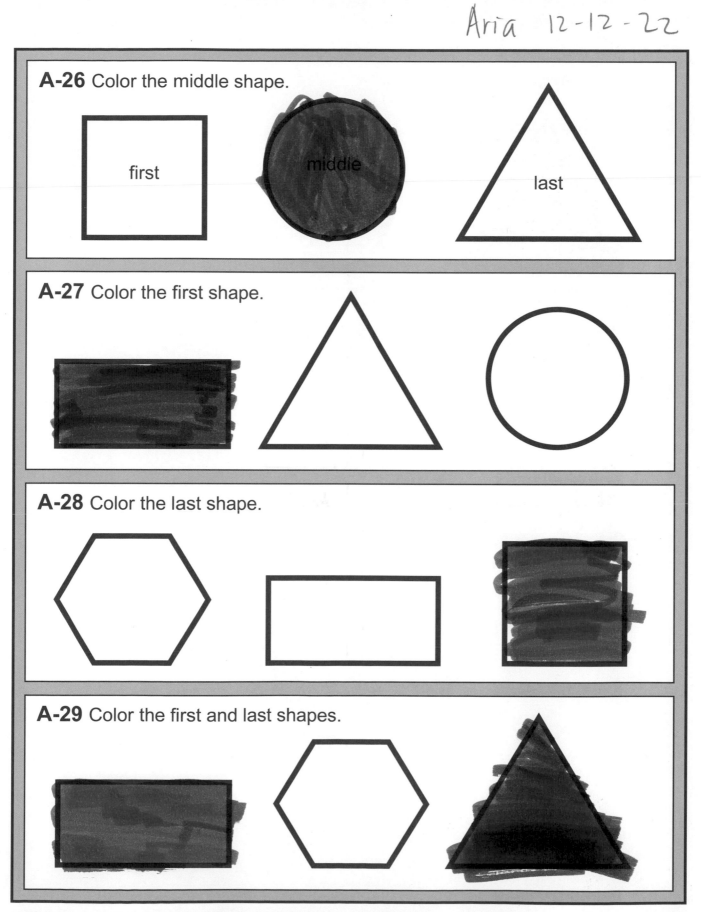

A-26 Color the middle shape.

first

middle

last

A-27 Color the first shape.

A-28 Color the last shape.

A-29 Color the first and last shapes.

FOLLOWING DIRECTIONS—IDENTIFY FIRST TO LAST

DIRECTIONS: Draw a line from each shape name to the word that describes its position. Draw a line from each shape name to the word that describes its color. Then trace each position and color word.

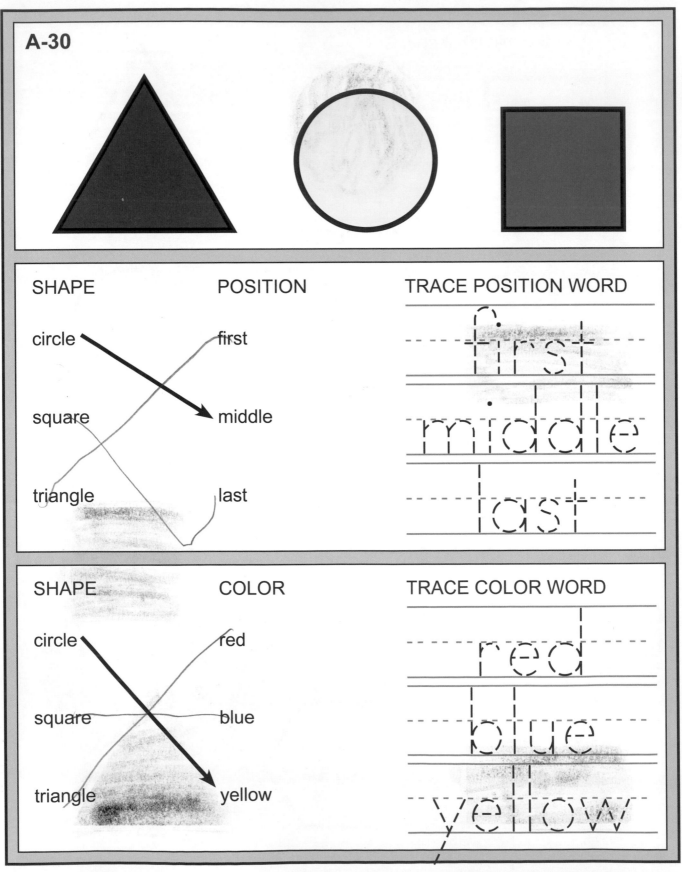

A-30

SHAPE | POSITION | TRACE POSITION WORD

circle

square

triangle

first

middle

last

first
middle
last

SHAPE | COLOR | TRACE COLOR WORD

circle

square

triangle

red

blue

yellow

red
blue
yellow

FOLLOWING DIRECTIONS—IDENTIFY FIRST TO LAST

DIRECTIONS: Using the words in the WORD BOX, write the color that describes each shape.

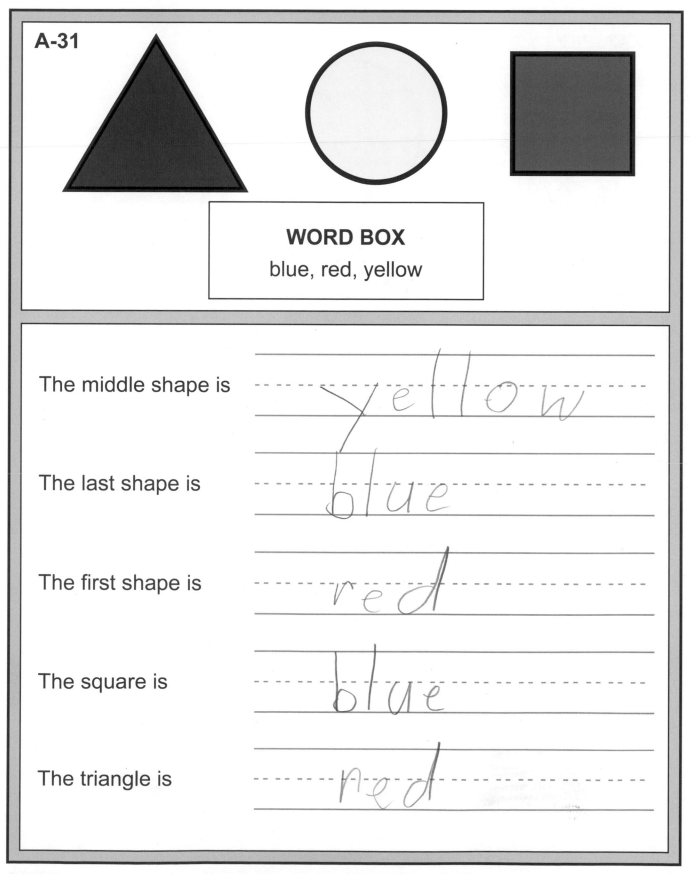

A-31

WORD BOX

blue, red, yellow

The middle shape is _yellow_

The last shape is _blue_

The first shape is _red_

The square is _blue_

The triangle is _red_

FOLLOWING DIRECTIONS—SELECT FIRST TO THIRD

DIRECTIONS: Follow the directions to color each shape.

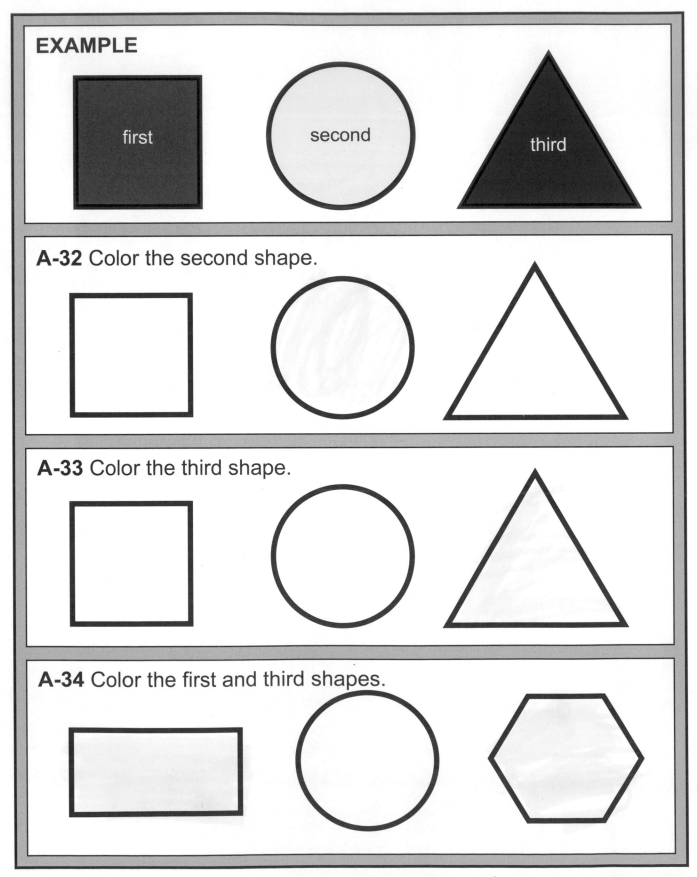

EXAMPLE

first   second   third

A-32 Color the second shape.

A-33 Color the third shape.

A-34 Color the first and third shapes.

FOLLOWING DIRECTIONS—IDENTIFY FIRST TO THIRD

DIRECTIONS: Draw a line from each shape name to the word that describes its position. Draw a line from each shape name to the word that describes its color. Then trace each position and color word.

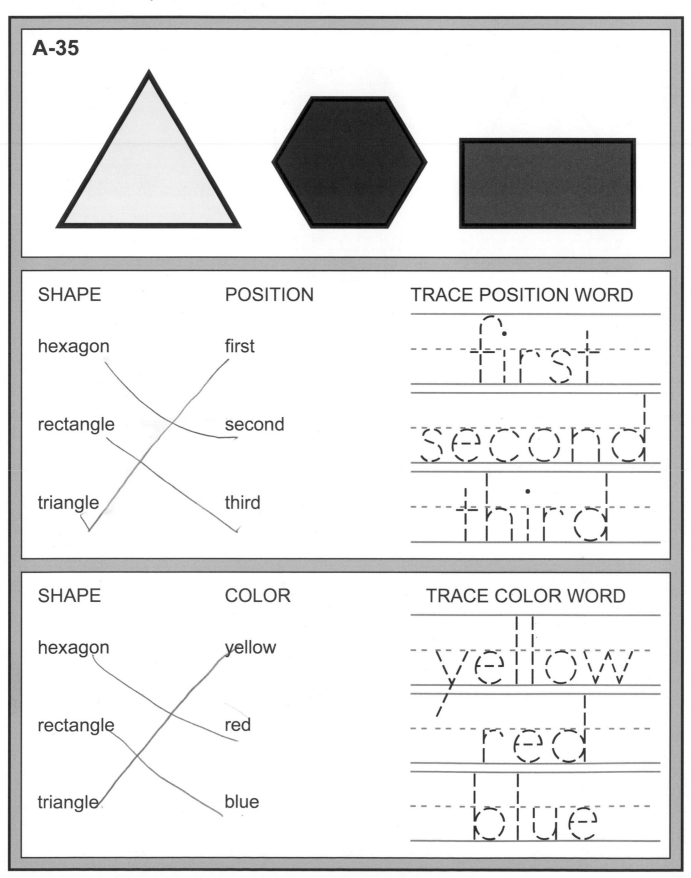

A-35

SHAPE	POSITION	TRACE POSITION WORD
hexagon	first	first
rectangle	second	second
triangle	third	third

SHAPE	COLOR	TRACE COLOR WORD
hexagon	yellow	yellow
rectangle	red	red
triangle	blue	blue

FOLLOWING DIRECTIONS—IDENTIFY FIRST TO THIRD

DIRECTIONS: Using the words in the WORD BOX, write the color that describes the position or name of each shape.

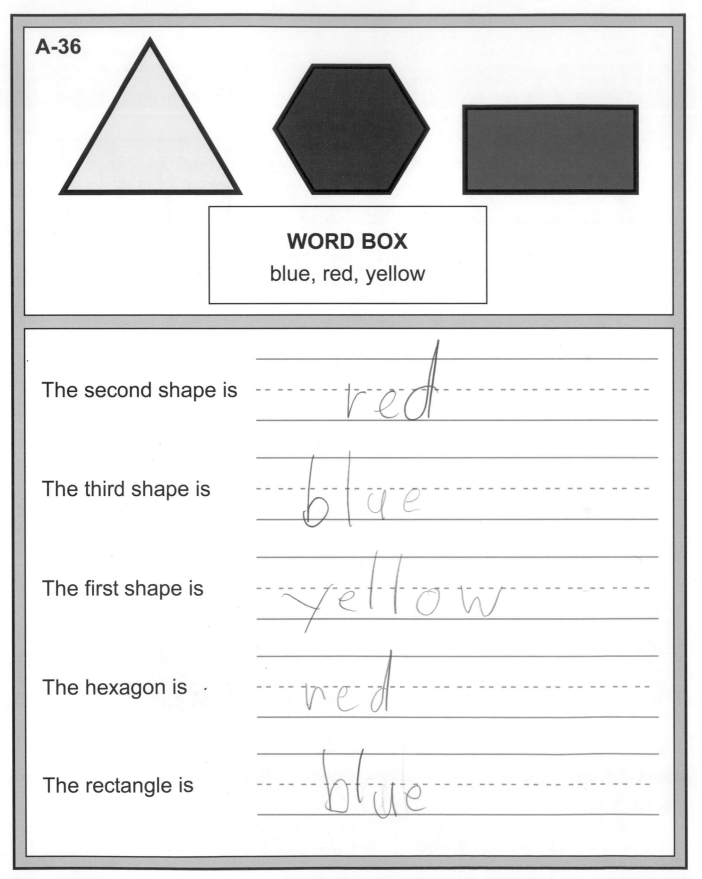

A-36

WORD BOX

blue, red, yellow

The second shape is _red_

The third shape is _blue_

The first shape is _yellow_

The hexagon is _red_

The rectangle is _blue_

FOLLOWING DIRECTIONS—IDENTIFY FIRST TO THIRD

DIRECTIONS: Using the words in the WORD BOX, write the shape name that describes the position or color of each shape.

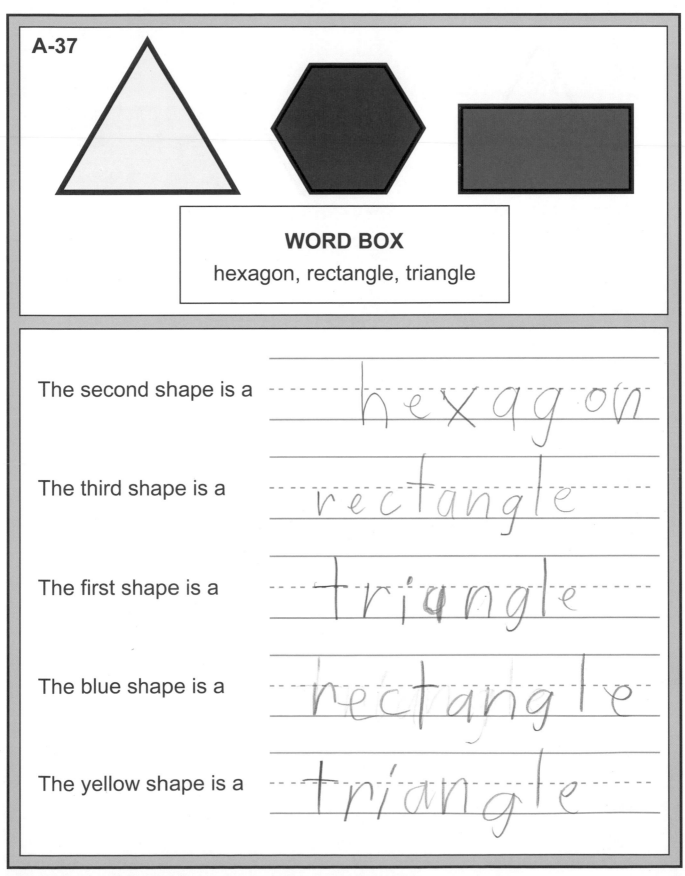

A-37

WORD BOX
hexagon, rectangle, triangle

The second shape is a ———— hexagon

The third shape is a ———— rectangle

The first shape is a ———— triangle

The blue shape is a ———— rectangle

The yellow shape is a ———— triangle

FOLLOWING DIRECTIONS—WRITING FIRST TO THIRD

DIRECTIONS: Trace each word that describes the position or color of each shape.

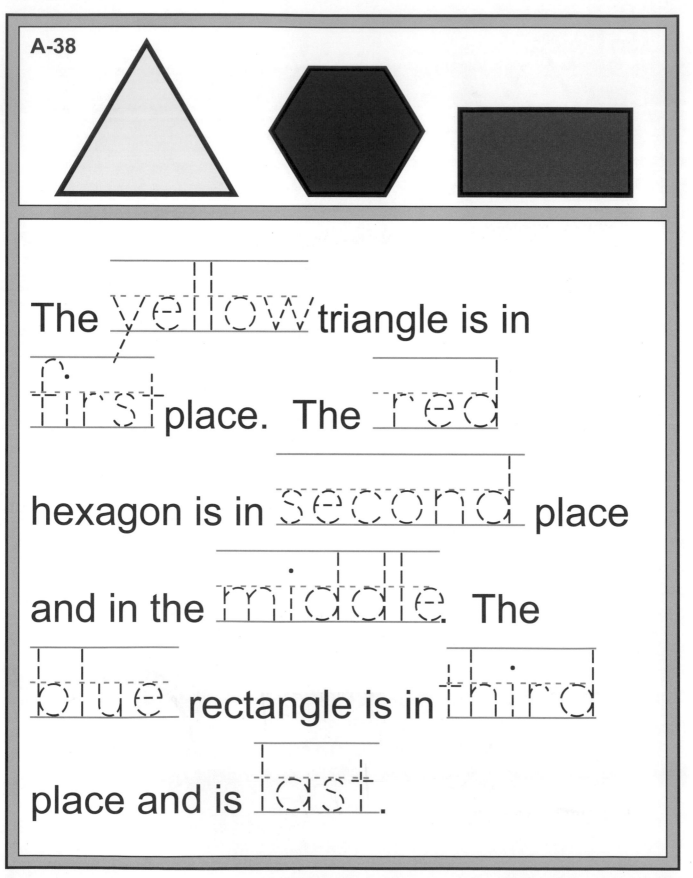

A-38

The _yellow_ triangle is in _first_ place. The _red_ hexagon is in _second_ place and in the _middle_. The _blue_ rectangle is in _third_ place and is _last_.

Aria R 1-10-23

FOLLOWING DIRECTIONS—SELECT LEFT OR RIGHT

DIRECTIONS: Follow the directions to color the shapes. Use any color.

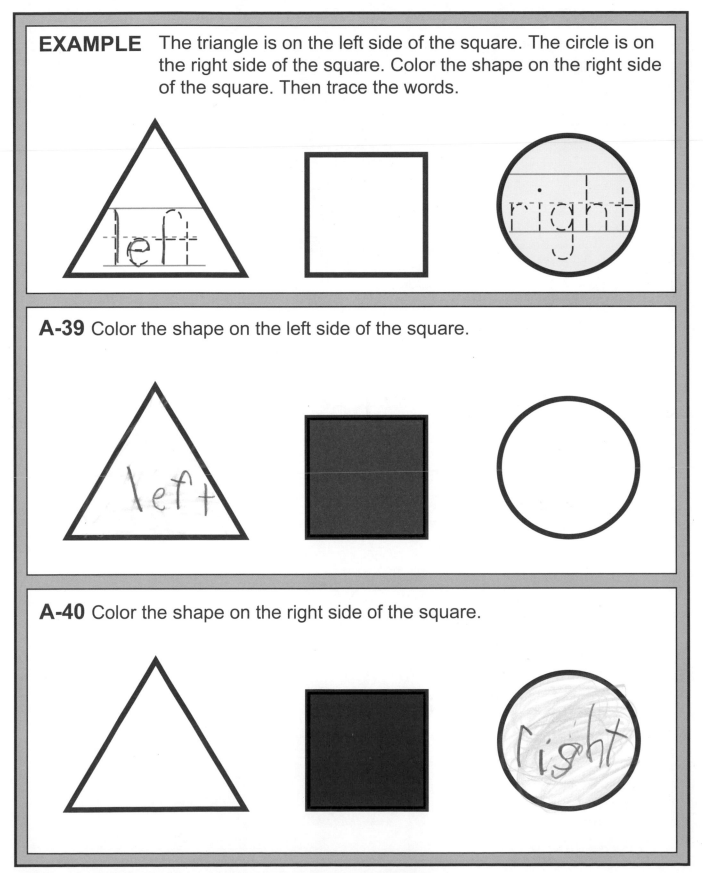

EXAMPLE The triangle is on the left side of the square. The circle is on the right side of the square. Color the shape on the right side of the square. Then trace the words.

A-39 Color the shape on the left side of the square.

A-40 Color the shape on the right side of the square.

FOLLOWING DIRECTIONS—SUPPLY LEFT OR RIGHT

DIRECTIONS: Follow the directions in each exercise using the attribute blocks.

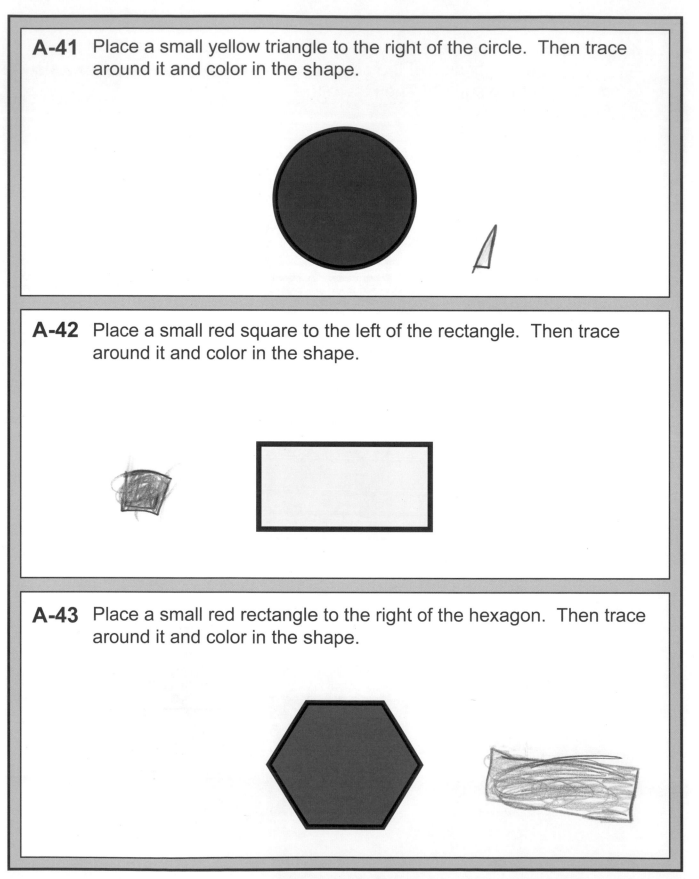

A-41   Place a small yellow triangle to the right of the circle. Then trace around it and color in the shape.

A-42   Place a small red square to the left of the rectangle. Then trace around it and color in the shape.

A-43   Place a small red rectangle to the right of the hexagon. Then trace around it and color in the shape.

FOLLOWING DIRECTIONS—SUPPLY LEFT OR RIGHT

DIRECTIONS: Follow the directions in each exercise using the attribute blocks.

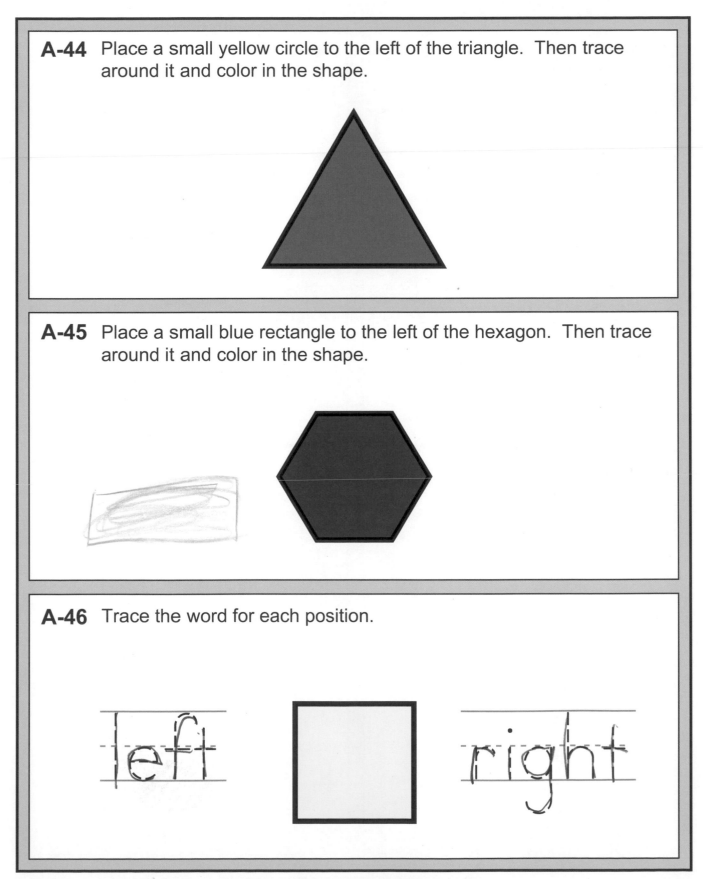

A-44 Place a small yellow circle to the left of the triangle. Then trace around it and color in the shape.

A-45 Place a small blue rectangle to the left of the hexagon. Then trace around it and color in the shape.

A-46 Trace the word for each position.

left   right

FOLLOWING DIRECTIONS—SELECT TOP TO BOTTOM

DIRECTIONS: Follow the directions to find the shape to color. Use any color.

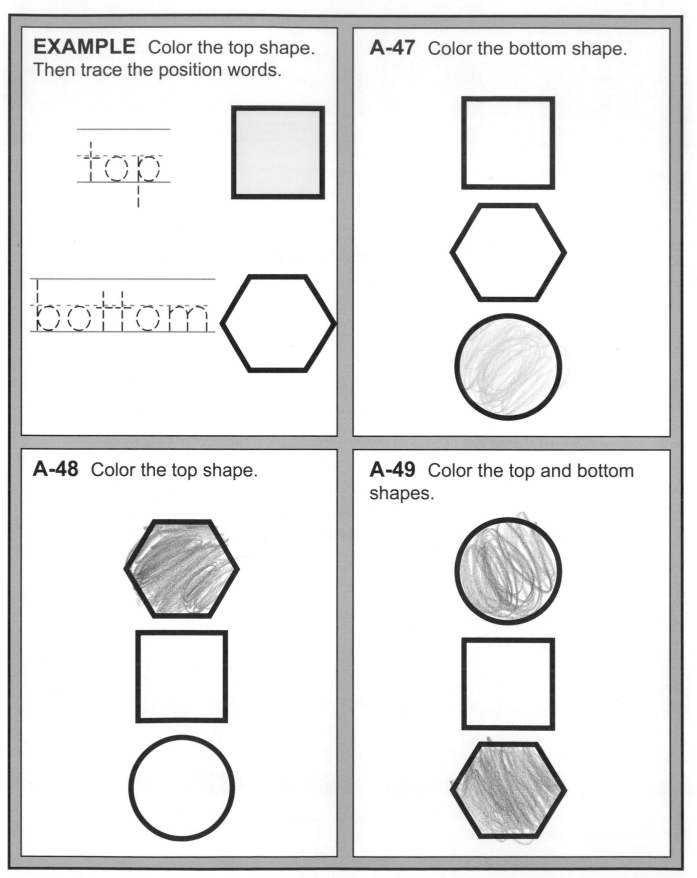

EXAMPLE Color the top shape. Then trace the position words.

top

bottom

A-47 Color the bottom shape.

A-48 Color the top shape.

A-49 Color the top and bottom shapes.

FOLLOWING DIRECTIONS—SUPPLY TOP TO BOTTOM

DIRECTIONS: Follow the directions in each exercise using the attribute blocks.

A-50 Place a small blue triangle on top. Then trace and color the shape.

A-51 Place a small red square on the bottom. Then trace and color the shape.

A-52 Place a small yellow rectangle on the top and a small red triangle on the bottom. Then trace and color the shapes.

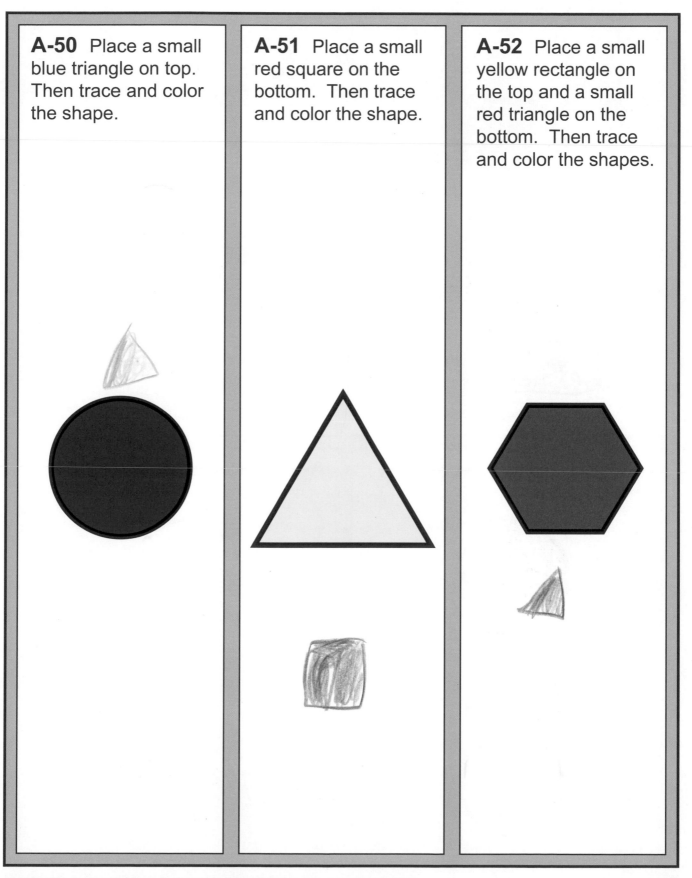

FOLLOWING DIRECTIONS—SELECT ABOVE OR BELOW

DIRECTIONS: Follow the directions to find the shape to color. Use any color.

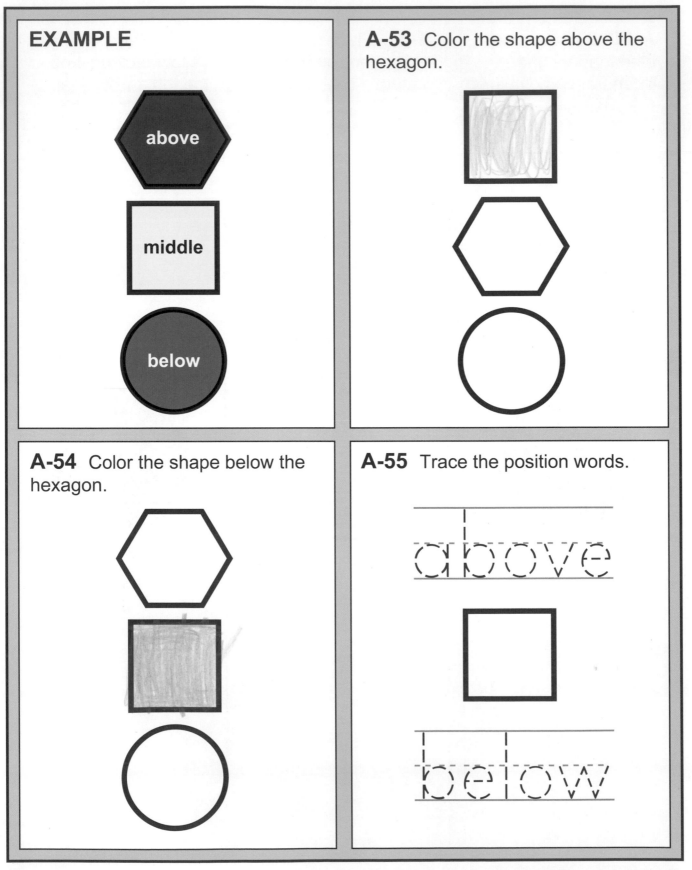

EXAMPLE

above

middle

below

A-53 Color the shape above the hexagon.

A-54 Color the shape below the hexagon.

A-55 Trace the position words.

above

below

FOLLOWING DIRECTIONS—SUPPLY ABOVE OR BELOW

DIRECTIONS: Follow the directions in each exercise using the attribute blocks.

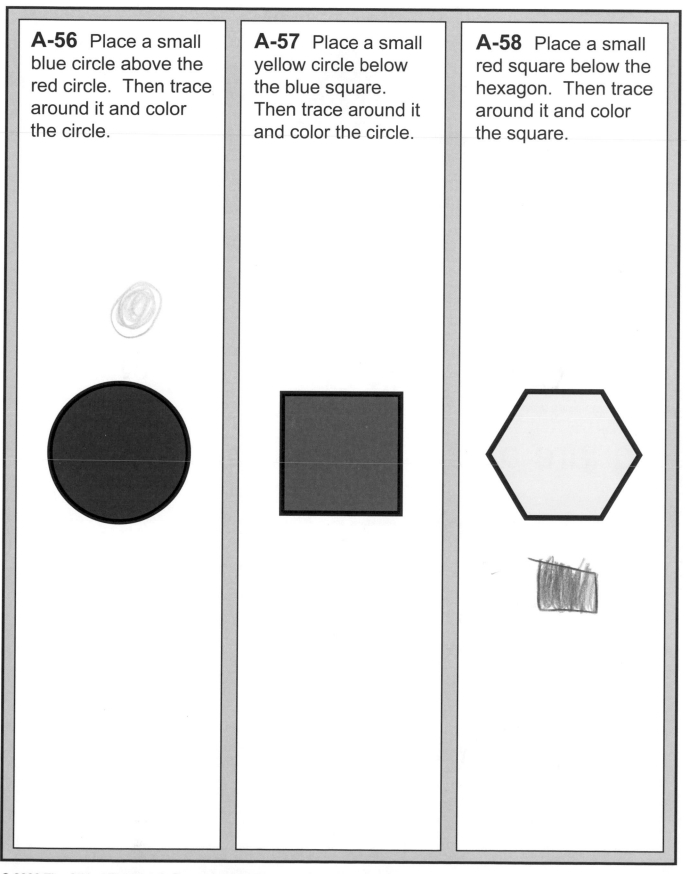

A-56 Place a small blue circle above the red circle. Then trace around it and color the circle.

A-57 Place a small yellow circle below the blue square. Then trace around it and color the circle.

A-58 Place a small red square below the hexagon. Then trace around it and color the square.

FOLLOWING DIRECTIONS—WRITING POSITION WORDS

DIRECTIONS: Trace the words that describe the position of the shapes.

A-59

The rectangle is <u>above</u> the square and <u>below</u> the triangle. The hexagon is on the <u>right</u> of the rectangle, and the circle is on the <u>left</u>. The triangle is at the <u>top</u> of the group, and the square is at the <u>bottom</u>.

NAMING SHAPES—SELECT AND WRITE

DIRECTIONS: Use the words from the WORD BOX to write each color and shape. Then trace the example answers.

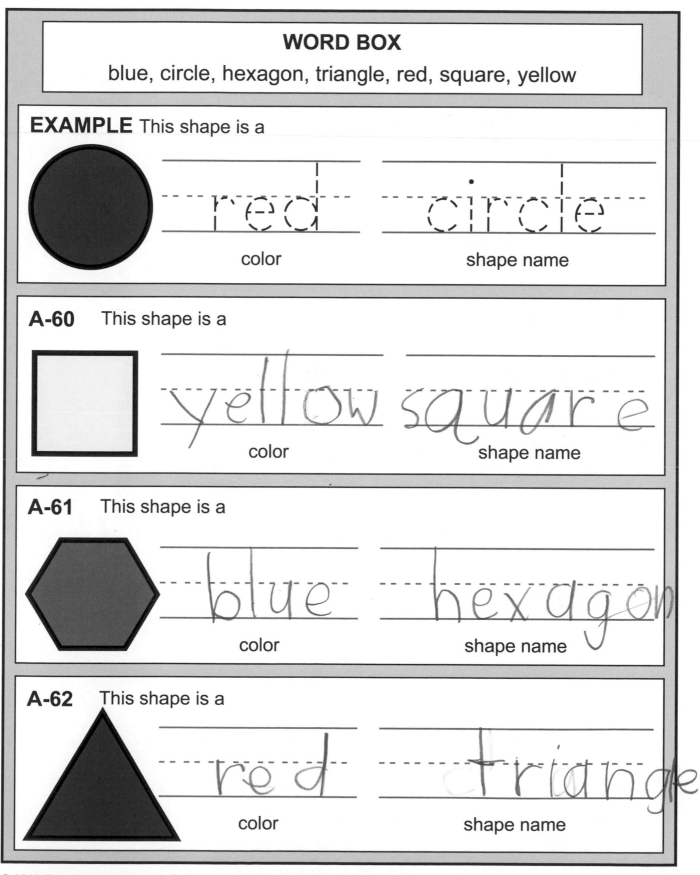

WORD BOX

blue, circle, hexagon, triangle, red, square, yellow

EXAMPLE This shape is a

red   circle

color   shape name

A-60   This shape is a

yellow   square

color   shape name

A-61   This shape is a

blue   hexagon

color   shape name

A-62   This shape is a

red   triangle

color   shape name

FOLLOWING DIRECTIONS—SELECT AND WRITE

DIRECTIONS: Use words from the WORD BOX to write each size and shape.

WORD BOX

large, rectangle, small, square

1

2

3

A-63   Shape 1 is a

_____   _____

- - - - - - - - - - - - - - -   - - - - - - - - - - - - - - - - -

_____   _____

size   shape name

A-64   Shape 2 is a

_____   _____

- - - - - - - - - - - - - - -   - - - - - - - - - - - - - - - - -

_____   _____

size   shape name

A-65   Shape 3 is a

_____   _____

- - - - - - - - - - - - - - -   - - - - - - - - - - - - - - - - -

_____   _____

size   shape name

FOLLOWING DIRECTIONS—SELECT AND WRITE

DIRECTIONS: Use words from the WORD BOX to write each size and shape.

WORD BOX
circle, hexagon, large, small, triangle

4

5

6

A-66   Shape 4 is a

_____   _____

- - - - - - - - - - - - - - -   - - - - - - - - - - - - - - -

_____   _____

size   shape name

A-67   Shape 5 is a

_____   _____

- - - - - - - - - - - - - - -   - - - - - - - - - - - - - - -

_____   _____

size   shape name

A-68   Shape 6 is a

_____   _____

- - - - - - - - - - - - - - -   - - - - - - - - - - - - - - -

_____   _____

size   shape name

DESCRIBING SHAPES—SELECT AND WRITE

DIRECTIONS: Use the words in the WORD BOX to complete the sentences. Then trace the example answers.

WORD BOX

three, four, six

EXAMPLE

This shape has _four_ sides and

four corners.

A-69

This shape has _____

sides and _____ corners.

A-70

This shape has _____

sides and _____ corners.

DESCRIBING SHAPES—EXPLAIN

DIRECTIONS: Write a sentence to describe each shape. Use the words in the WORD BOX to write your sentence. Then trace the example answer.

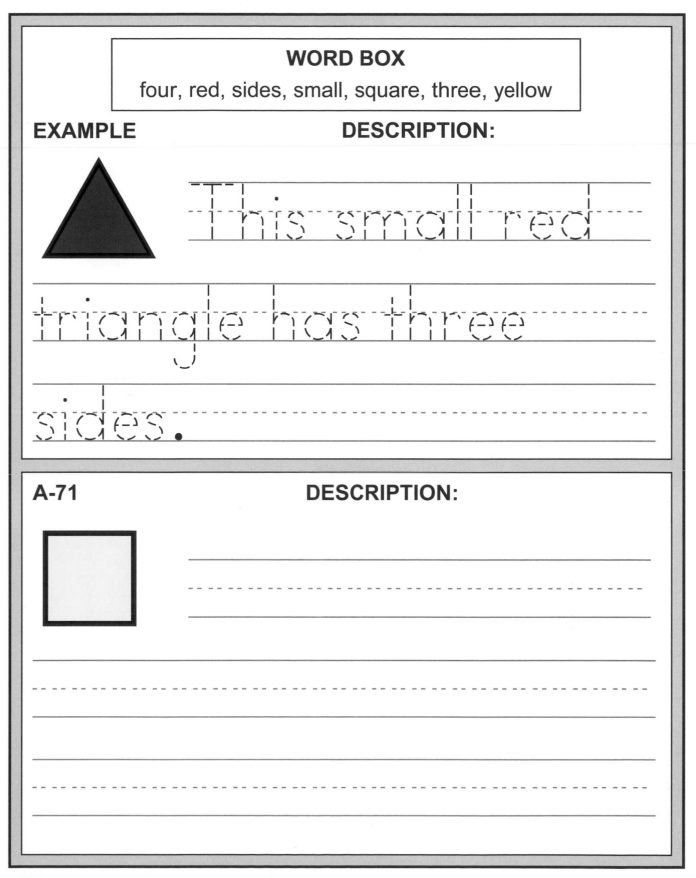

WORD BOX
four, red, sides, small, square, three, yellow

EXAMPLE   **DESCRIPTION:**

This small red triangle has three sides.

A-71   **DESCRIPTION:**

DESCRIBING SHAPES—EXPLAIN

DIRECTIONS: Using the words in the WORD BOX, write a sentence to describe each shape.

WORD BOX
blue, circle, corner, four, hexagon, red, sides, six

A-72   DESCRIPTION:

A-73   DESCRIPTION:

Chapter Two
Figural Similarities and Differences

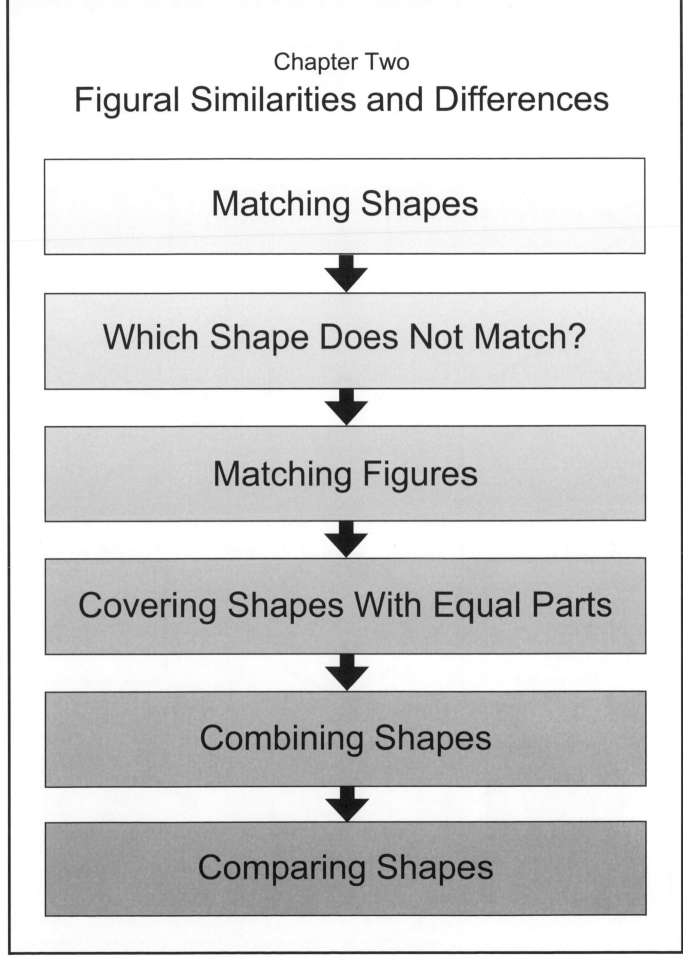

Matching Shapes

Which Shape Does Not Match?

Matching Figures

Covering Shapes With Equal Parts

Combining Shapes

Comparing Shapes

MATCHING SHAPES

DIRECTIONS: Color the matching shape. Use any color.

MATCHING SHAPES

DIRECTIONS: Color the matching shape. Use any color.

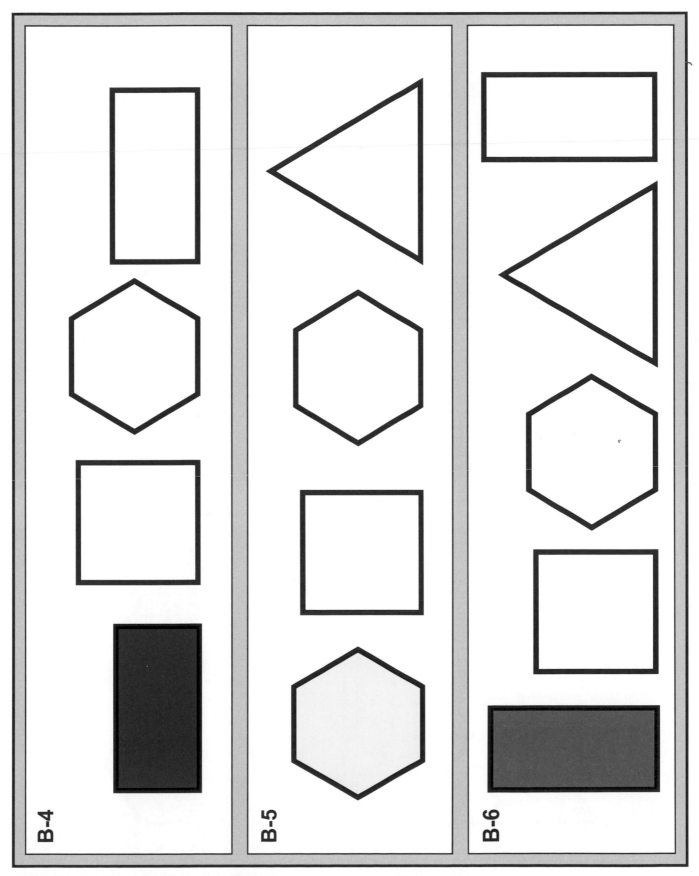

B-4

B-5

B-6

MATCHING BLOCKS BY SHAPE AND COLOR

DIRECTIONS: Draw a line from each shape to the one that has the same shape and color.

Aria 1-30 23

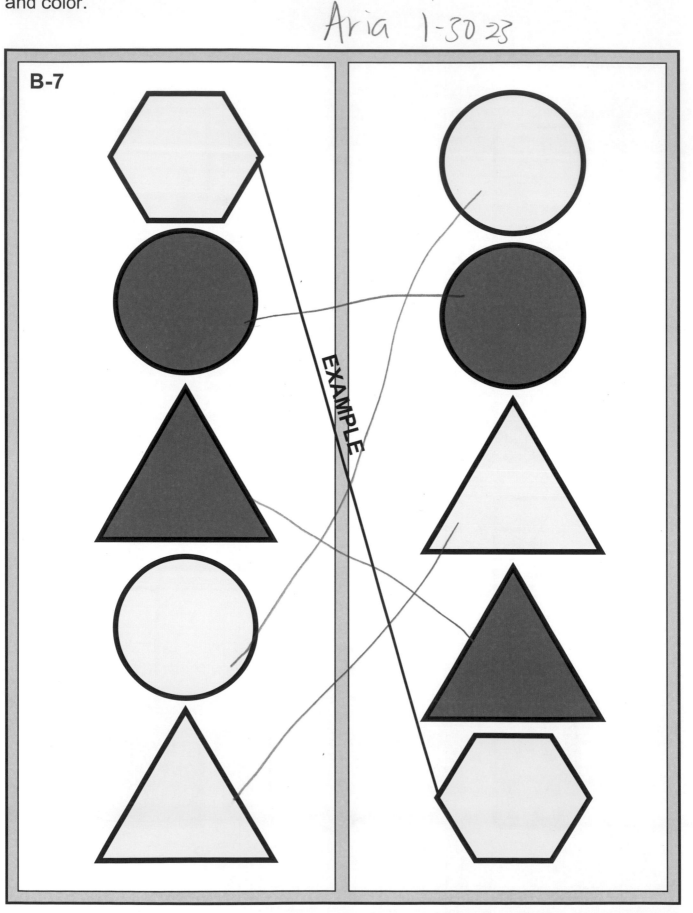

MATCHING BLOCKS BY SHAPE AND COLOR

DIRECTIONS: Draw a line from each shape to the one that has the same shape and color.

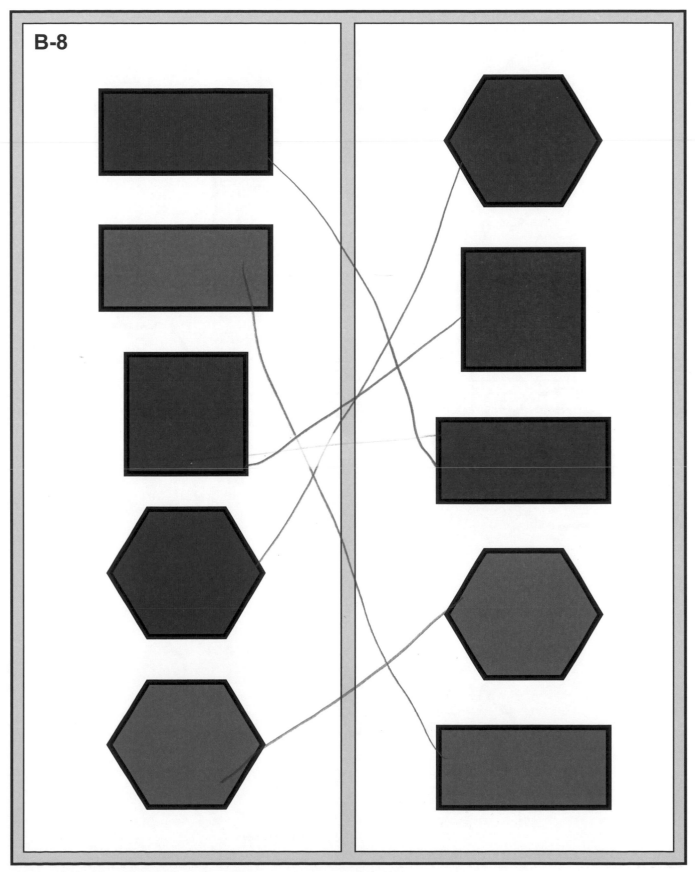

WHICH SHAPE DOES NOT MATCH THE BLOCK?

DIRECTIONS: Place an attribute block on the colored shape. Move the block until you find the shape that does NOT match. Then cross it out.

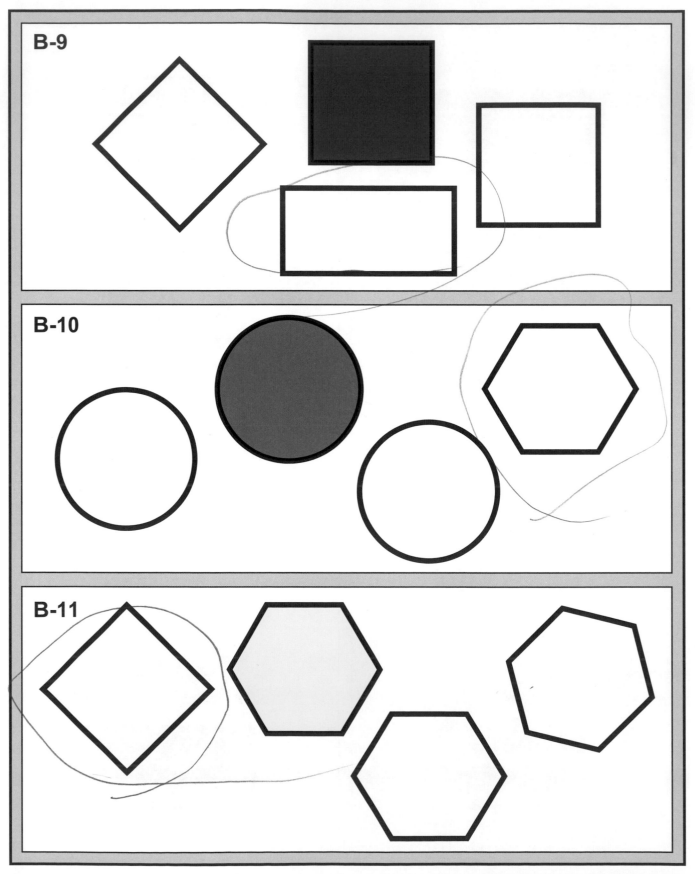

WHICH SHAPE DOES NOT MATCH THE BLOCK?

DIRECTIONS: Place an attribute block on the colored shape. Move the block until you find the shape that does NOT match. Then cross it out.

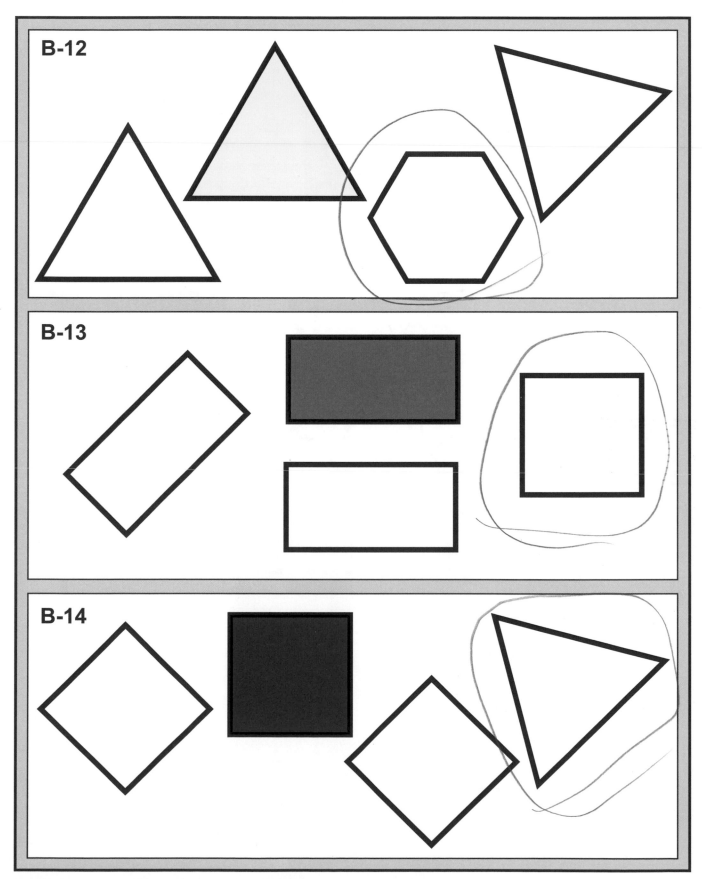

MATCHING FIGURES

DIRECTIONS: Use interlocking cubes to make a figure to match the colored one. Move your figure to find those that match the one you made. Color them. Then draw an "X" through the ones you CANNOT match.

EXAMPLE

Build this one.   Color this one.

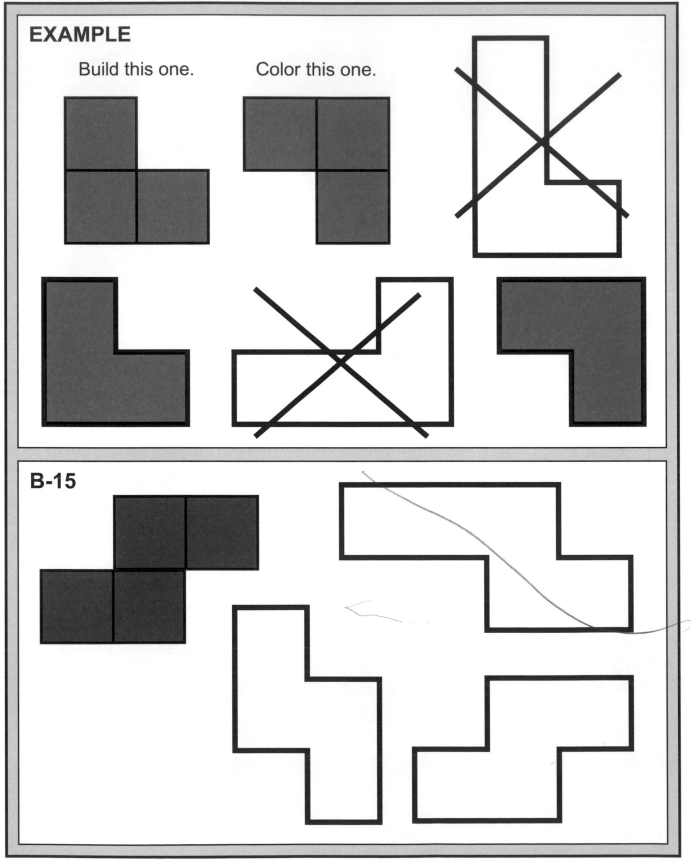

B-15

COMBINING ATTRIBUTE BLOCKS

DIRECTIONS: Using the attribute blocks, find the figures below that can be made by combining the two blocks. Color the figures you can make. Then draw an "X" through the ones you CANNOT make.

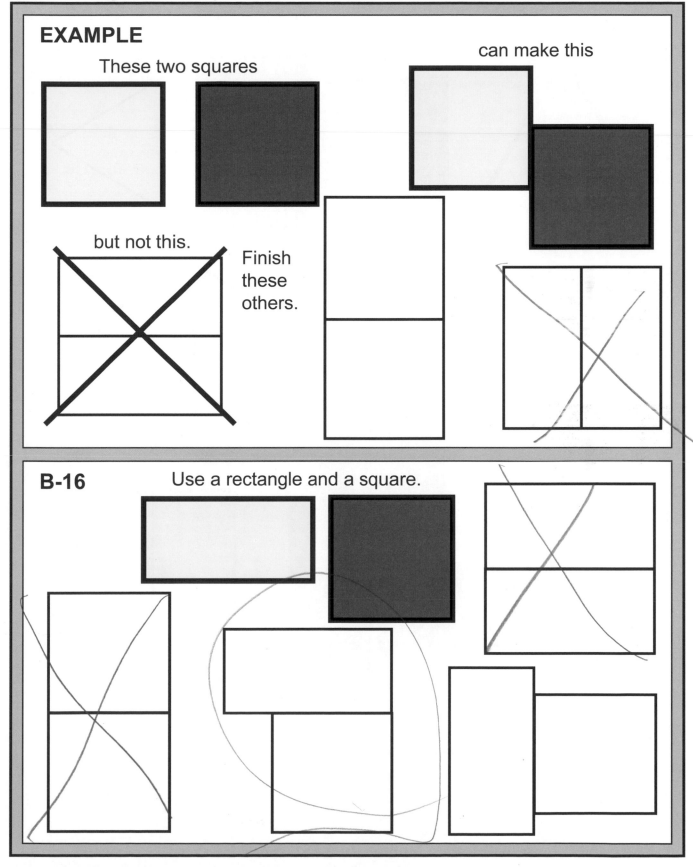

EXAMPLE

These two squares

can make this

but not this.

Finish these others.

B-16   Use a rectangle and a square.

43

COMBINING ATTRIBUTE BLOCKS

DIRECTIONS: Using the attribute blocks, find the figures below that can be made by combining the two blocks. Color the figures you can make. Then draw an "X" through the ones you CANNOT make.

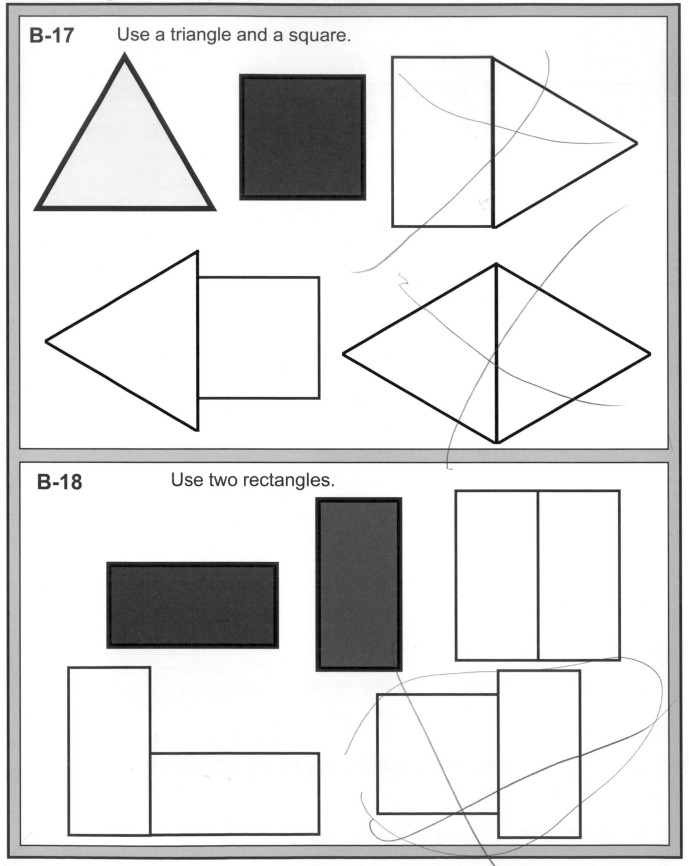

B-17   Use a triangle and a square.

B-18   Use two rectangles.

COMBINING INTERLOCKING CUBES

DIRECTIONS: Find the figures that can be made by combining two red interlocking cubes and two blue interlocking cubes. Circle the figures you can make. Then draw an "X" through the ones you CANNOT make.

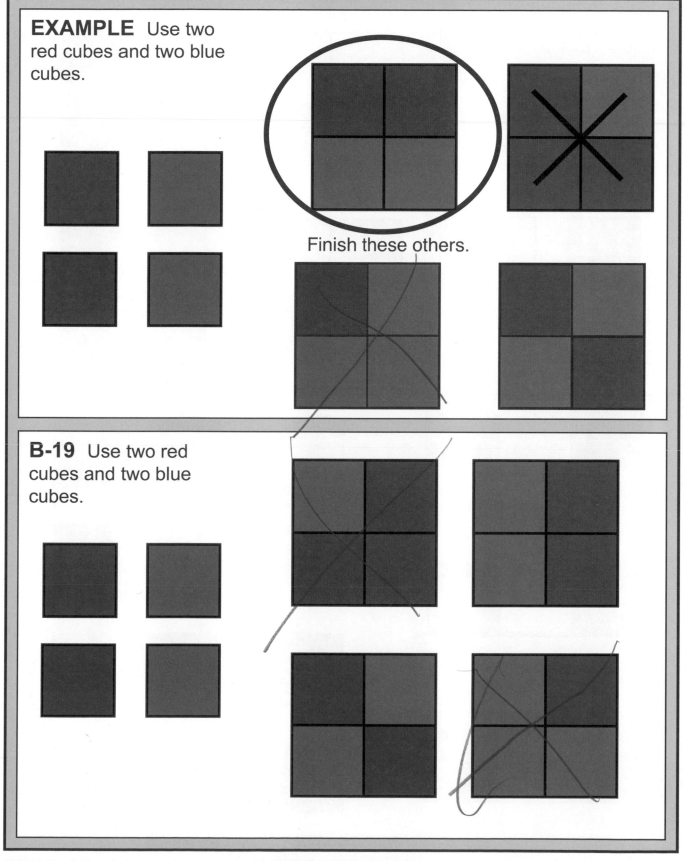

EXAMPLE Use two red cubes and two blue cubes.

Finish these others.

B-19 Use two red cubes and two blue cubes.

COMBINING INTERLOCKING CUBES

DIRECTIONS: Find the figures that can be made by combining two red interlocking cubes and two yellow interlocking cubes. Circle the figures you can make. Then draw an "X" through the ones you CANNOT make.

B-20 Use two red cubes and two yellow cubes.

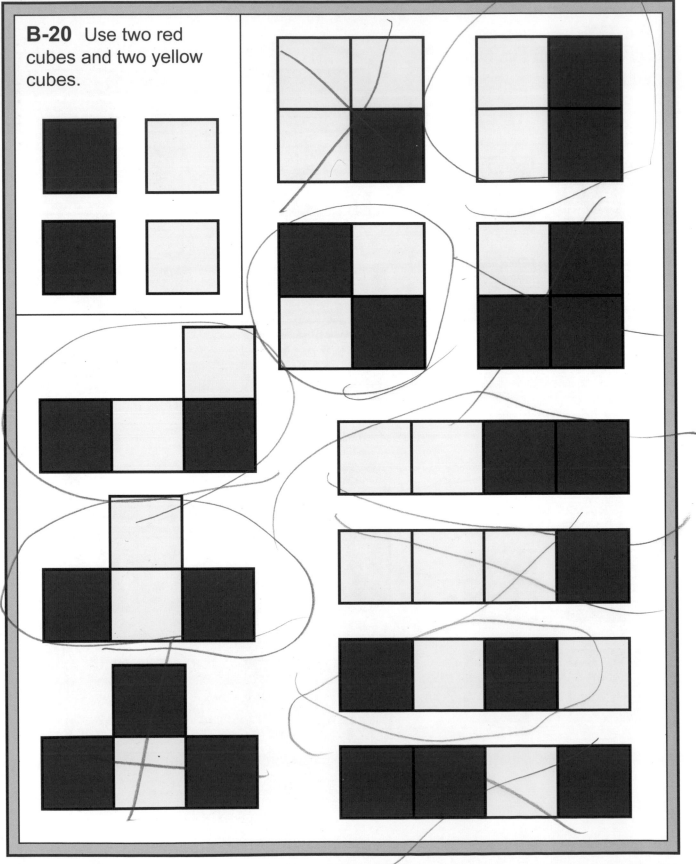

COMBINING INTERLOCKING CUBES

DIRECTIONS: Find the figures that can be made by combining five interlocking cubes. Circle the figures you can make. Then draw an "X" through the ones you CANNOT make.

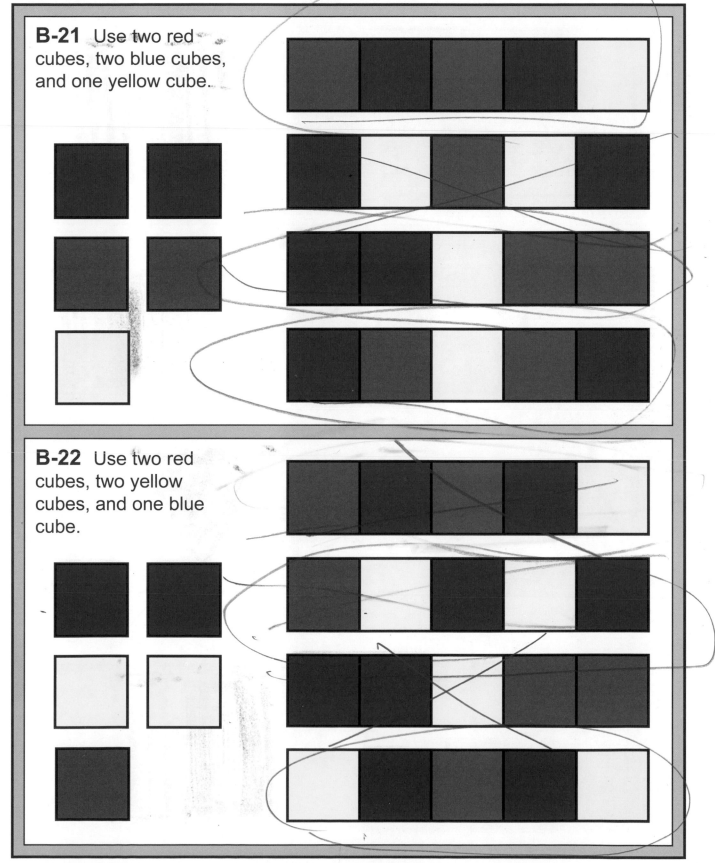

B-21 Use two red cubes, two blue cubes, and one yellow cube.

B-22 Use two red cubes, two yellow cubes, and one blue cube.

COVERING SHAPES WITH EQUAL PARTS—BLOCKS

DIRECTIONS: Place attribute blocks on each pair of shapes. Then use the two blocks to cover the figure on the right and color it to match.

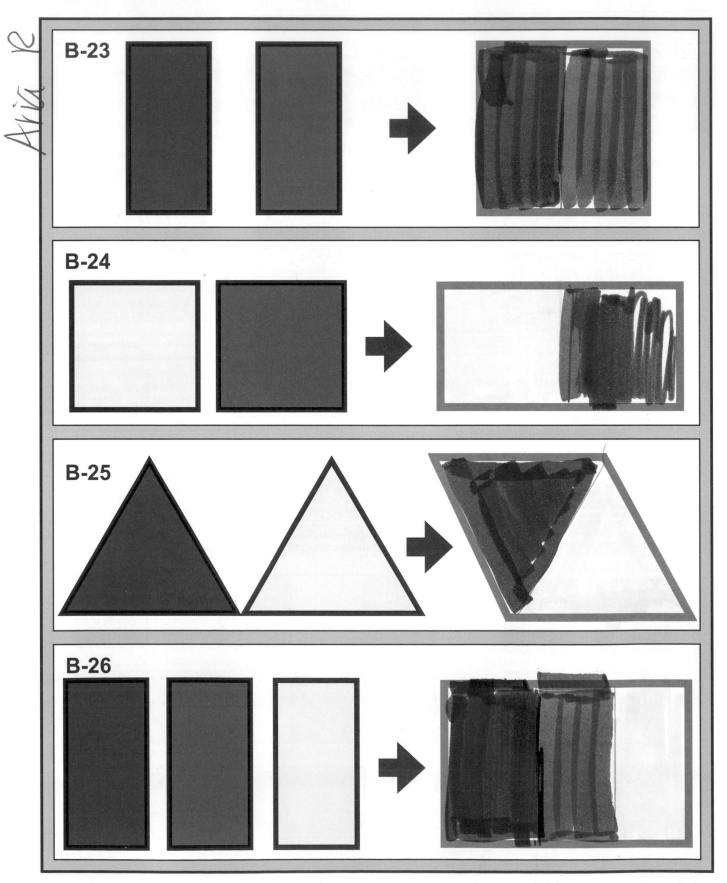

COVERING SHAPES WITH EQUAL PARTS—BLOCKS

DIRECTIONS: Place an attribute block on each of the three shapes on the left. Then use the three blocks to cover the figure on the right and color it to match.

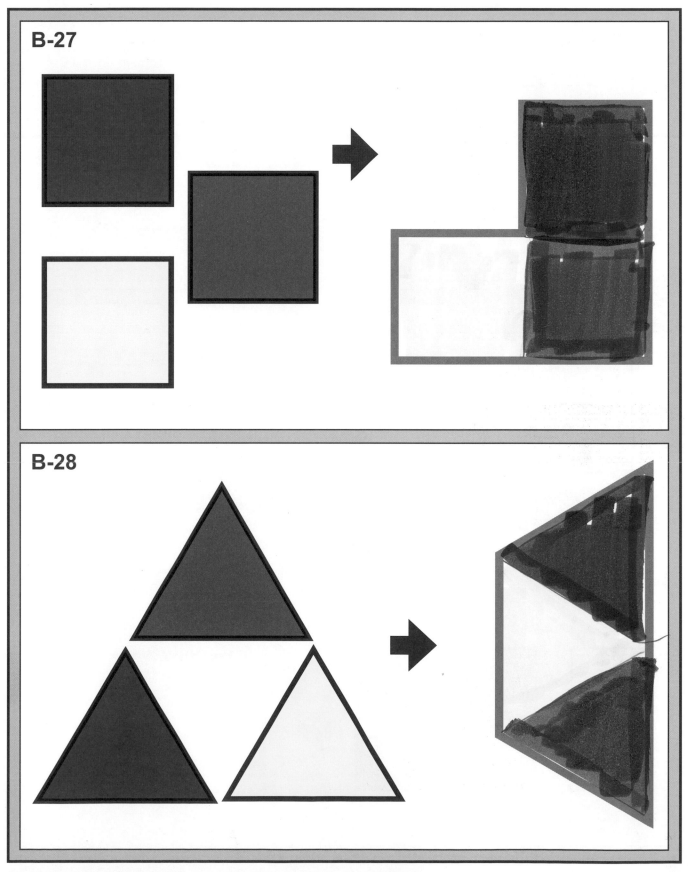

B-27

B-28

COVERING SHAPES WITH EQUAL PARTS—CUBES

DIRECTIONS: Build the equal parts with interlocking cubes. Use the parts to cover the figure on the right. Then color it to match.

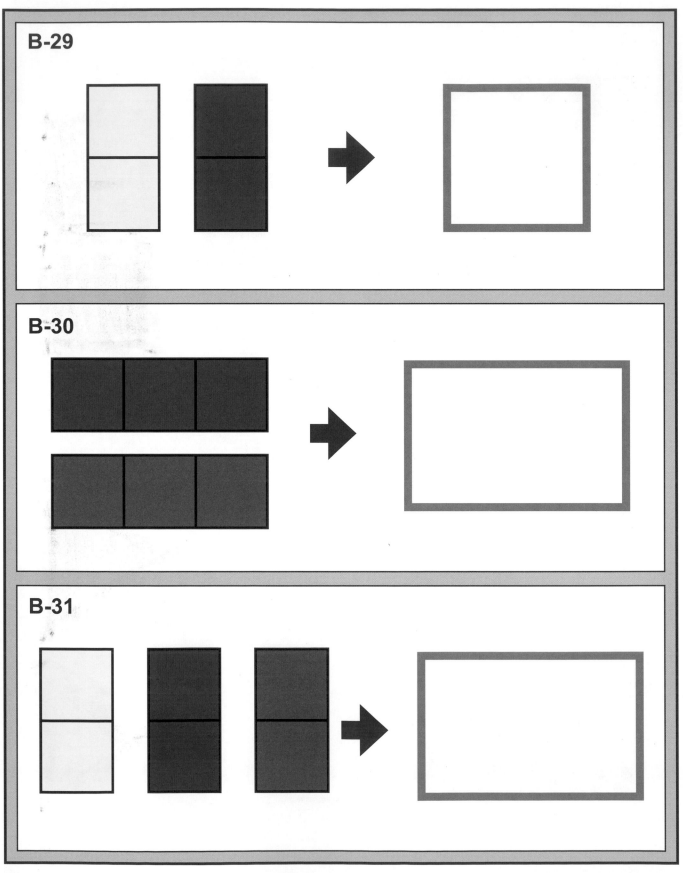

B-29

B-30

B-31

COVERING SHAPES WITH EQUAL PARTS—CUBES

DIRECTIONS: Build the equal parts with interlocking cubes. Use the parts to cover the figure on the right. Then color it to match.

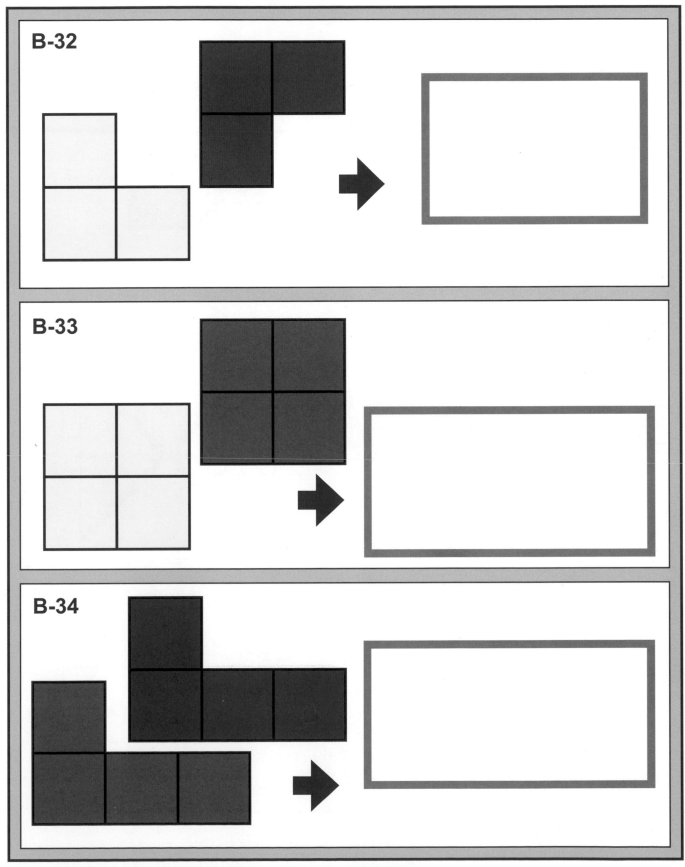

COVERING SHAPES MADE WITH CUBES

DIRECTIONS: Make each figure by joining colored interlocking cubes. Then find the figures that can be made by combining the ones that you made. Color the ones you can make. Then draw an "X" through the figures you CANNOT make.

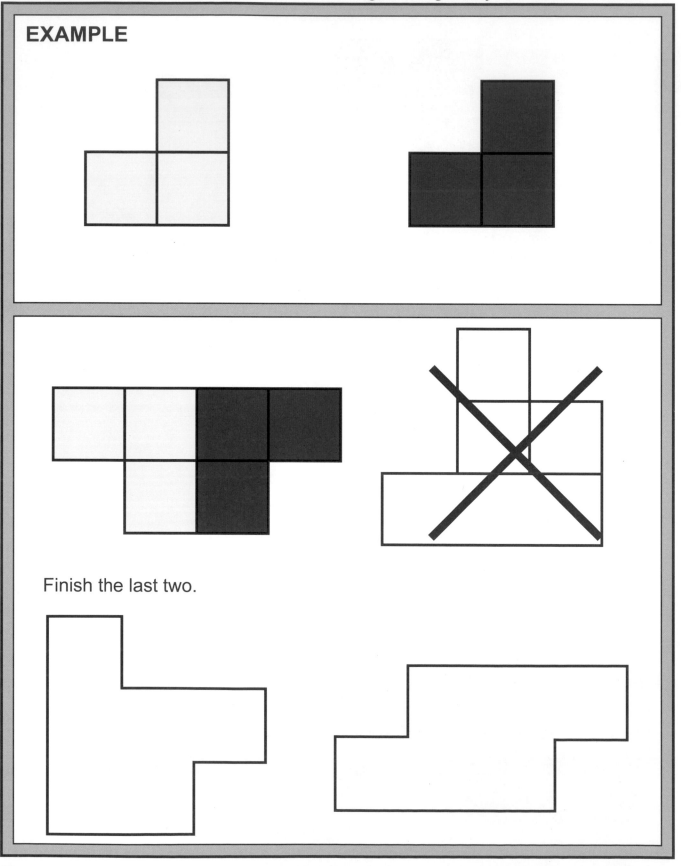

EXAMPLE

Finish the last two.

COVERING SHAPES MADE WITH CUBES

DIRECTIONS: Make each figure by joining colored interlocking cubes. Then find the figures that can be made by combining the ones that you made. Color the ones you can make. Then draw an "X" through the figures you CANNOT make.

B-35

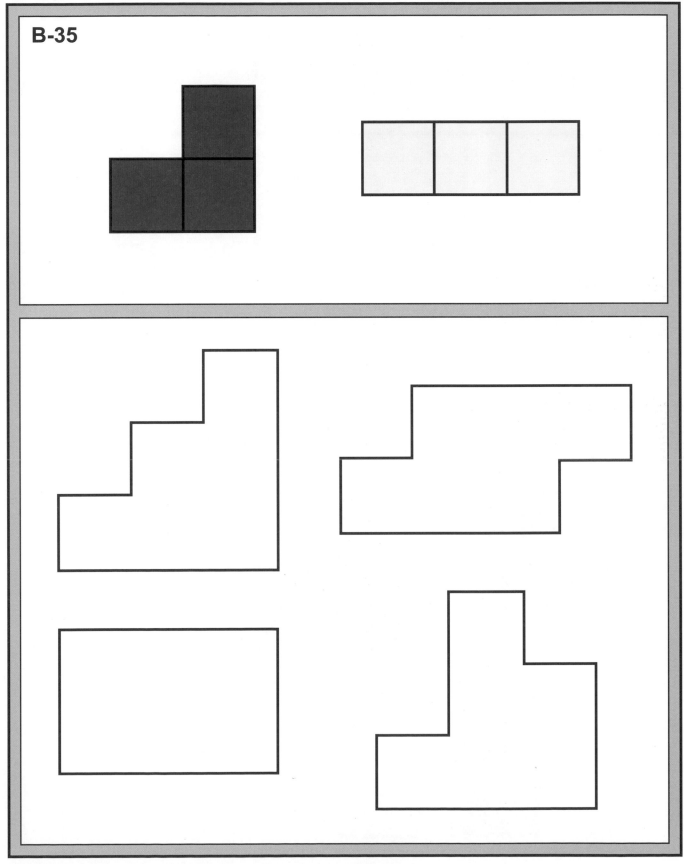

COMPARING ONE CHARACTERISTIC

DIRECTIONS: Write "S" for same or "D" for different for color, shape, and size.

EXAMPLE

COLOR: _____ S _____

SHAPE: _____ S _____

SIZE: _____ D _____

B-36

COLOR: _____

SHAPE: _____

SIZE: _____

B-37

COLOR: _____

SHAPE: _____

SIZE: _____

B-38

COLOR: _____

SHAPE: _____

SIZE: _____

COMPARING ONE CHARACTERISTIC

DIRECTIONS: Write "S" for same or "D" for different for color, shape, and size.

B-39

COLOR: _____

SHAPE: _____

SIZE: _____

B-40

COLOR: _____

SHAPE: _____

SIZE: _____

B-41

COLOR: _____

SHAPE: _____

SIZE: _____

B-42

COLOR: _____

SHAPE: _____

SIZE: _____

CHANGING ONE CHARACTERISTIC—COLOR

DIRECTIONS: In each dotted box, place an attribute block with the same SIZE and SHAPE but a different COLOR as the one on the left. Then trace the block and color it to match.

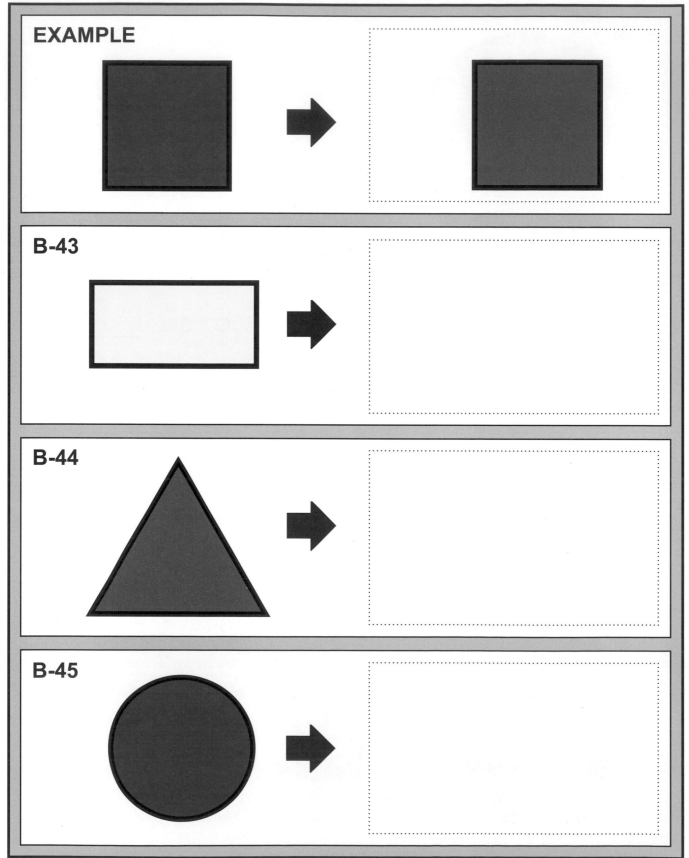

CHANGING ONE CHARACTERISTIC—SIZE

DIRECTIONS: In each dotted box, place an attribute block with the same COLOR and SHAPE but a different SIZE as the one on the left. Then trace the block and color it to match.

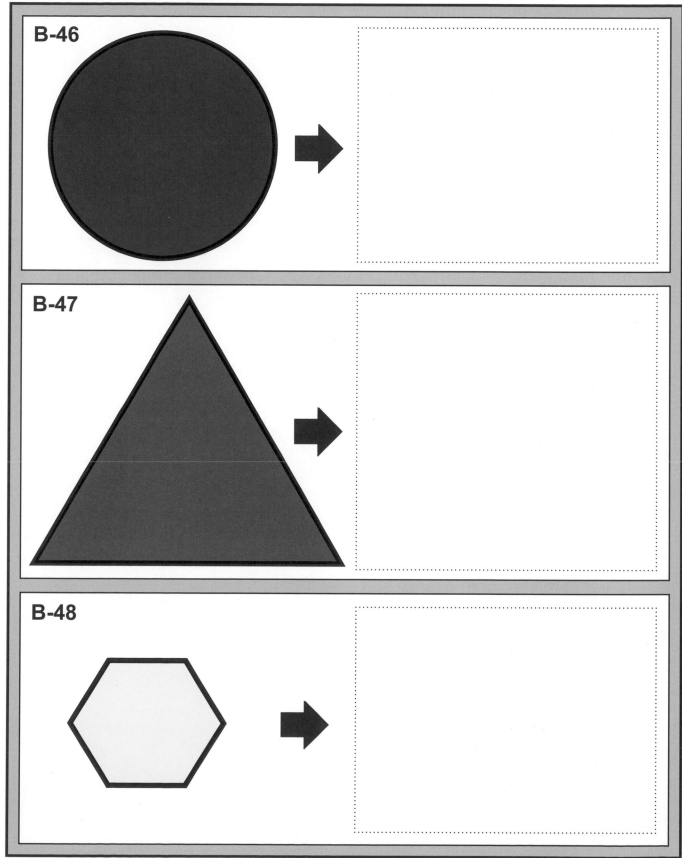

B-46

B-47

B-48

CHANGING ONE CHARACTERISTIC—SHAPE

DIRECTIONS: In each dotted box, place an attribute block with the same SIZE and COLOR but a different SHAPE as the one on the left. Trace the block and color it to match.

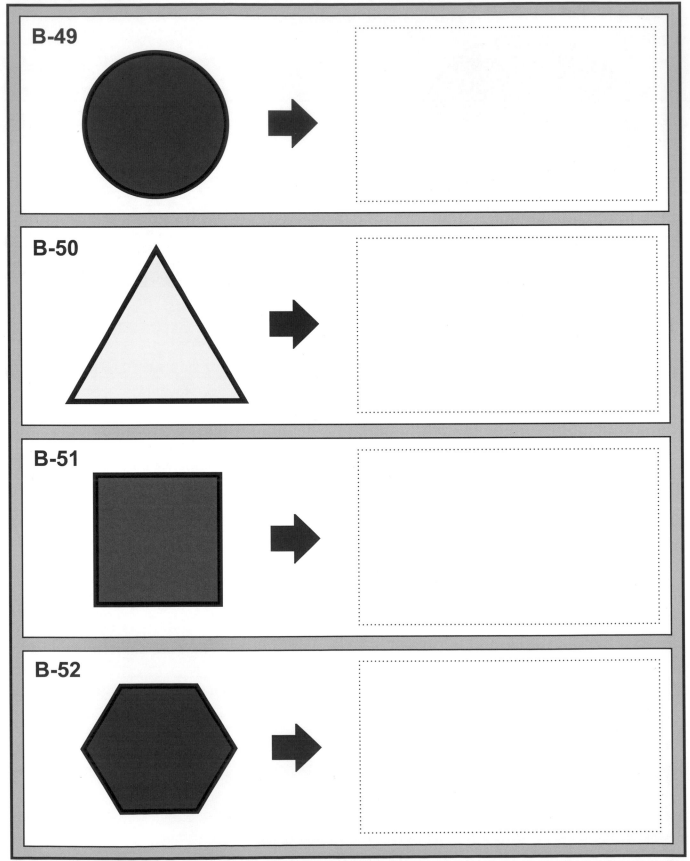

COMPARING SHAPES—EXPLAIN

DIRECTIONS: Using the words in the WORD BOX, write a sentence that describes how the shapes are ALIKE. Then trace the example.

EXAMPLE

WORD BOX
blue, circle, hexagon, small

The circle and hexagon are small and blue.

B-53

WORD BOX
red, small, square, triangle

COMPARING SHAPES—EXPLAIN

DIRECTIONS: Using the words in the WORD BOX, write a sentence that describes how the shapes are DIFFERENT.

B-54

WORD BOX

blue, red, other, square

B-55

WORD BOX

red, yellow, square, triangle

COMPARING SHAPES—EXPLAIN

DIRECTIONS: Using the words in the WORD BOX, explain how the square and triangle are alike and how they are different.

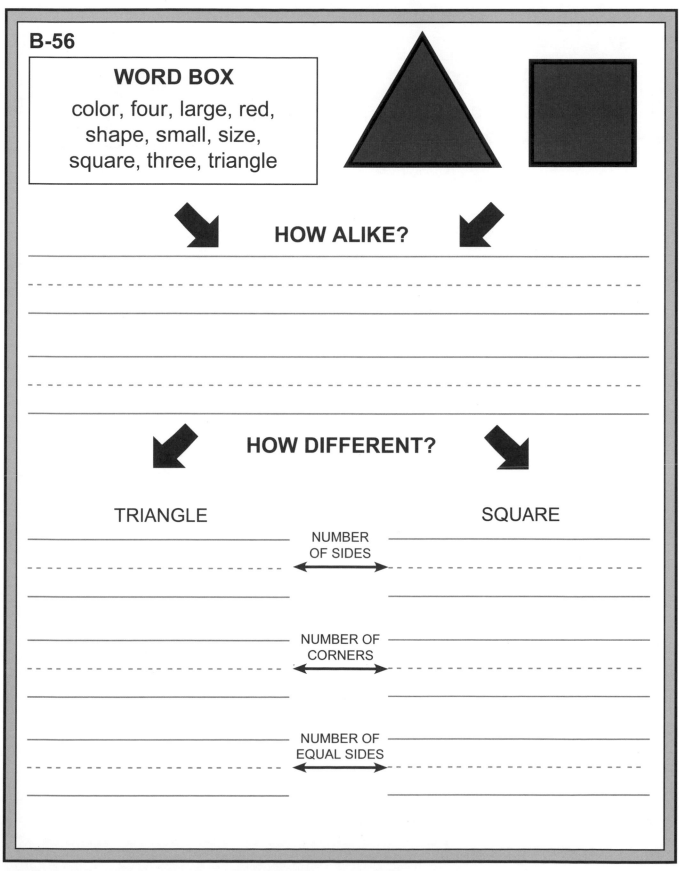

B-56

WORD BOX
color, four, large, red, shape, small, size, square, three, triangle

HOW ALIKE?

_____
- - - - - - - - - - - - - - - - - - - -
_____
- - - - - - - - - - - - - - - - - - - -
_____

HOW DIFFERENT?

TRIANGLE   SQUARE

_____ NUMBER _____
- - - - - - - - - - OF SIDES - - - - - - - - - -
_____ ←——→ _____

_____ NUMBER OF _____
- - - - - - - - - - CORNERS - - - - - - - - - -
_____ ←——→ _____

_____ NUMBER OF _____
- - - - - - - - - - EQUAL SIDES - - - - - - - - - -
_____ ←——→ _____

COMPARING SHAPES—EXPLAIN

DIRECTIONS: Using the words in the WORD BOX, explain how the two squares are alike and how they are different.

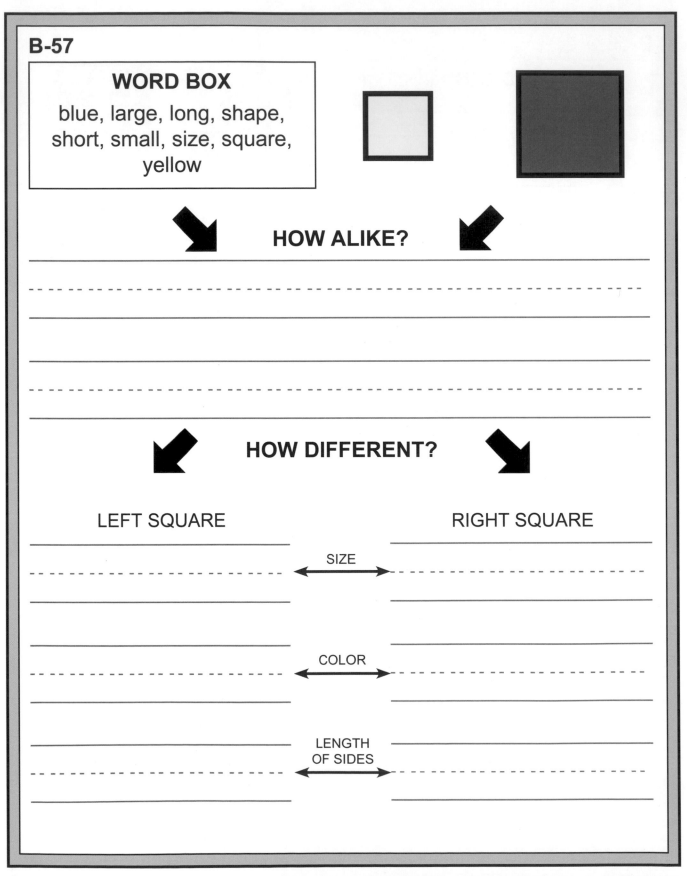

B-57

WORD BOX
blue, large, long, shape,
short, small, size, square,
yellow

HOW ALIKE?

HOW DIFFERENT?

LEFT SQUARE   RIGHT SQUARE

SIZE

COLOR

LENGTH
OF SIDES

Chapter Three
Figural Sequences

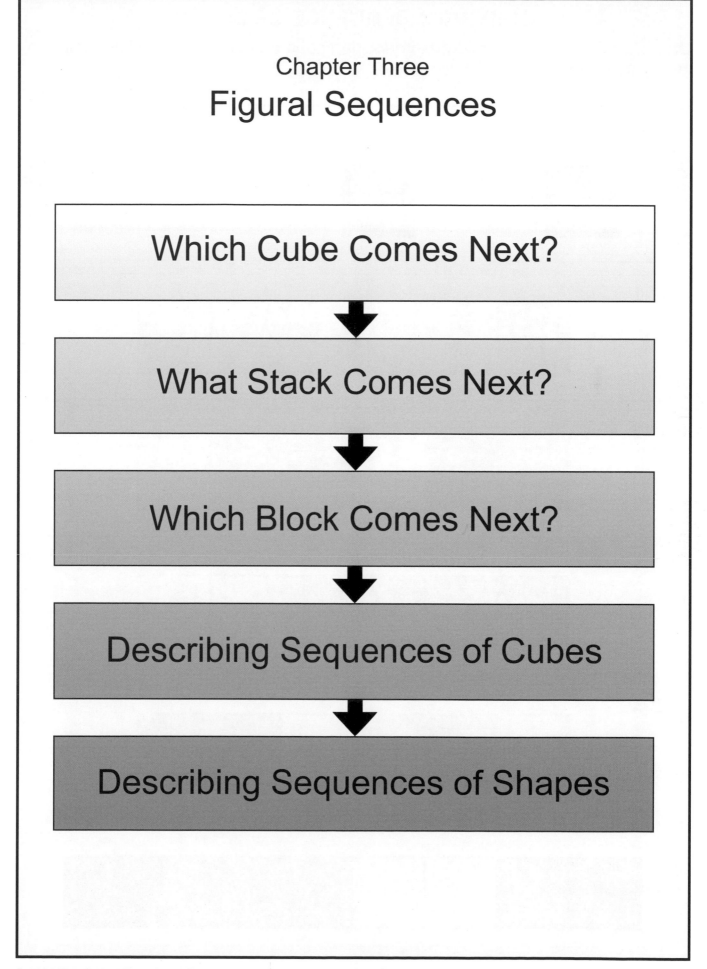

Which Cube Comes Next?

What Stack Comes Next?

Which Block Comes Next?

Describing Sequences of Cubes

Describing Sequences of Shapes

COPYING A SEQUENCE OF CUBES

DIRECTIONS: Place a colored interlocking cube on each square. Then join the cubes together to make the sequence.

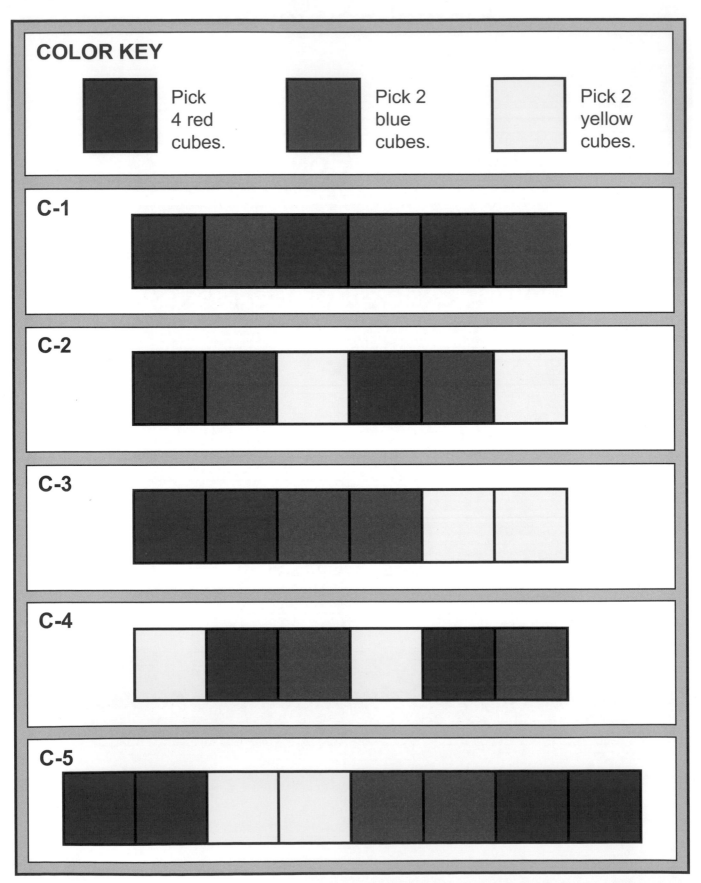

© 2008 The Critical Thinking Co™ • www.CriticalThinking.com • 800-458-4849

WHICH CUBE COMES NEXT?

DIRECTIONS: Make each sequence with interlocking cubes. Add a cube that comes next in the sequence. Then color the last space to match the cube you added.

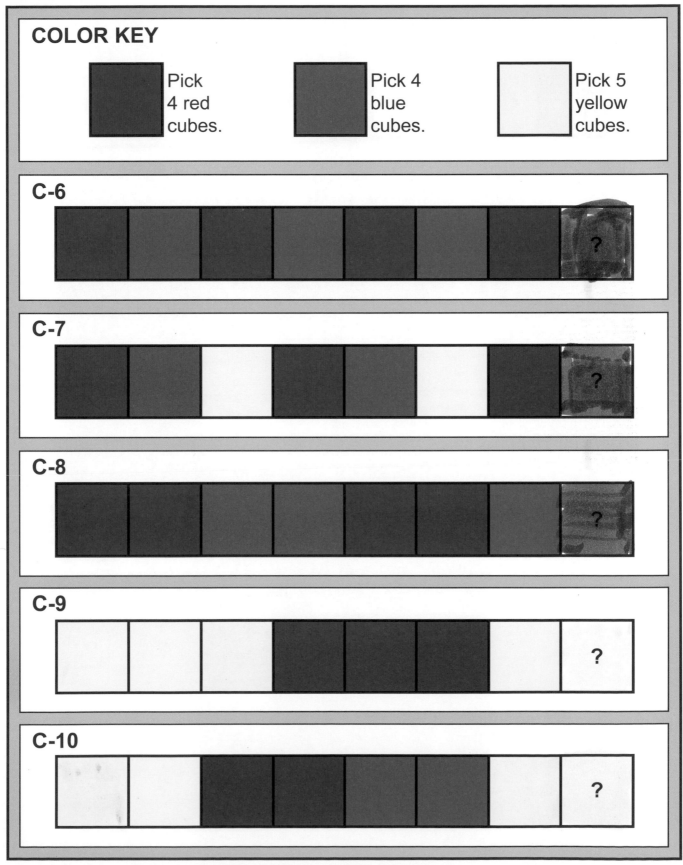

COLOR KEY

Pick 4 red cubes.

Pick 4 blue cubes.

Pick 5 yellow cubes.

C-6

C-7

C-8

C-9

C-10

WHICH CUBE COMES NEXT?

DIRECTIONS: Make each sequence with interlocking cubes. Add the cubes that come next in the sequence. Then color the last two spaces to match the cubes you added.

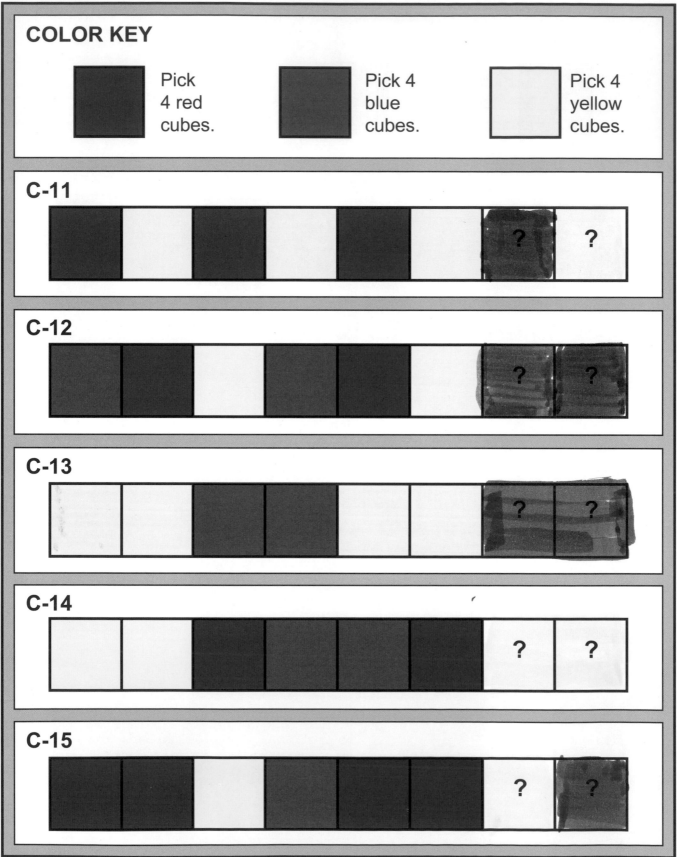

COLOR KEY

Pick 4 red cubes.

Pick 4 blue cubes.

Pick 4 yellow cubes.

C-11

C-12

C-13

C-14

C-15

WHICH STACK COMES NEXT?

DIRECTIONS: Using interlocking cubes, make the first stack of cubes. Add or take away the cube that comes next. Then draw your stacks in the blank boxes.

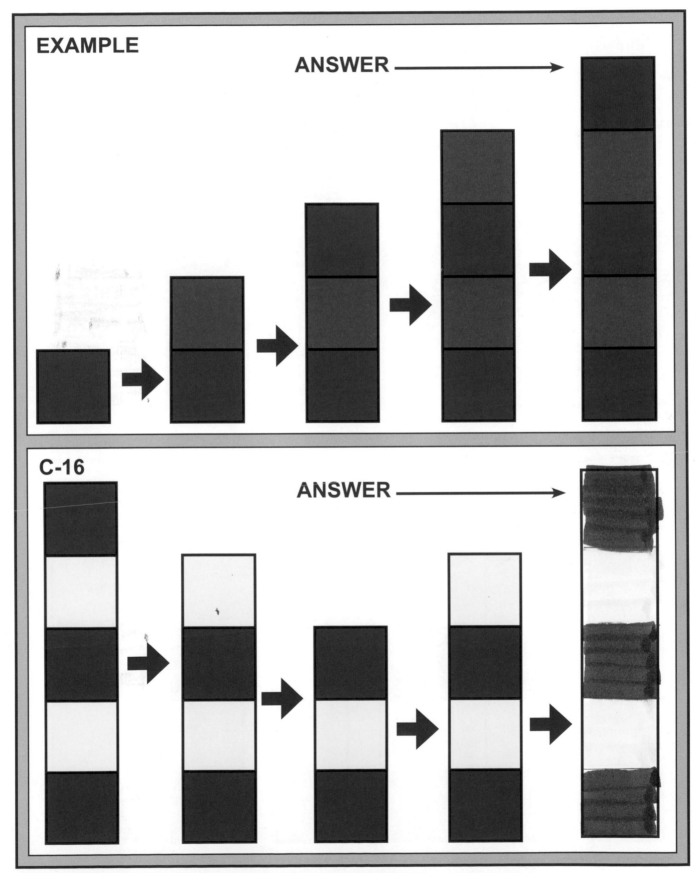

EXAMPLE

ANSWER ———————————➤

C-16

ANSWER ———————————➤

WHICH STACK COMES NEXT?

DIRECTIONS: Using interlocking cubes, make the first stack of cubes. Add or take away the cube that comes next. Then draw your stacks in the blank boxes.

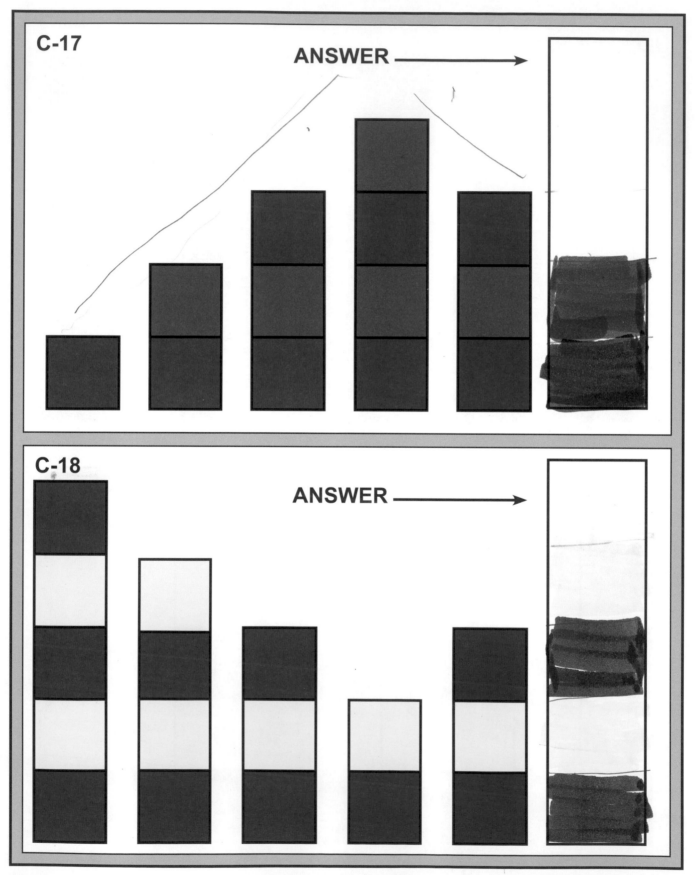

WHICH STACK COMES NEXT?

DIRECTIONS: Using interlocking cubes, make the first stack of cubes. Add or take away the cube that comes next. Then draw your stacks in the blank boxes.

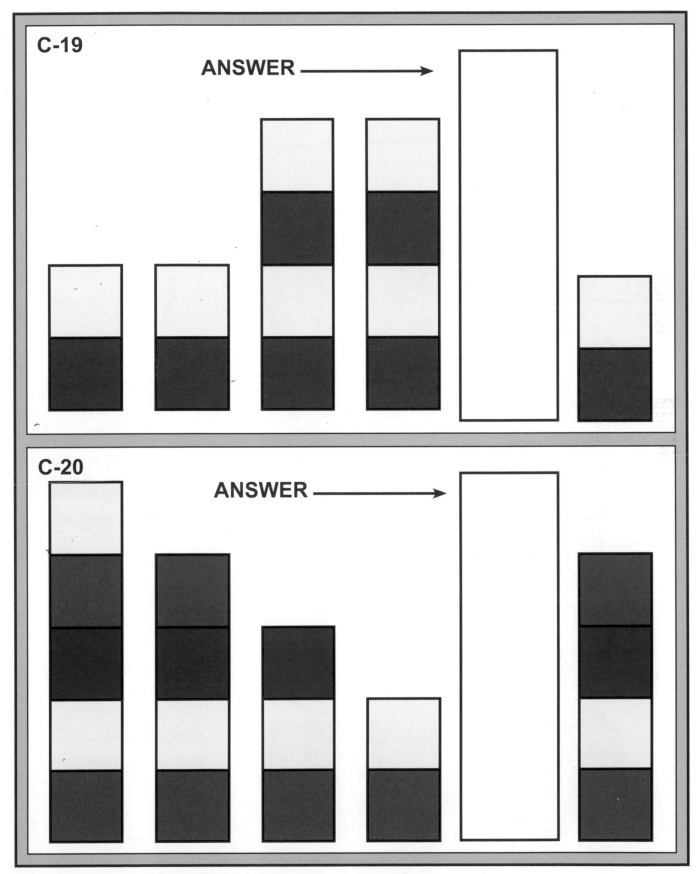

WHICH BLOCK COMES NEXT?

DIRECTIONS: Find the attribute block that comes next. Place it in the empty space. Then trace around the block and color it the same color.

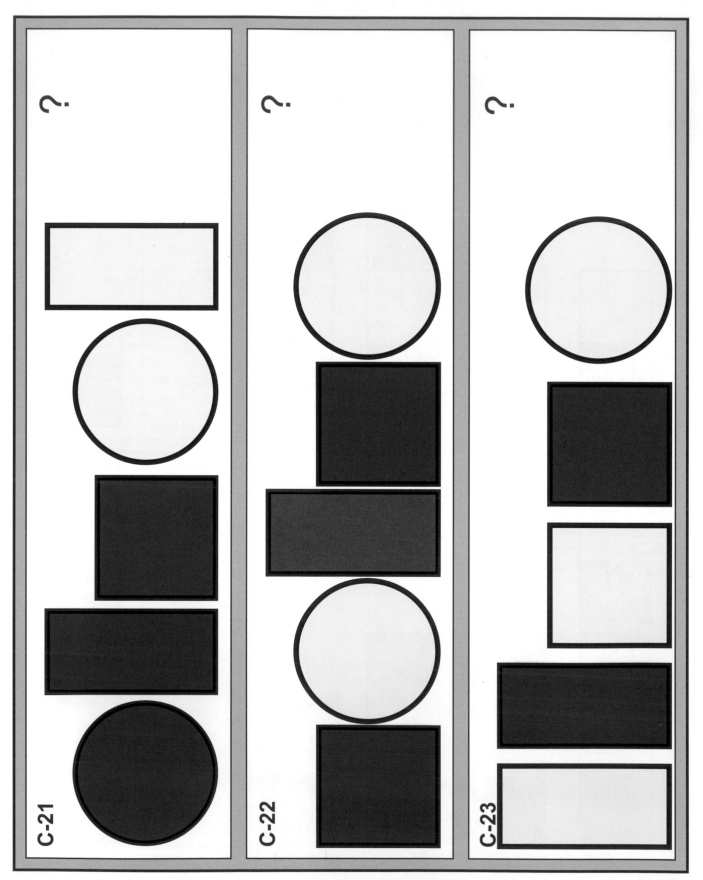

C-21

C-22

C-23

WHICH BLOCK COMES NEXT?

DIRECTIONS: Find the attribute block that comes next. Place it in the empty space. Then trace around the block and color it the same color.

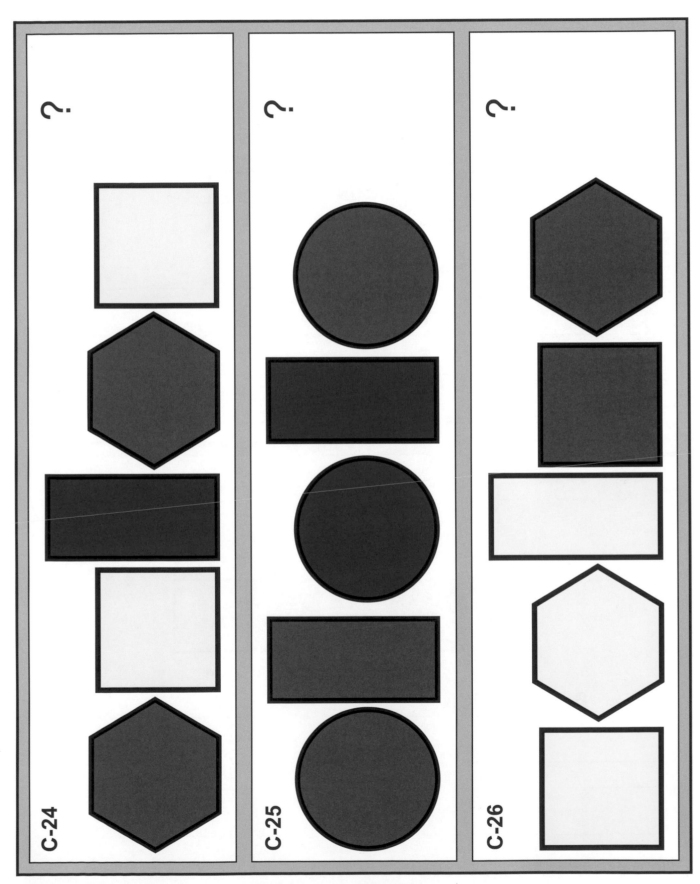

DESCRIBING SEQUENCES OF CUBES

DIRECTIONS: Using the words in the WORD BOX, describe the sequence. Then trace the example.

EXAMPLE

WORD BOX

blue, sequence, red

DESCRIPTION:

This sequence is red, blue, red, blue.

C-27

WORD BOX

red, sequence, yellow

DESCRIPTION:

DESCRIBING SEQUENCES OF CUBES

DIRECTIONS: Using the words in the WORD BOX, describe the sequence.

C-28

WORD BOX

blue, red, sequence, yellow

DESCRIPTION:

C-29

WORD BOX

blue, red, sequence, yellow

DESCRIPTION:

DESCRIBING SEQUENCES OF SHAPES

DIRECTIONS: Using the words in the WORD BOX, write a sentence that describes the sequence. Then trace the example.

EXAMPLE

WORD BOX

yellow, sequence, circle, square

DESCRIPTION:

This sequence of yellow shapes is square, circle, square, circle.

C-30

WORD BOX

red, sequence, square, triangle

DESCRIPTION:

DESCRIBING SEQUENCES OF SHAPES

DIRECTIONS: Using the words in the WORD BOX, write a sentence that describes the sequence.

C-31

WORD BOX
circle, red,
sequence, yellow

DESCRIPTION:

C-32

WORD BOX
blue, large, sequence, small, square

DESCRIPTION:

DESCRIBING SEQUENCES OF SHAPES

DIRECTIONS: Using the words in the WORD BOX, write a sentence that describes the sequence.

C-33

WORD BOX

blue, circle, large, sequence, small, yellow

DESCRIPTION:

C-34

WORD BOX

circle, large, red, sequence, square, yellow

DESCRIPTION:

DESCRIBING SEQUENCES OF SHAPES

DIRECTIONS: Using the words in the WORD BOX, write a sentence that describes the sequence.

C-31

WORD BOX
circle, red,
sequence, yellow

DESCRIPTION:

_____

- -

_____

- -

_____

- -

C-32

WORD BOX
blue, large, sequence, small, square

DESCRIPTION:

- -

_____

- -

_____

- -

DESCRIBING SEQUENCES OF SHAPES

DIRECTIONS: Using the words in the WORD BOX, write a sentence that describes the sequence.

C-33

WORD BOX

blue, circle, large, sequence, small, yellow

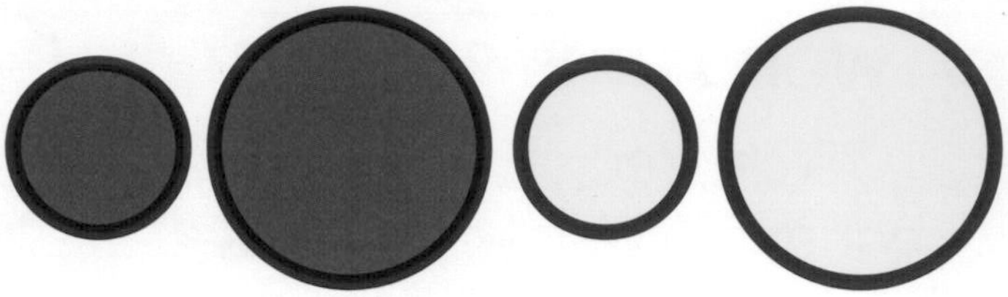

DESCRIPTION:

C-34

WORD BOX

circle, large, red, sequence, square, yellow

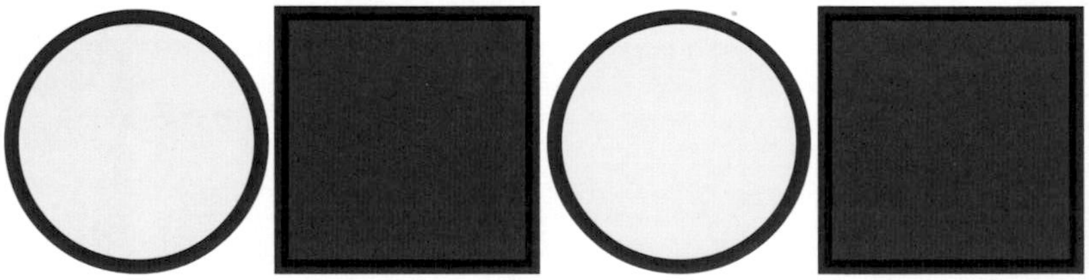

DESCRIPTION:

Chapter Four
Figural Classifications

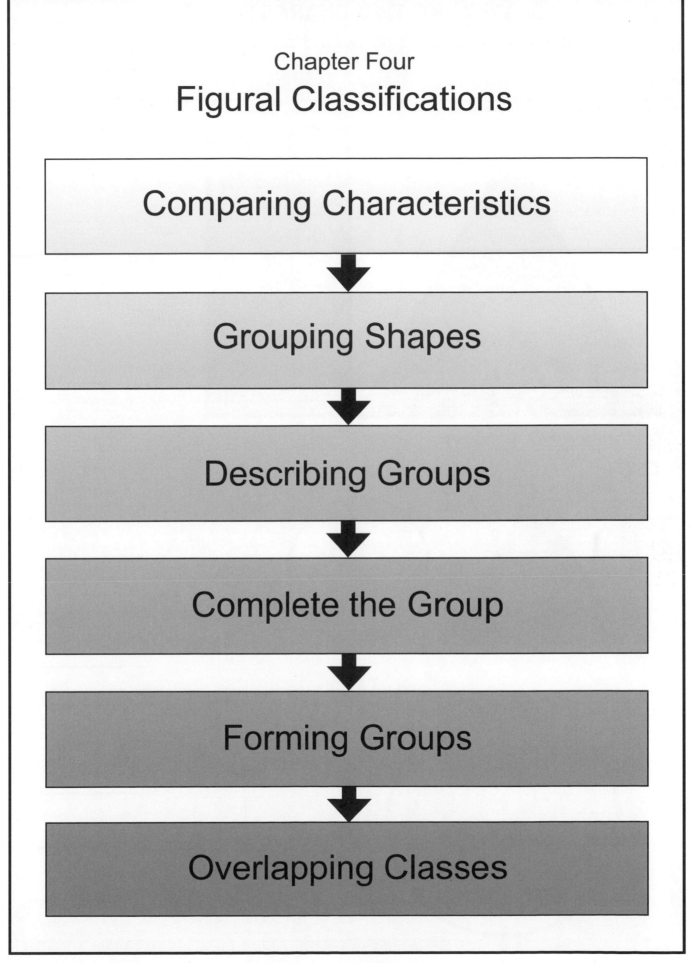

Comparing Characteristics

Grouping Shapes

Describing Groups

Complete the Group

Forming Groups

Overlapping Classes

COMPARING TWO CHARACTERISTICS

DIRECTIONS: Write "S" for same or "D" for different for color, shape, and size.

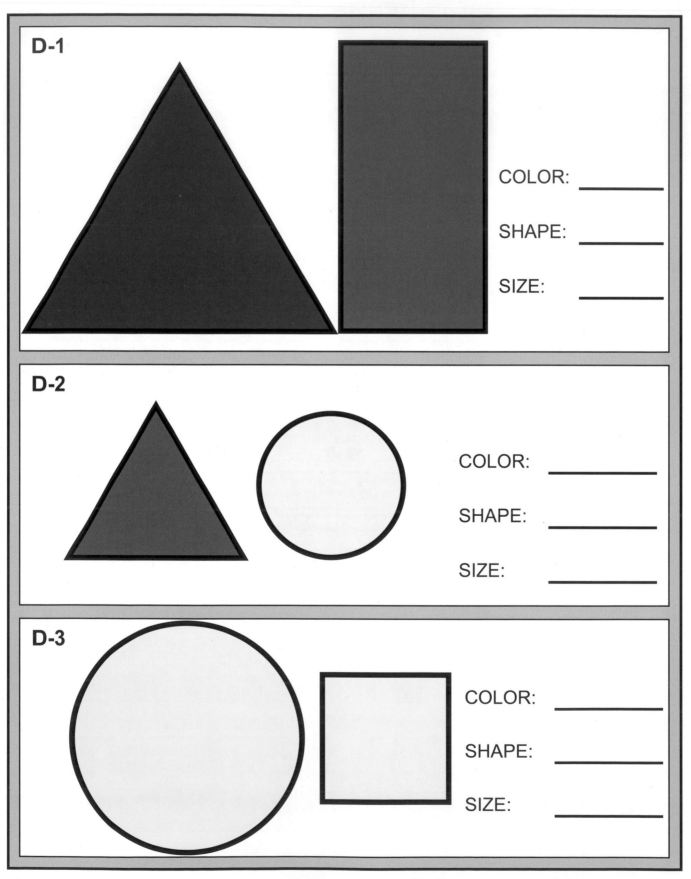

D-1

COLOR: _____

SHAPE: _____

SIZE: _____

D-2

COLOR: _____

SHAPE: _____

SIZE: _____

D-3

COLOR: _____

SHAPE: _____

SIZE: _____

COMPARING TWO CHARACTERISTICS

DIRECTIONS: Write "S" for same or "D" for different for color, shape, and size.

D-4

COLOR: _____

SHAPE: _____

SIZE: _____

D-5

COLOR: _____

SHAPE: _____

SIZE: _____

D-6

COLOR: _____

SHAPE: _____

SIZE: _____

D-7

COLOR: _____

SHAPE: _____

SIZE: _____

CHANGING TWO CHARACTERISTICS—COLOR AND SHAPE

DIRECTIONS: In each dotted box, place an attribute block with a different COLOR and a different SHAPE. Then trace the block and color the drawing to match.

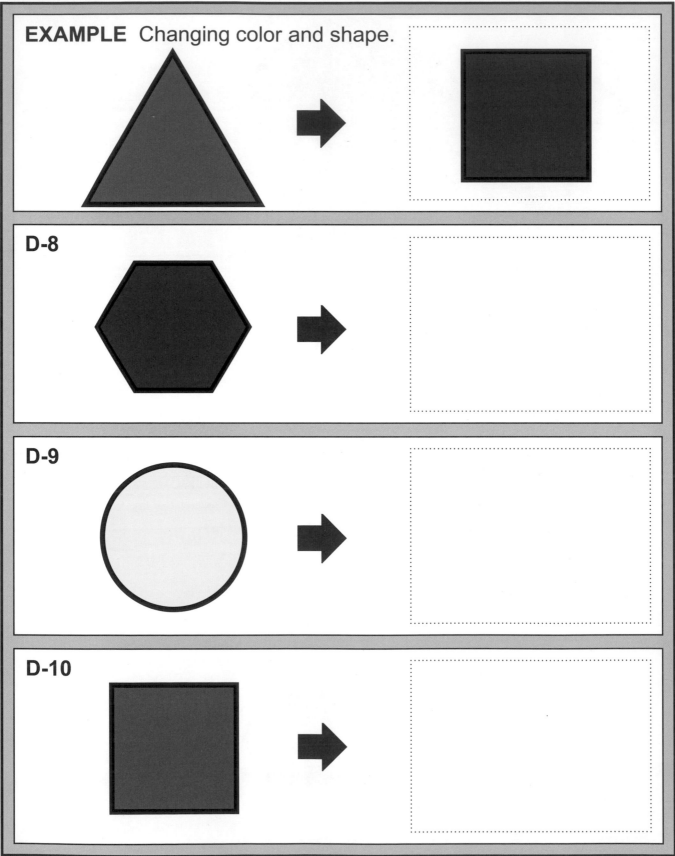

EXAMPLE Changing color and shape.

D-8

D-9

D-10

CHANGING TWO CHARACTERISTICS—SIZE AND SHAPE

DIRECTIONS: In each dotted box, place an attribute block with a different SIZE and a different SHAPE. Then trace the block and color the drawing to match.

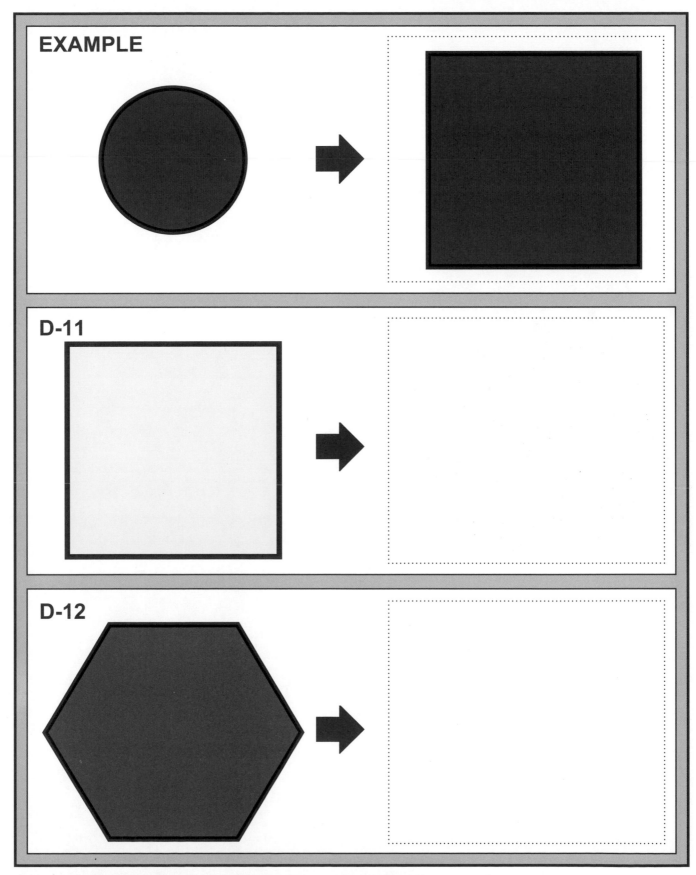

EXAMPLE

D-11

D-12

CHANGING TWO CHARACTERISTICS—SIZE AND SHAPE

DIRECTIONS: In each dotted box, place an attribute block with a different SIZE and a different SHAPE. Then trace the block and color the drawing to match.

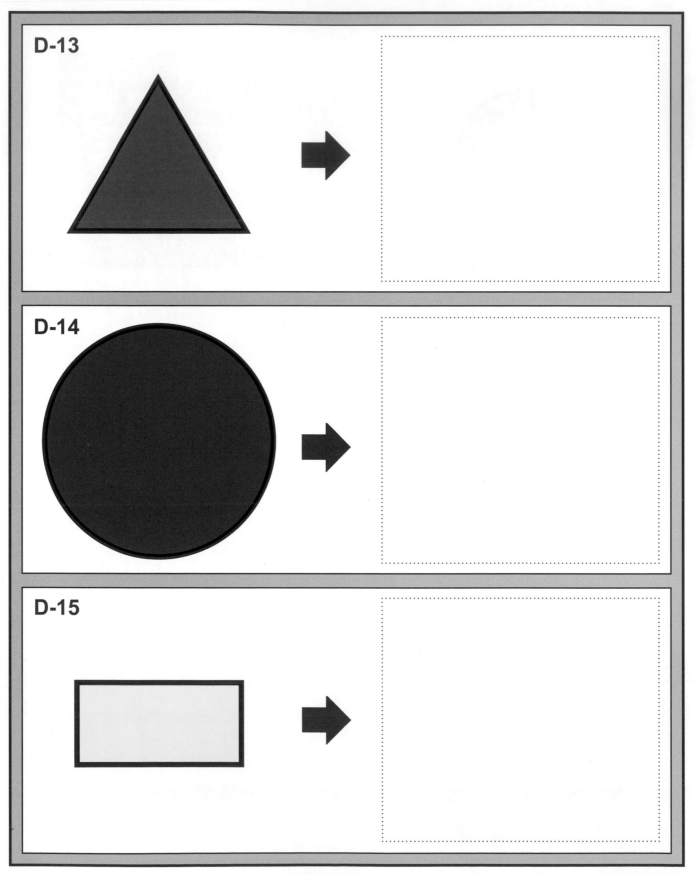

CHANGING TWO CHARACTERISTICS—SIZE AND COLOR

DIRECTIONS: In each dotted box, place an attribute block with a different SIZE and a different COLOR. Then trace the block and color the drawing to match.

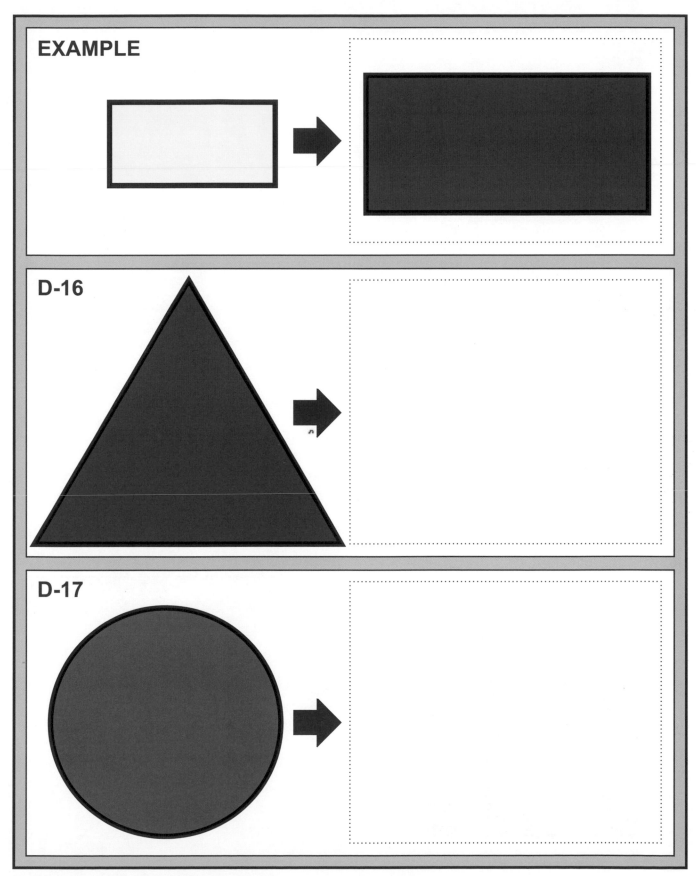

EXAMPLE

D-16

D-17

CHANGING TWO CHARACTERISTICS—SIZE AND COLOR

DIRECTIONS: In each dotted box, place an attribute block with a different SIZE and a different COLOR. Then trace the block and color the drawing to match.

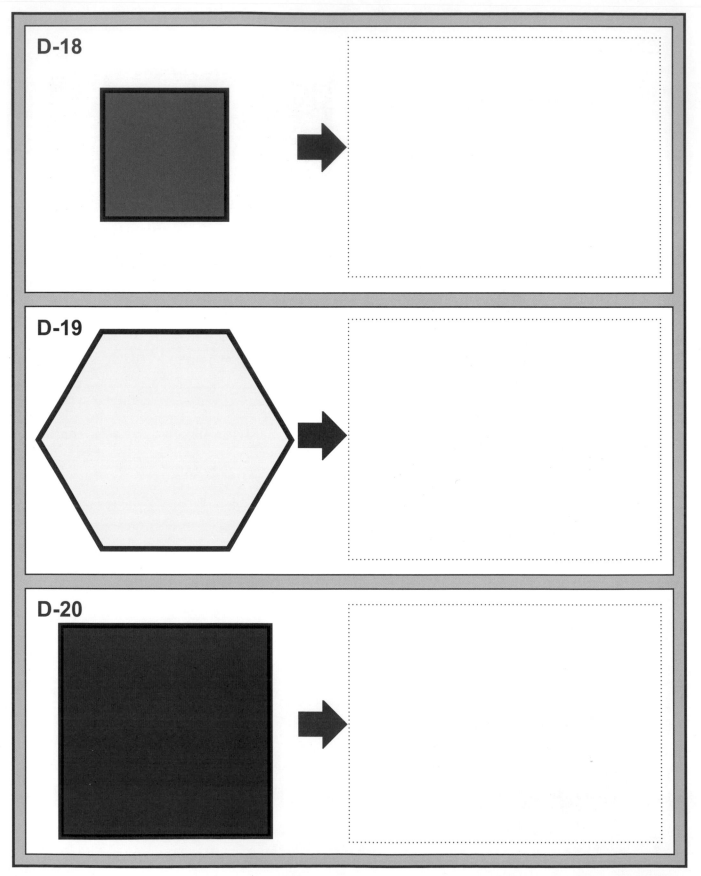

D-18

D-19

D-20

GROUPING BY SHAPE

DIRECTIONS: In each box, place two other attribute blocks that are the SAME SHAPE. Then trace around the blocks and color the drawings to match.

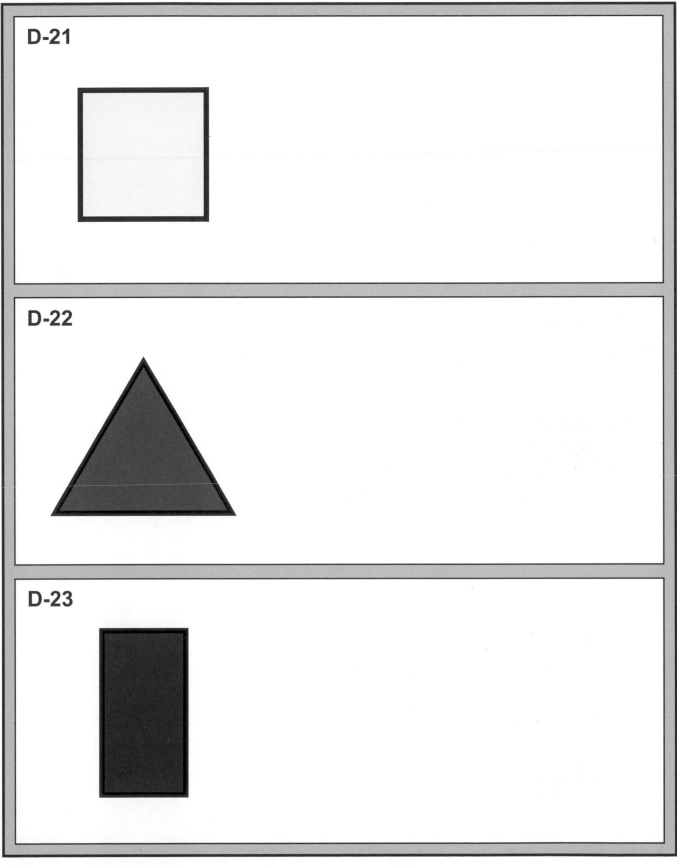

D-21

D-22

D-23

GROUPING BY COLOR

DIRECTIONS: In each box, place two other attribute blocks that are the SAME COLOR. Then trace around the blocks and color the drawings to match.

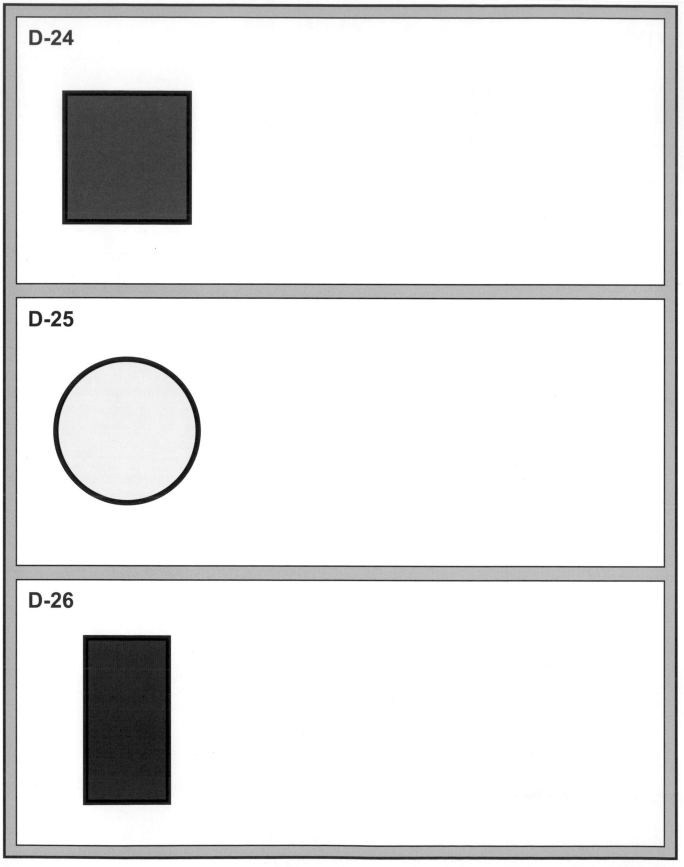

D-24

D-25

D-26

GROUPING BY SIZE

DIRECTIONS: In each box, place two other attribute blocks that are the SAME SIZE. Then trace around the blocks and color the drawings to match.

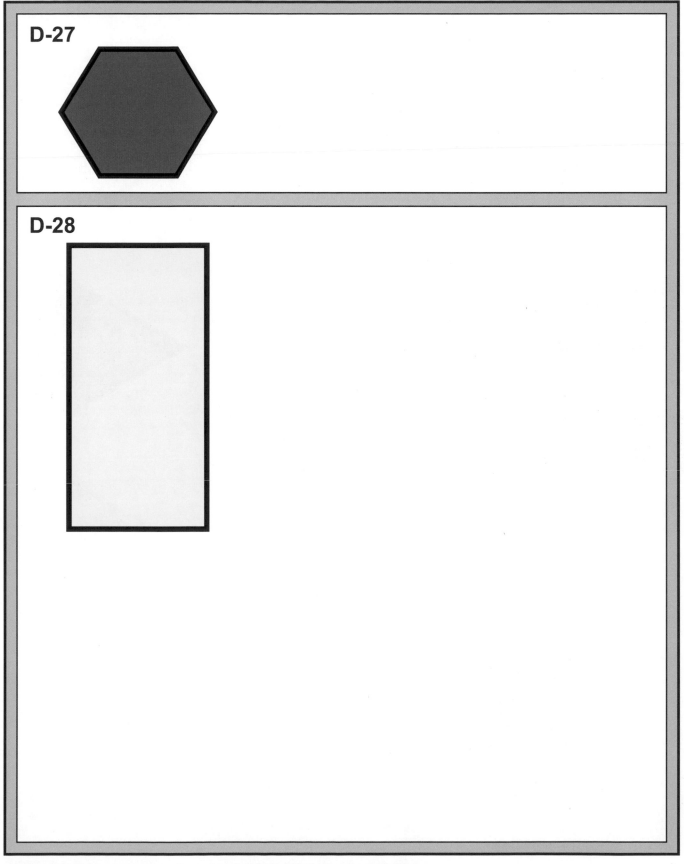

D-27

D-28

DESCRIBING A GROUP—WHAT BELONGS?

DIRECTIONS: Draw a line from each block on the right to the group in which it belongs.

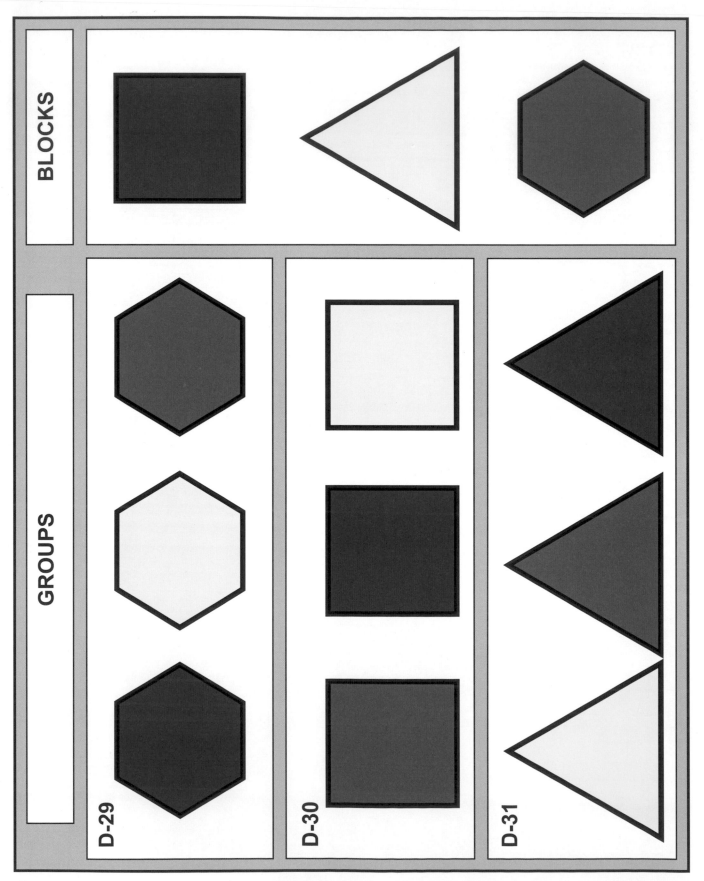

BLOCKS

GROUPS

D-29

D-30

D-31

© 2008 The Critical Thinking Co™ • www.CriticalThinking.com • 800-458-4849

DESCRIBING A GROUP—WHAT BELONGS?

DIRECTIONS: Draw a line from each block on the right to the group in which it belongs.

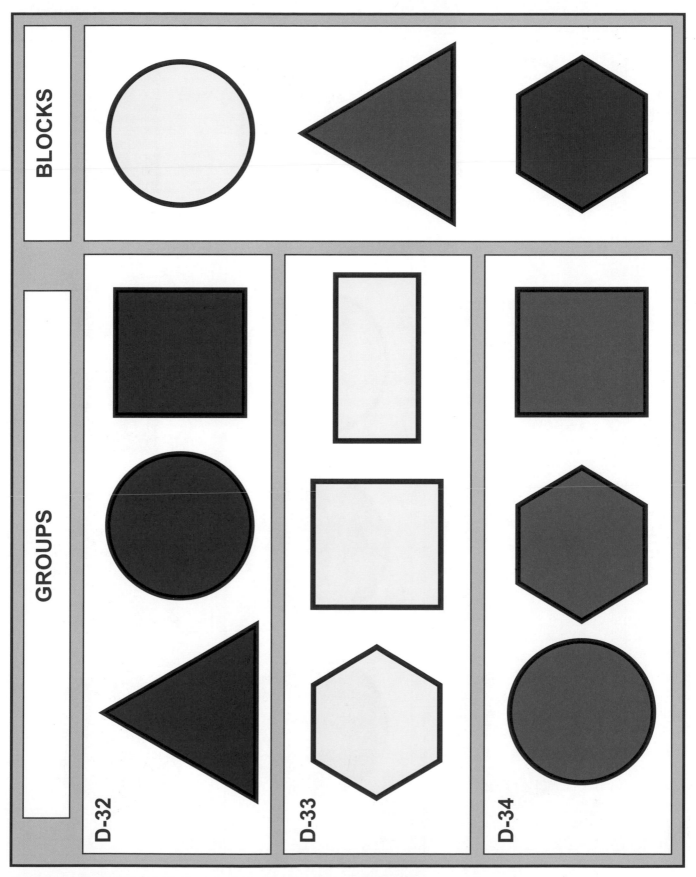

BLOCKS

GROUPS

D-32

D-33

D-34

DESCRIBING A GROUP—WHAT BELONGS?

DIRECTIONS: Draw a line from each block on the right to the group in which it belongs.

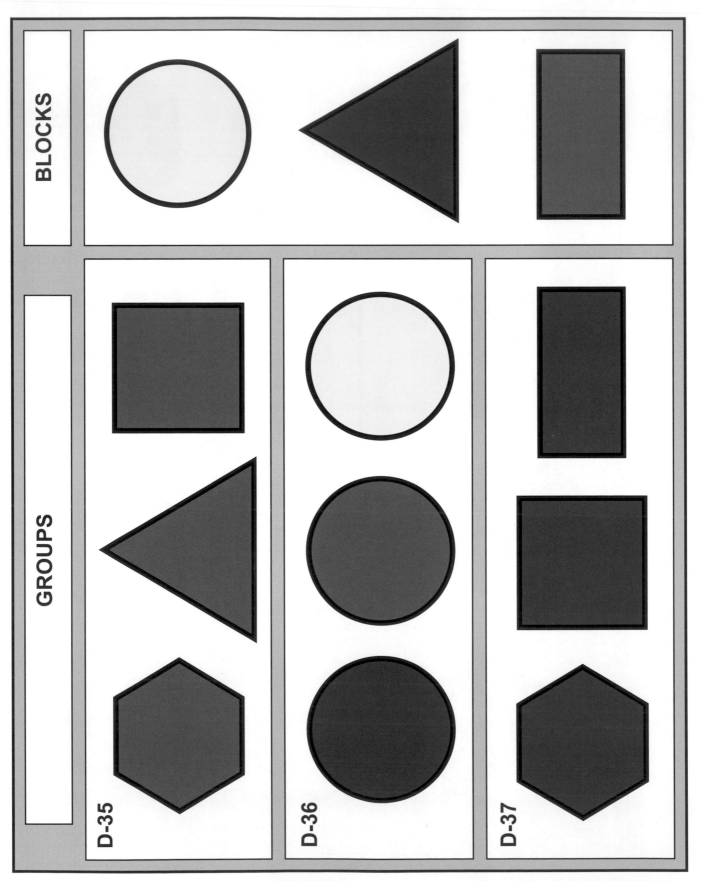

BLOCKS

GROUPS

D-35

D-36

D-37

WHICH BLOCK DOES NOT BELONG?

DIRECTIONS: Draw an "X" through the drawing of the block that DOES NOT belong to the group.

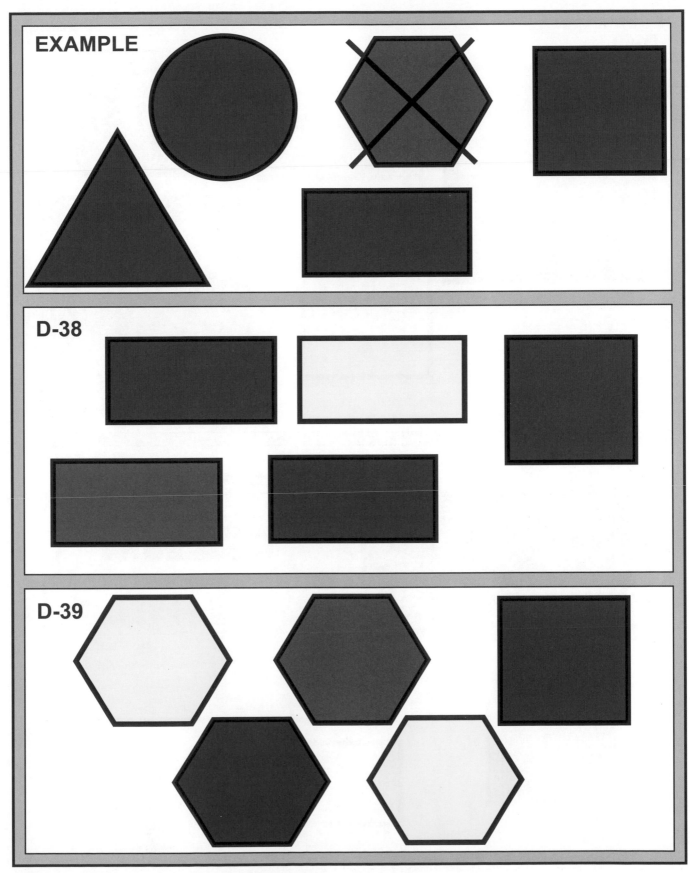

EXAMPLE

D-38

D-39

WHICH BLOCK DOES NOT BELONG?

DIRECTIONS: Draw an "X" through the drawing of the block that DOES NOT belong to the group.

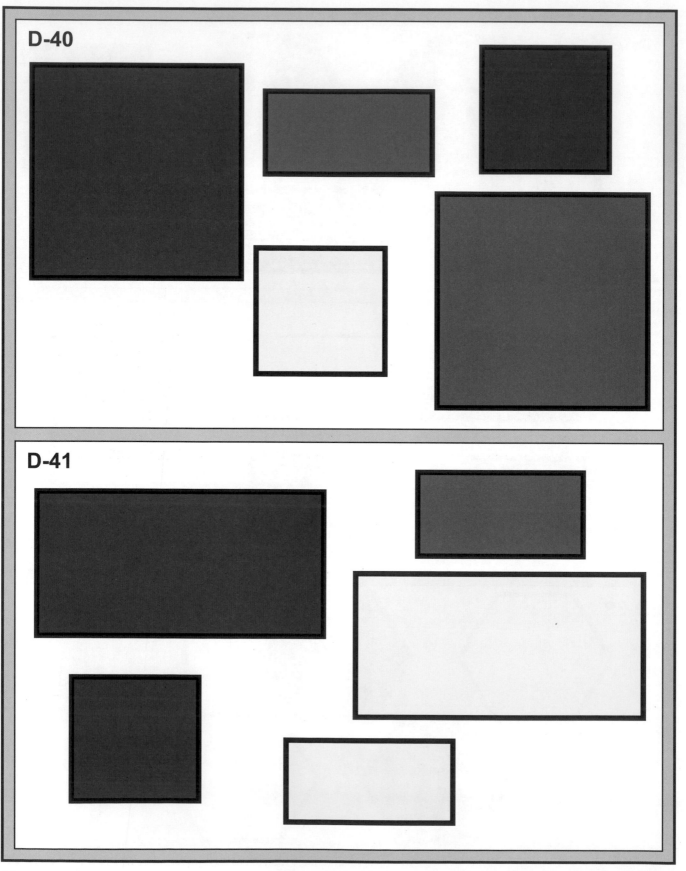

DESCRIBING A GROUP—ADDING SHAPES

DIRECTIONS: In each box, add one more attribute block that belongs to the group. Then trace the block you add and color the drawing to match.

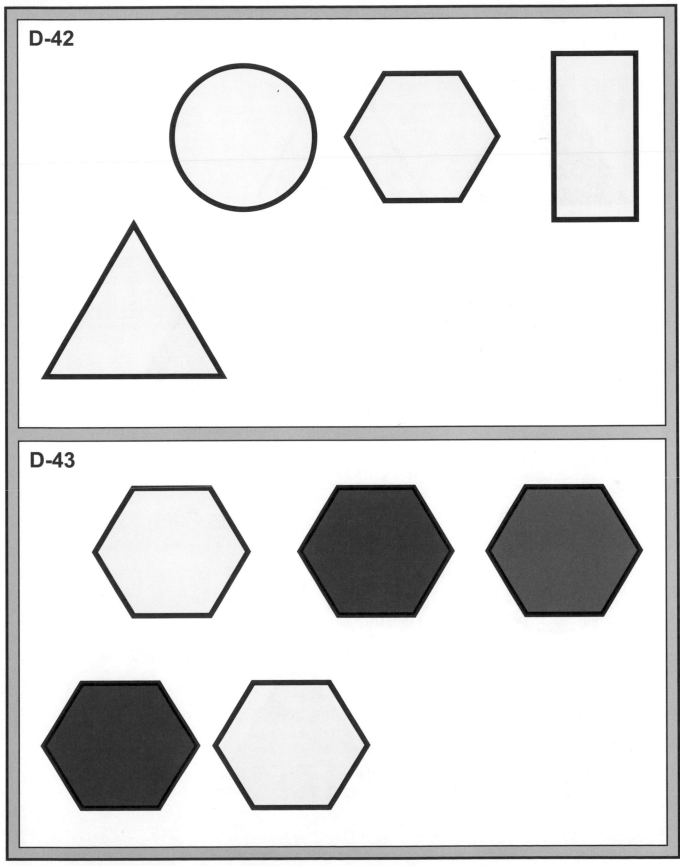

DESCRIBING A GROUP—ADDING SHAPES

DIRECTIONS: In each box, add one more attribute block that belongs to the group. Then trace the block you add and color the drawing to match.

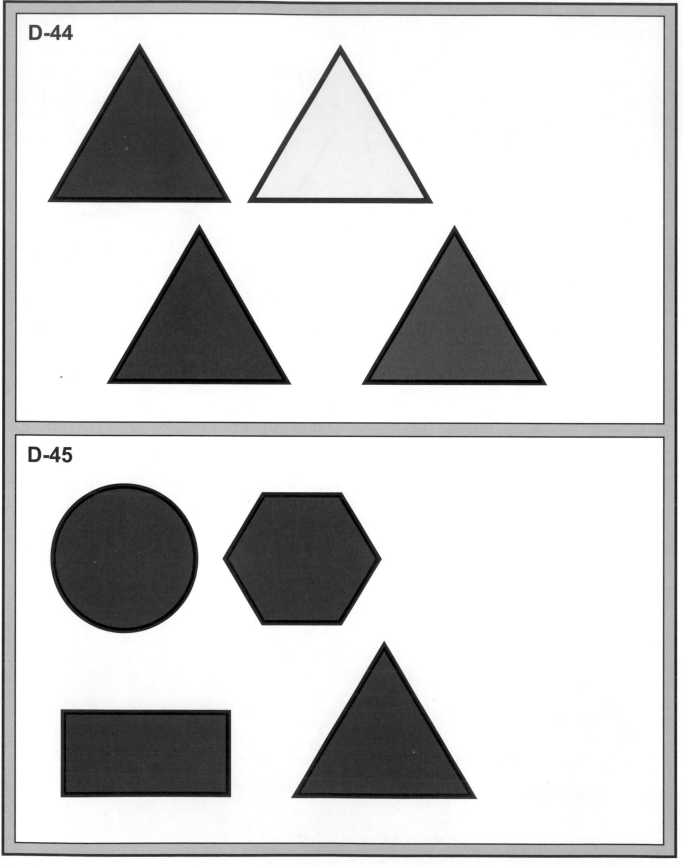

D-44

D-45

DESCRIBING A GROUP—WHAT BELONGS?

DIRECTIONS: Draw a line from each block to the group in which it belongs.

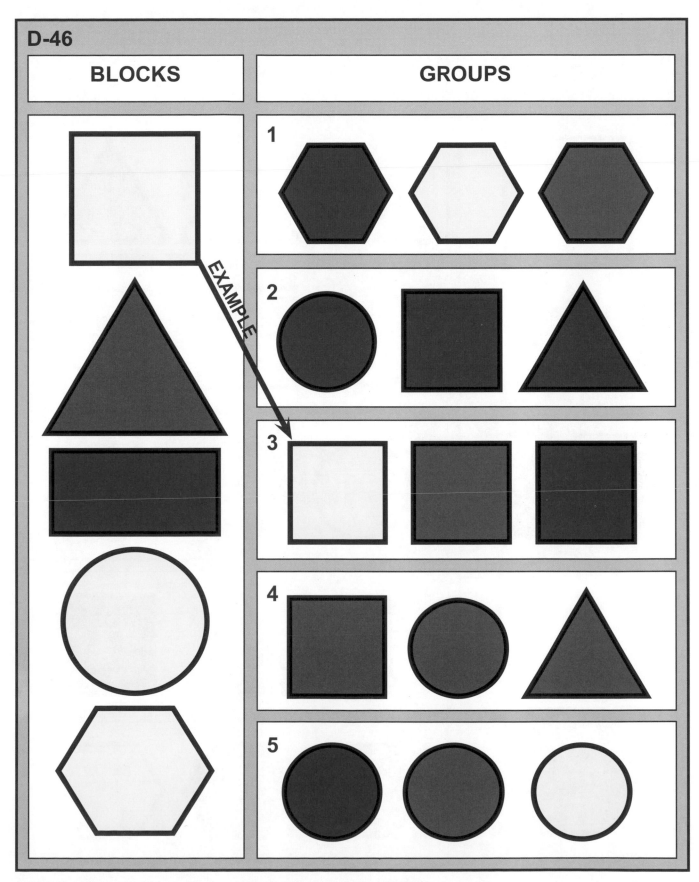

DESCRIBING A GROUP—WHAT BELONGS?

DIRECTIONS: Draw a line from each block to the group in which it belongs.

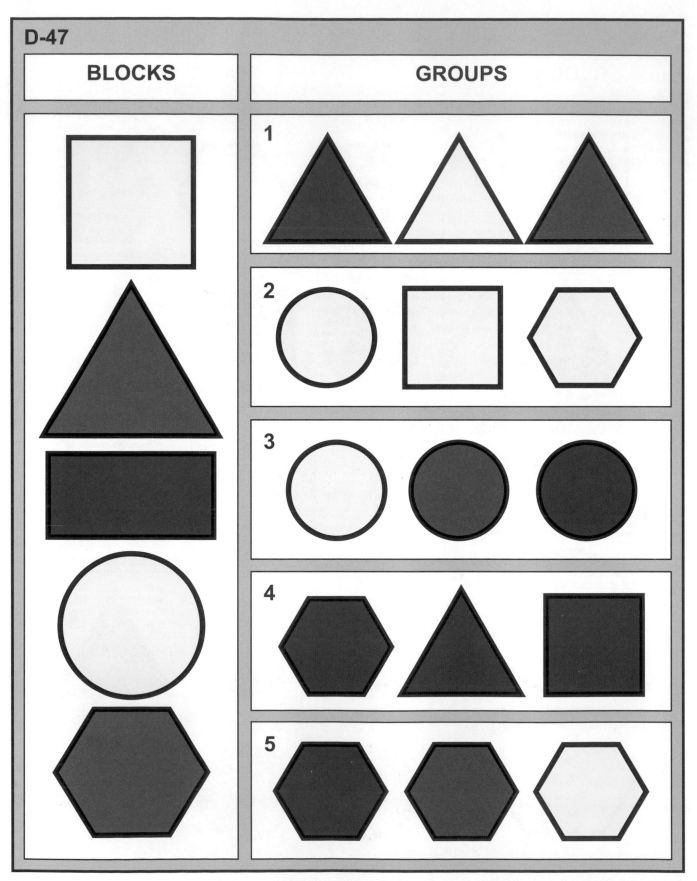

DESCRIBING A GROUP—WHAT BELONGS?

DIRECTIONS: Draw a line from each block to the group in which it belongs.

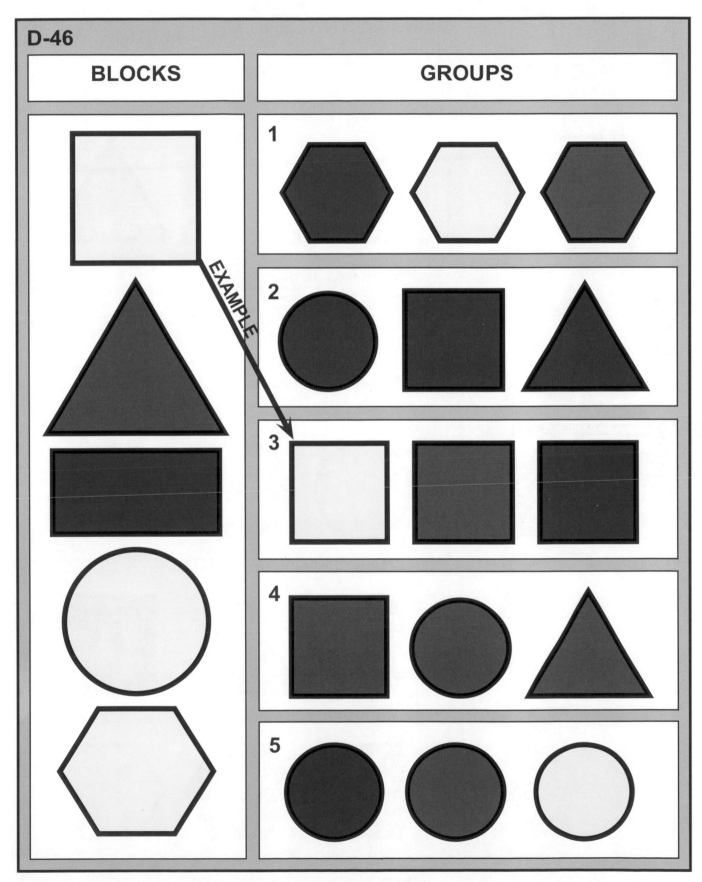

DESCRIBING A GROUP—WHAT BELONGS?

DIRECTIONS: Draw a line from each block to the group in which it belongs.

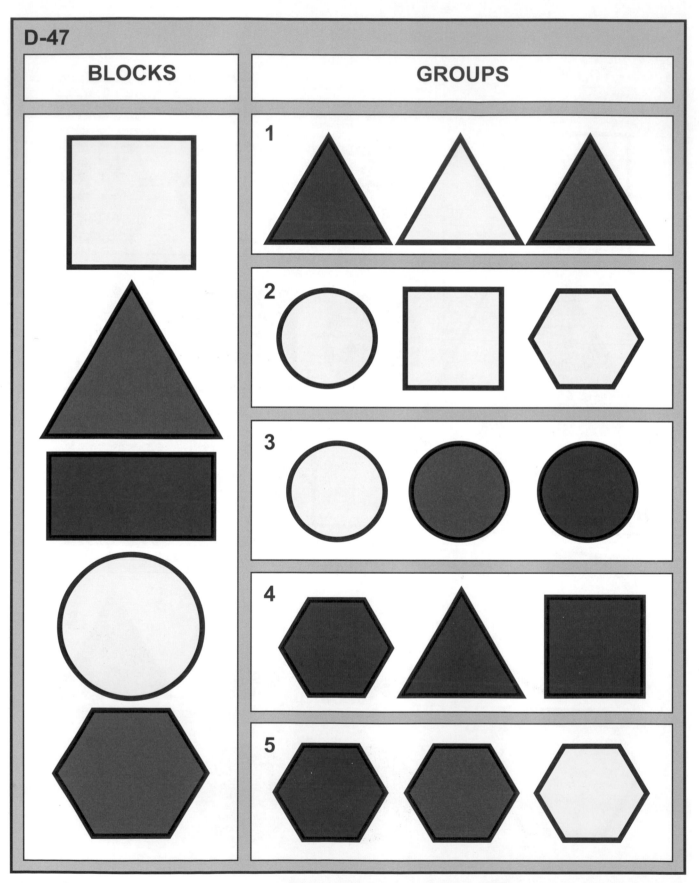

SORTING BLOCKS

DIRECTIONS: Place attribute blocks on the shapes in the top box. Move all the red shapes into the left box and the blue shapes into the right box. Then trace and color them to match.

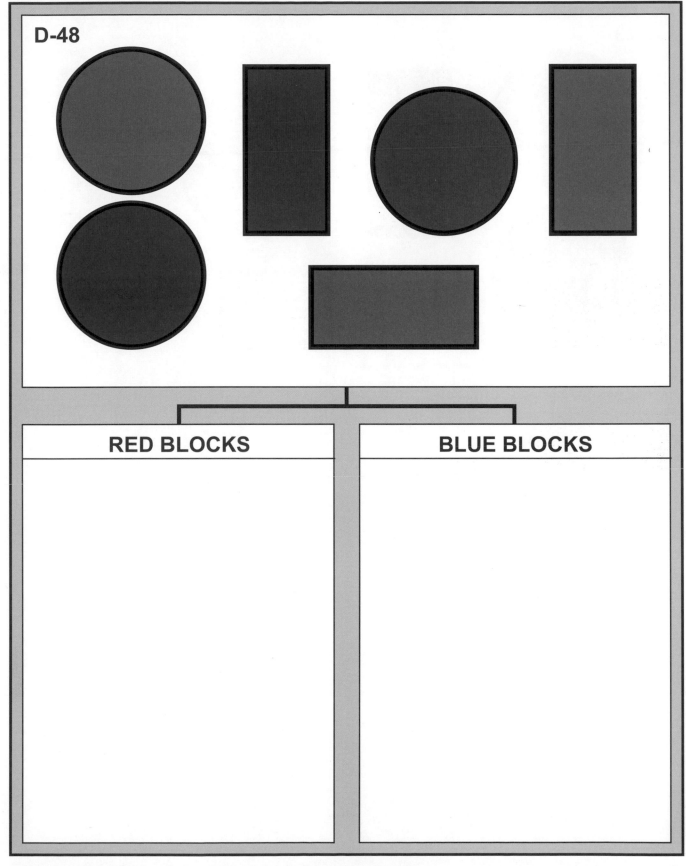

D-48

RED BLOCKS

BLUE BLOCKS

SORTING BLOCKS

DIRECTIONS: Place attribute blocks on the shapes in the top box. Move all the circles into the left box and the rectangles into the right box. Then trace and color them to match.

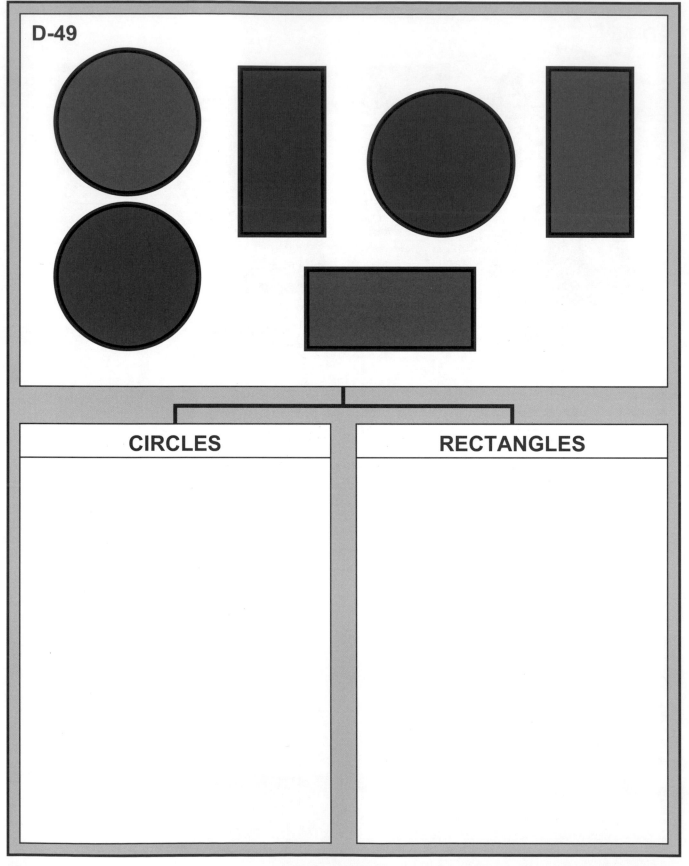

D-49

CIRCLES

RECTANGLES

SORTING BLOCKS

DIRECTIONS: Place attribute blocks on the shapes in the top box. Move all the circles into the left box, all the hexagons into the middle box, and all the squares into the right box. Then trace and color them to match.

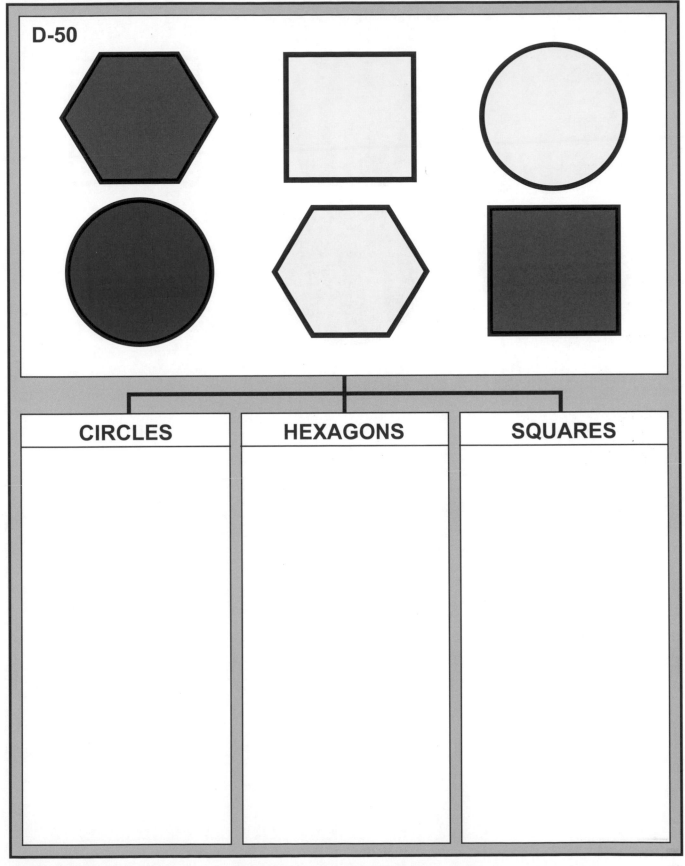

D-50

CIRCLES	HEXAGONS	SQUARES

SORTING BLOCKS

DIRECTIONS: Place attribute blocks on the shapes in the top box. Move the blue shapes into the left box, the red shapes into the middle box, and the yellow shapes into the right box. Then trace and color them to match.

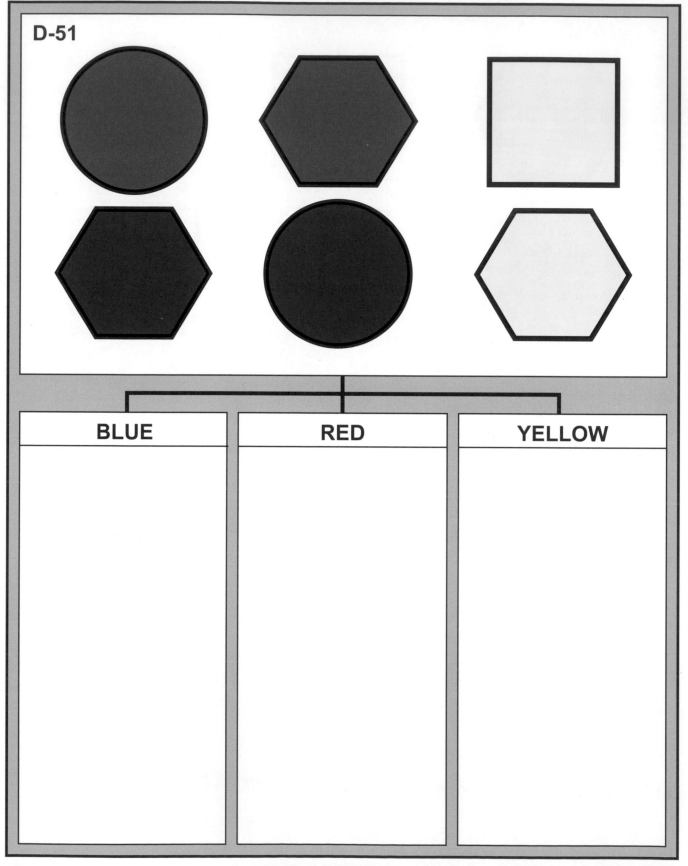

D-51

BLUE	RED	YELLOW

FIND THE ONE THAT IS DIFFERENT

DIRECTIONS: Place interlocking cubes on the shapes in each box. Make an "X" through the figure that is not like the others.

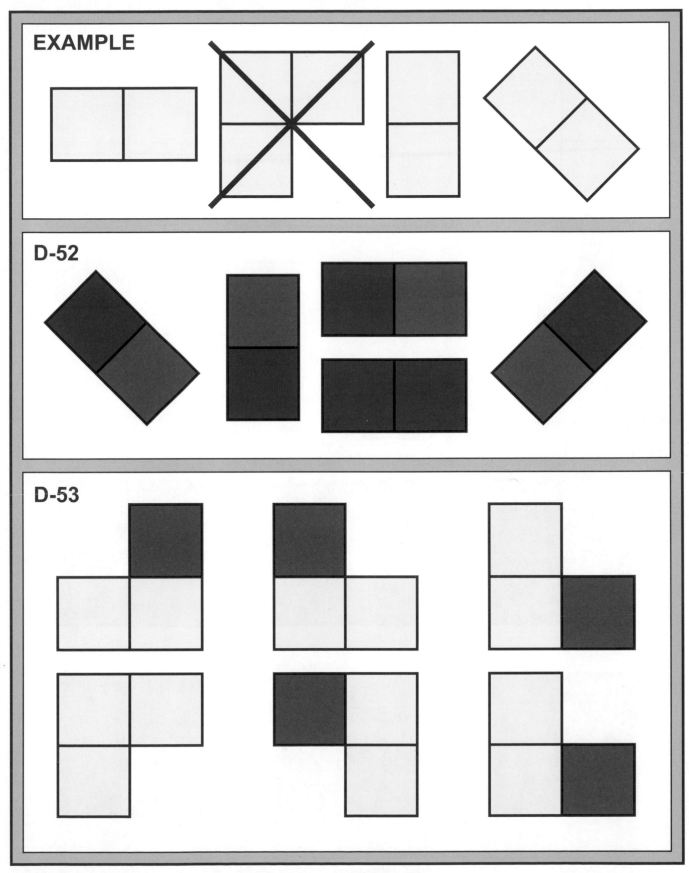

EXAMPLE

D-52

D-53

FIND THE ONE THAT IS DIFFERENT

DIRECTIONS: Place interlocking cubes on the shapes in each box. Make an "X" through the figure that is not like the others.

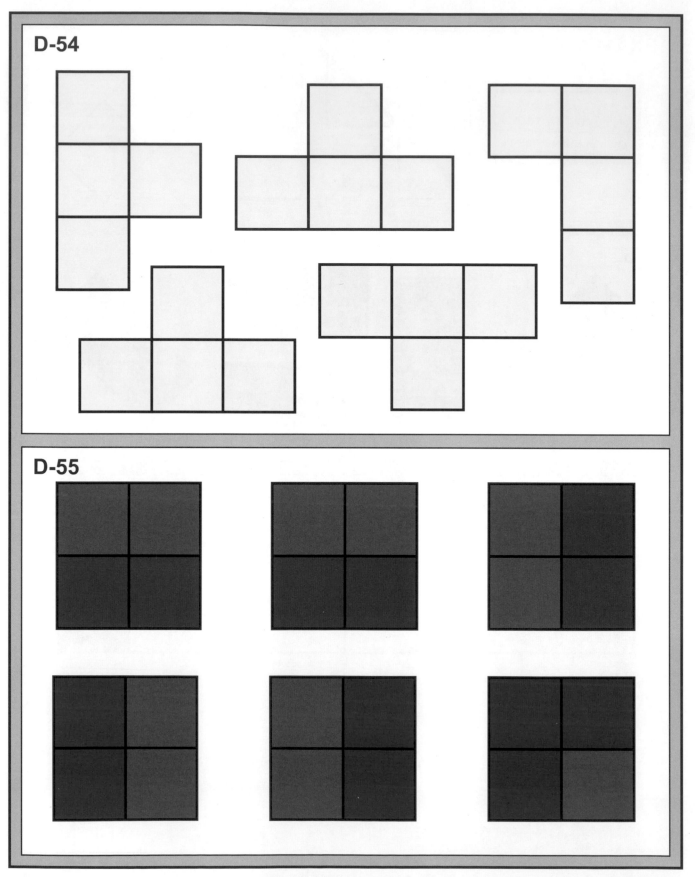

SORTING FIGURES

DIRECTIONS: Make each figure with colored interlocking cubes. Place each figure in the box that describes it. Then trace and color each figure.

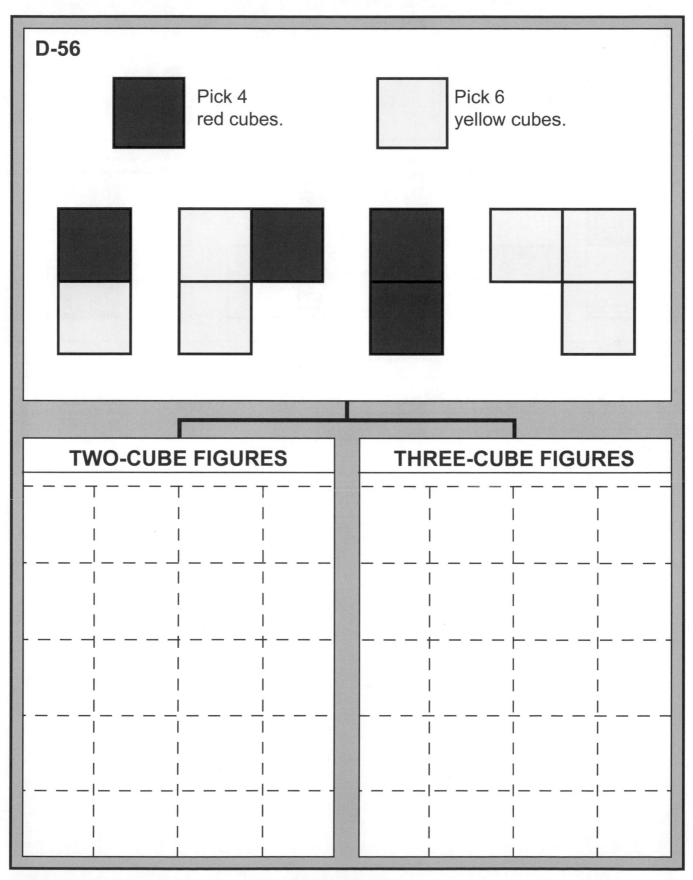

D-56

Pick 4 red cubes.

Pick 6 yellow cubes.

TWO-CUBE FIGURES

THREE-CUBE FIGURES

SORTING FIGURES

DIRECTIONS: Make each figure with colored interlocking cubes. Place each figure in the box that describes it. Then trace and color each figure.

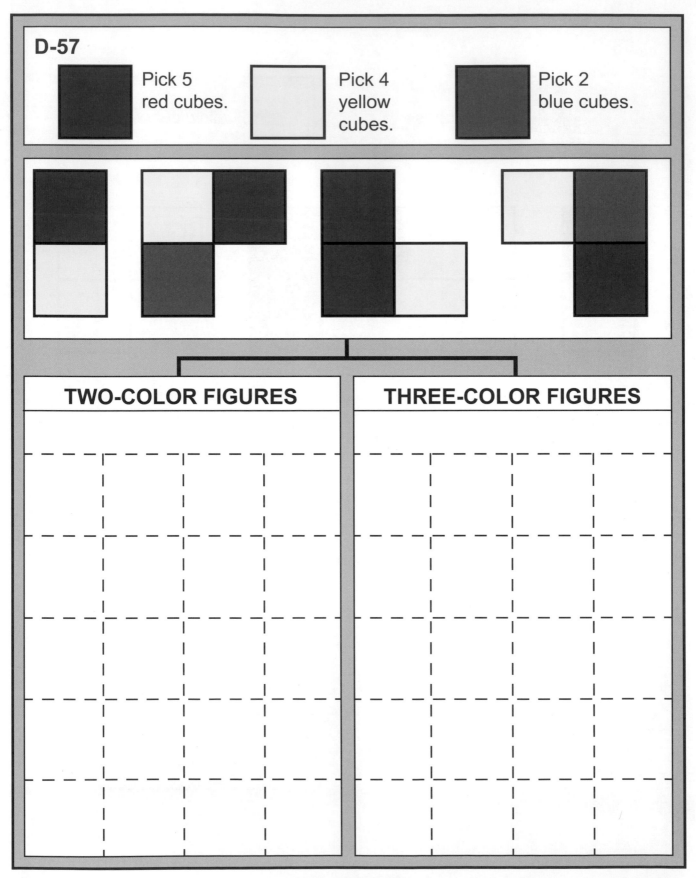

D-57

Pick 5 red cubes.

Pick 4 yellow cubes.

Pick 2 blue cubes.

TWO-COLOR FIGURES	THREE-COLOR FIGURES

SORTING FIGURES

DIRECTIONS: Make each figure with colored interlocking cubes. Place each figure in the box that describes it. Then trace and color each figure.

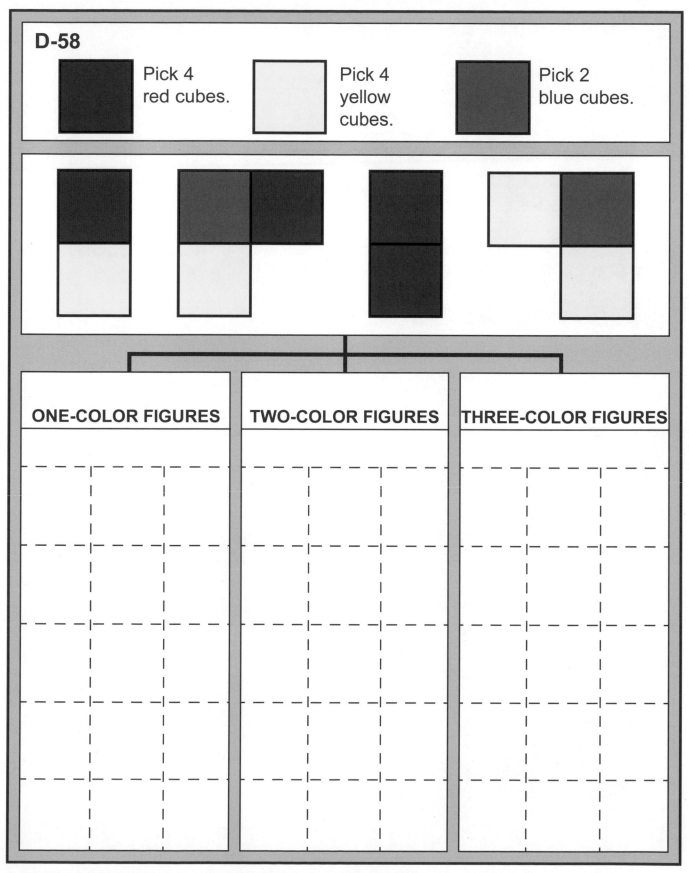

D-58

Pick 4 red cubes.

Pick 4 yellow cubes.

Pick 2 blue cubes.

ONE-COLOR FIGURES

TWO-COLOR FIGURES

THREE-COLOR FIGURES

FORMING GROUPS

DIRECTIONS: This example shows how to sort blocks. The shapes drawn with dashed lines show where the blocks should be placed.

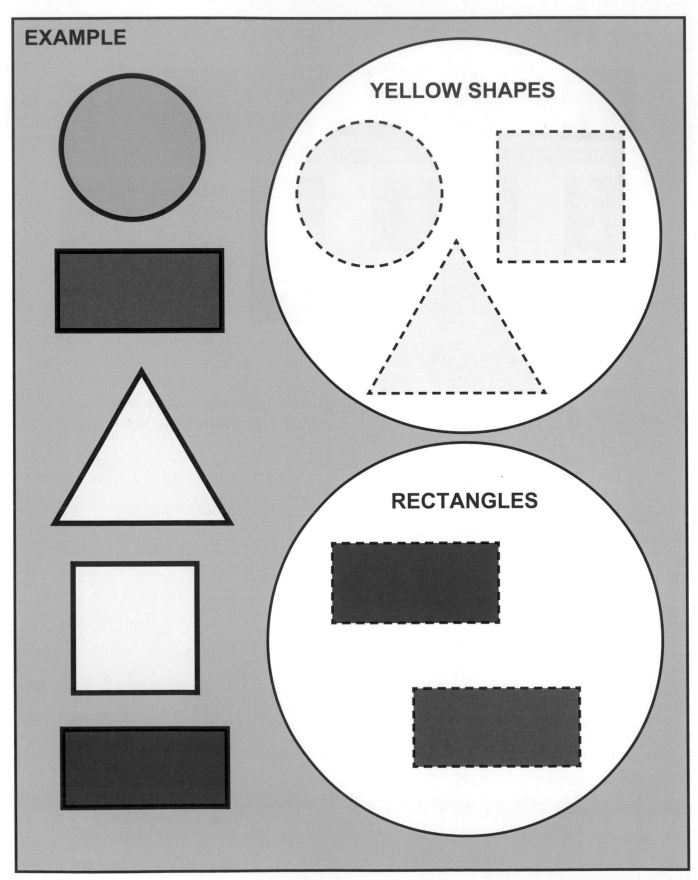

FORMING GROUPS

DIRECTIONS: Place an attribute block on each of the shapes. Move the blocks into the grouping circles. Then trace and color your answers.

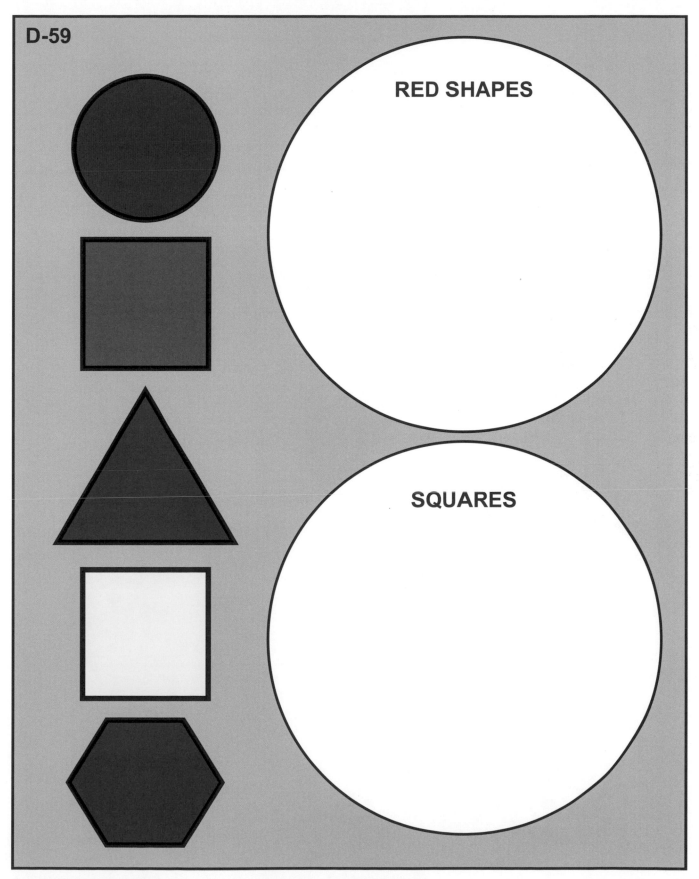

D-59

RED SHAPES

SQUARES

FORMING GROUPS

DIRECTIONS: Place an attribute block on each of the shapes. Move the blocks into the grouping circles. Then trace and color your answers.

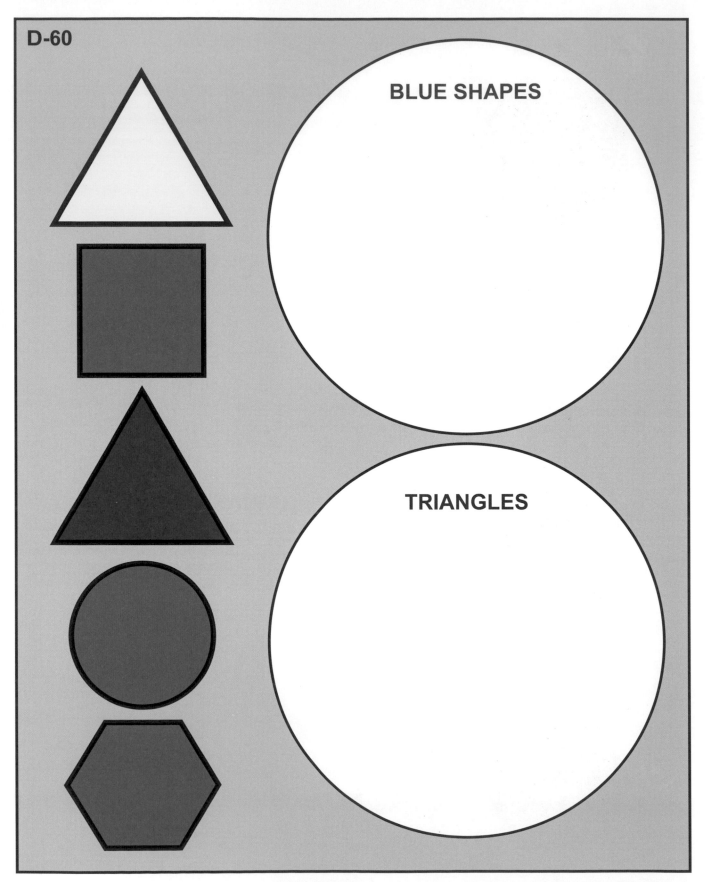

D-60

BLUE SHAPES

TRIANGLES

FORMING OVERLAPPING GROUPS

DIRECTIONS: Notice that the yellow rectangle is in the overlapping part of the grouping circles. It is inside the circle for yellow shapes and also inside the circle for rectangles.

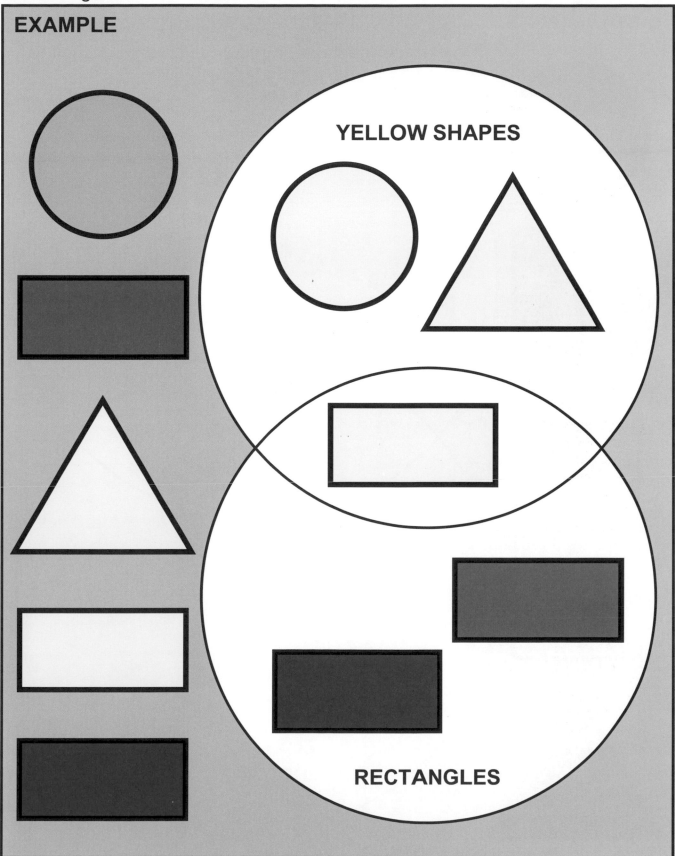

EXAMPLE

YELLOW SHAPES

RECTANGLES

FORMING OVERLAPPING GROUPS

DIRECTIONS: Place an attribute block on each of the small shapes. Move the blocks into the grouping circles. Then trace and color your answers.

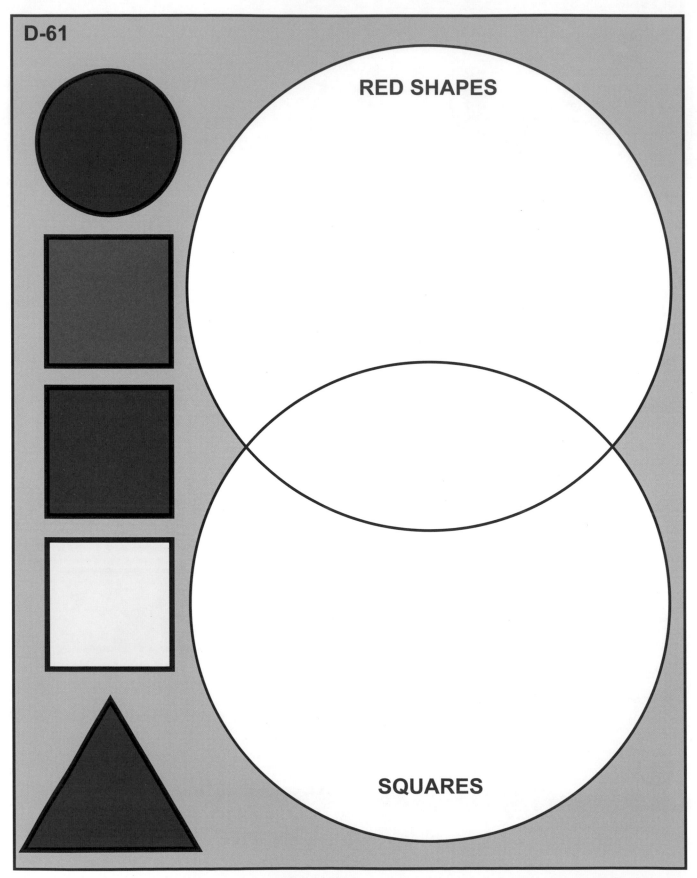

ROWS AND COLUMNS

DIRECTIONS: Look up and down the columns. Notice that the shape is the same. Look across the rows. Notice that the color is the same.

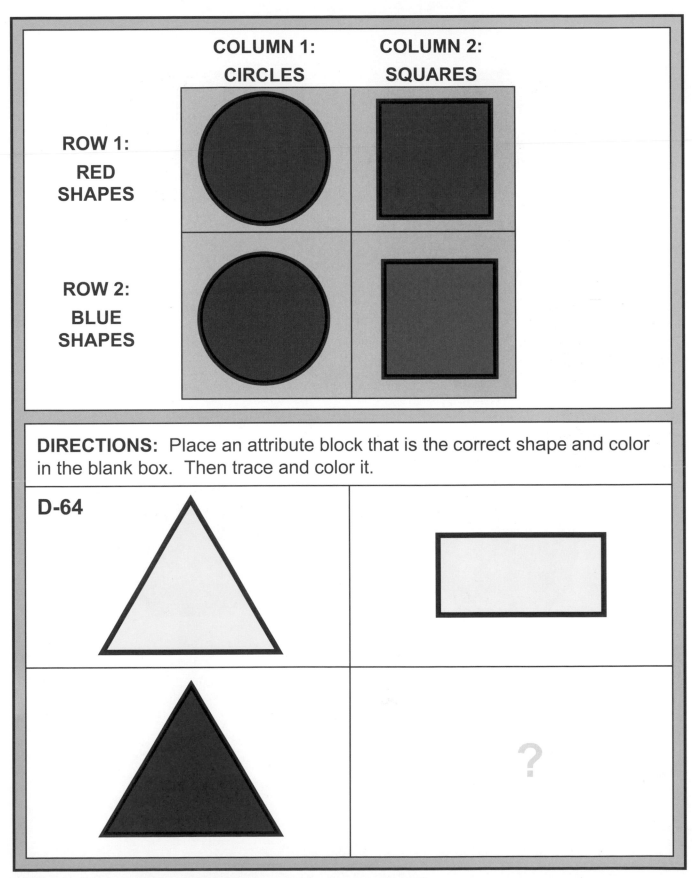

DIRECTIONS: Place an attribute block that is the correct shape and color in the blank box. Then trace and color it.

D-64

OVERLAPPING CLASSES—ROWS AND COLUMNS

DIRECTIONS: Place an attribute block that is the correct shape and color in the blank box. Then trace and color your answers.

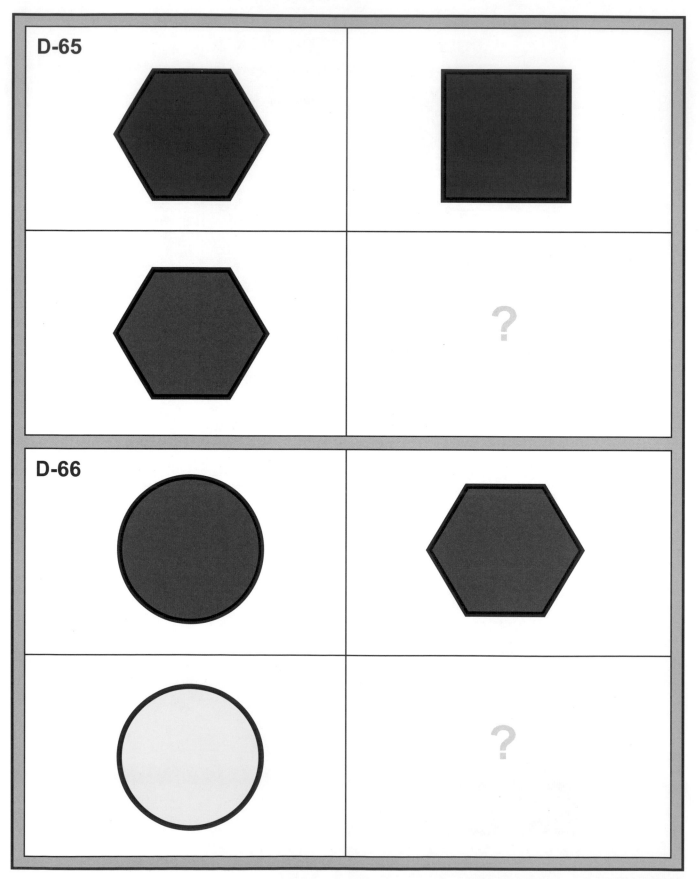

OVERLAPPING CLASSES—ROWS AND COLUMNS

DIRECTIONS: Place an attribute block that is the correct shape and color in the blank box. Then trace and color your answers.

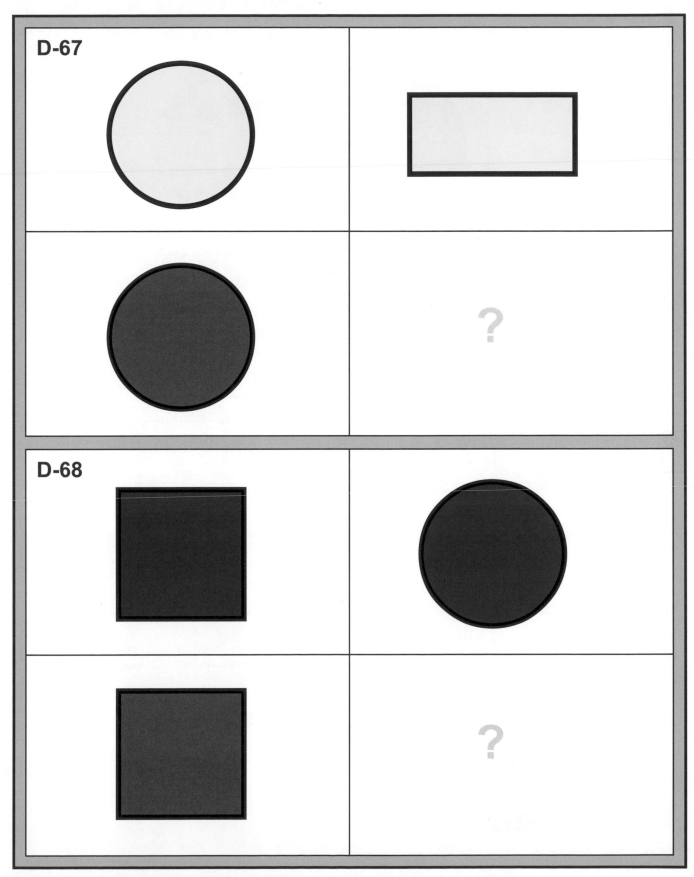

ROWS AND COLUMNS

DIRECTIONS: Blocks in the same column have the same color. Blocks in the same row have the same shape.

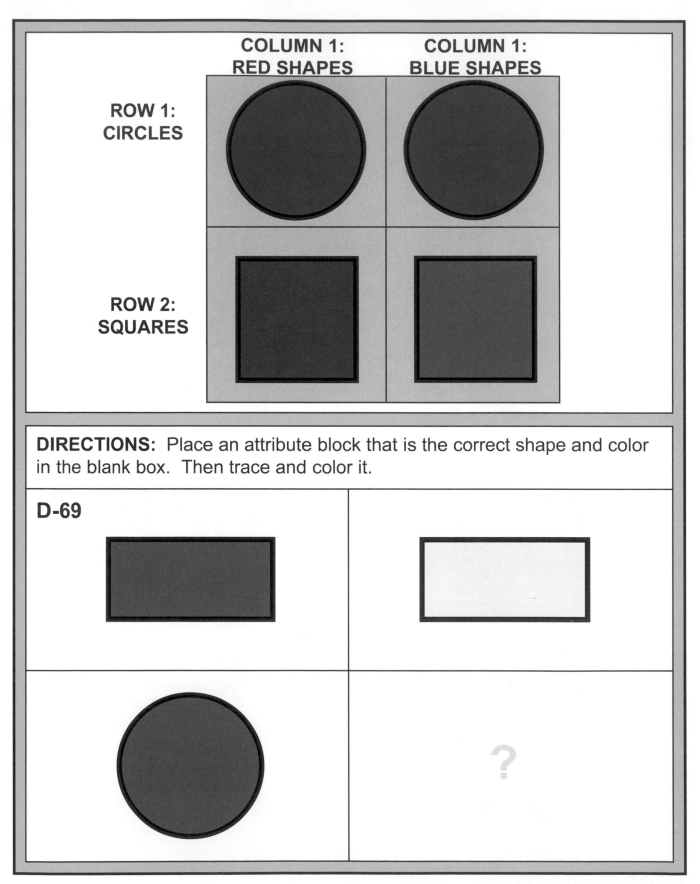

	COLUMN 1: RED SHAPES	COLUMN 1: BLUE SHAPES
ROW 1: CIRCLES		
ROW 2: SQUARES		

DIRECTIONS: Place an attribute block that is the correct shape and color in the blank box. Then trace and color it.

D-69

?

OVERLAPPING CLASSES—ROWS AND COLUMNS

DIRECTIONS: In each exercise, place an attribute block that is the correct shape and color in the blank box. Then trace and color it.

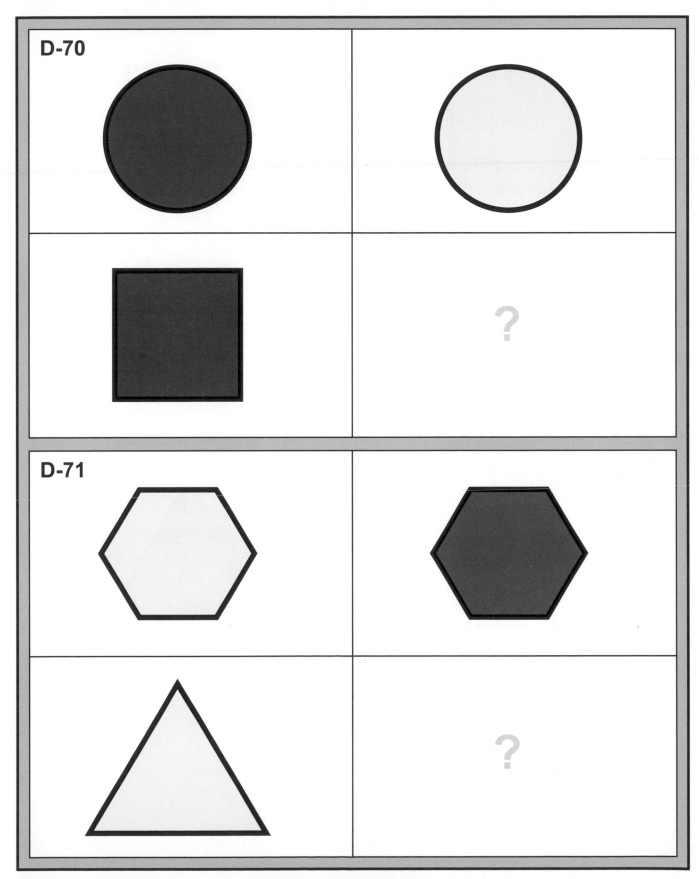

D-70

D-71

OVERLAPPING CLASSES—ROWS AND COLUMNS

DIRECTIONS: In each exercise, place an attribute block that is the correct shape and color in the blank box. Then trace and color it.

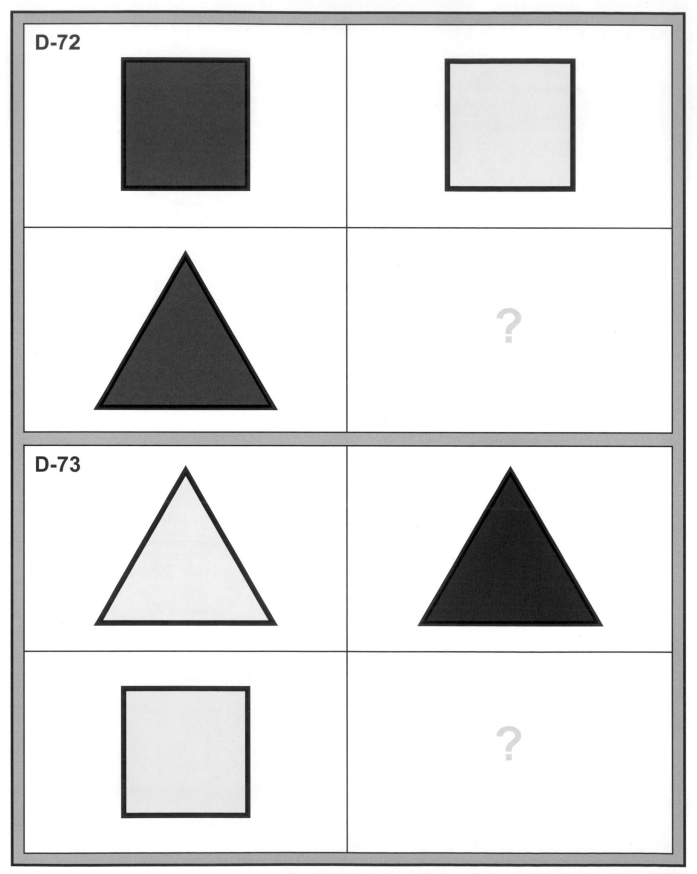

ROWS AND COLUMNS

DIRECTIONS: Look at the columns. All the blocks have the same attribute of shape. Look at the rows. All the blocks have the same attribute of color.

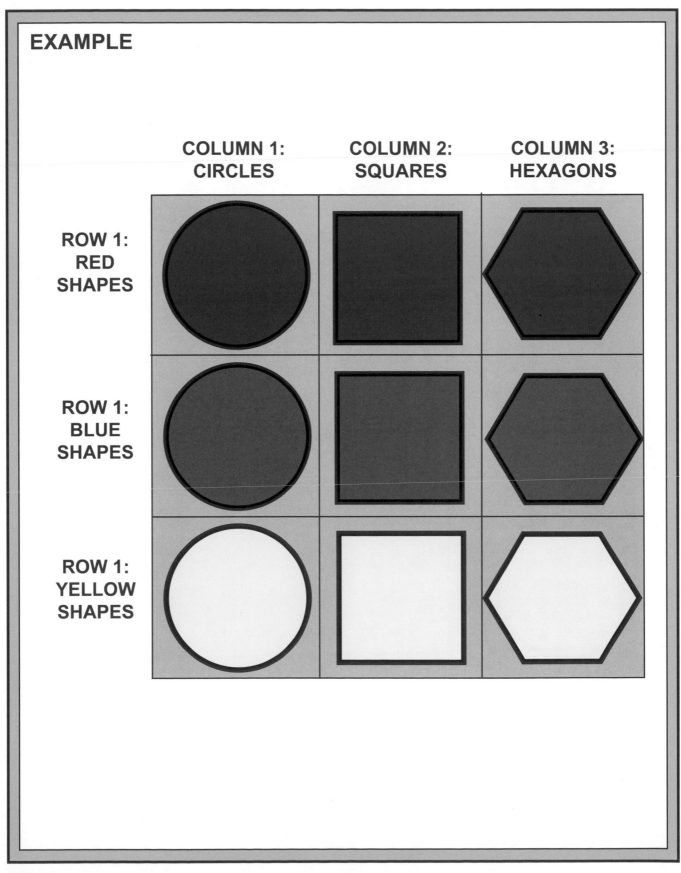

EXAMPLE

	COLUMN 1: CIRCLES	COLUMN 2: SQUARES	COLUMN 3: HEXAGONS
ROW 1: RED SHAPES			
ROW 1: BLUE SHAPES			
ROW 1: YELLOW SHAPES			

OVERLAPPING CLASSES—ROWS AND COLUMNS

DIRECTIONS: In each blank box, place an attribute block that is the correct shape and color. Then trace and color your answers.

D-74

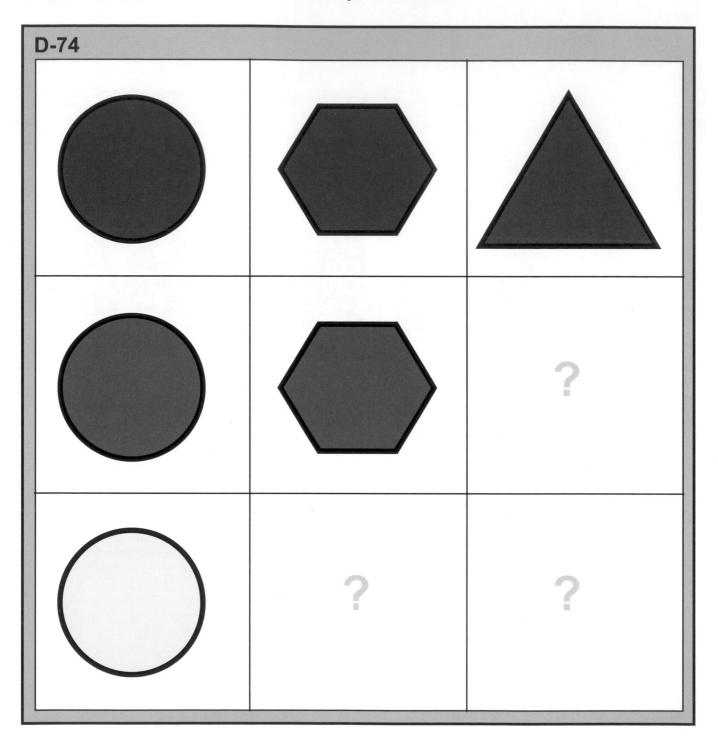

© 2008 The Critical Thinking Co™ • www.CriticalThinking.com • 800-458-4849

OVERLAPPING CLASSES—ROWS AND COLUMNS

DIRECTIONS: In each blank box, place an attribute block that is the correct shape and color. Then trace and color your answers.

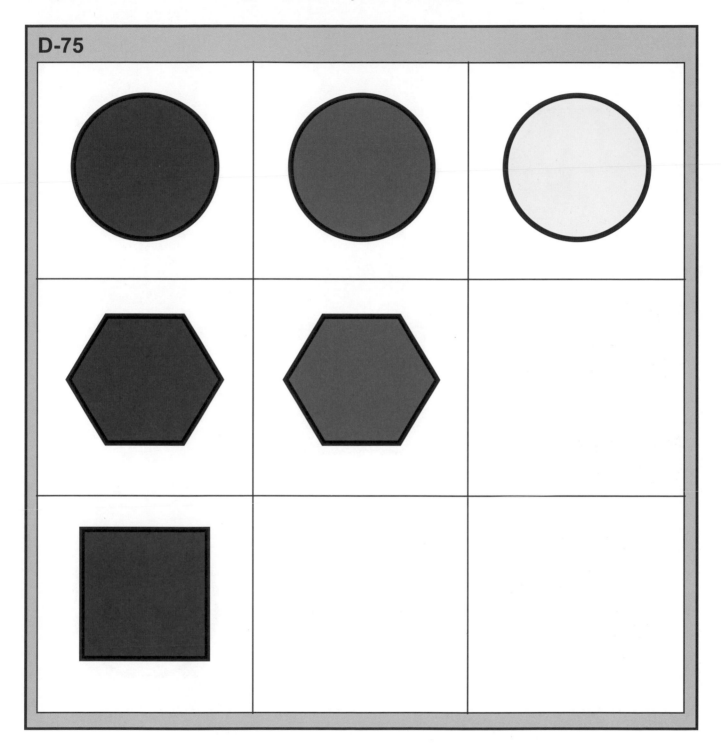

D-75

OVERLAPPING CLASSES—ROWS AND COLUMNS

DIRECTIONS: In each blank box, place an attribute block that is the correct shape and color. Then trace and color your answers.

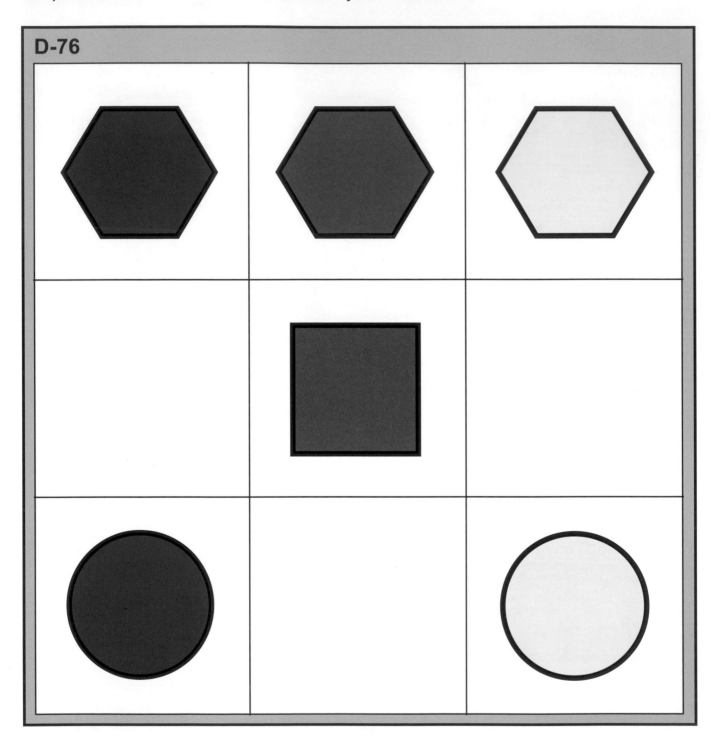

Chapter Five
Thinking About Family Members

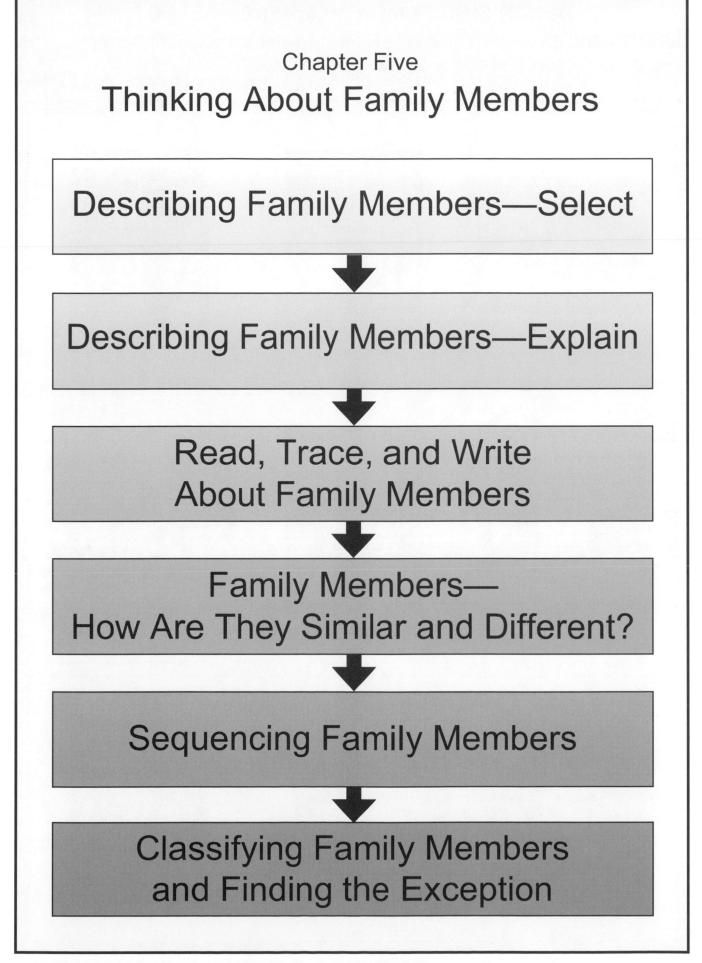

Describing Family Members—Select

Describing Family Members—Explain

Read, Trace, and Write
About Family Members

Family Members—
How Are They Similar and Different?

Sequencing Family Members

Classifying Family Members
and Finding the Exception

DESCRIBING FAMILY MEMBERS—SELECT

DIRECTIONS: Circle the picture of the family member that your teacher describes. (Teacher: see page 262.)

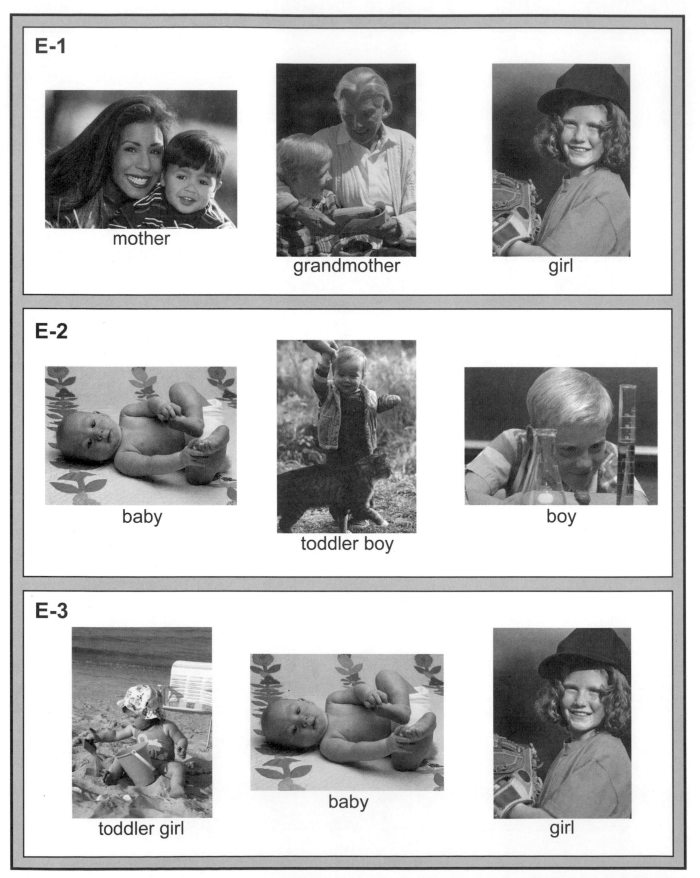

E-1

mother

grandmother

girl

E-2

baby

toddler boy

boy

E-3

toddler girl

baby

girl

CHARACTERISTICS OF FAMILY MEMBERS

DIRECTIONS: Some of these family members are young and some are old. Trace and copy each word. Then draw lines from each picture to the word that describes that person.

E-4

baby

grandmother

grandfather

girl

toddler

EXAMPLE

EXAMPLE

Trace the word.

old

Copy the word.

Trace the word.

young

Copy the word.

CHARACTERISTICS OF FAMILY MEMBERS

DIRECTIONS: Some of these family members are men and some are women. Trace and copy each word. Then draw lines from each picture to the word that describes that person.

E-5

father

grandmother

mother

grandfather

Trace the word.

man

Copy the word.

Trace the word.

woman

Copy the word.

CHARACTERISTICS OF FAMILY MEMBERS

DIRECTIONS: Some of these family members are children and some are adults. Mothers and fathers are adults. Trace and copy each word. Then draw lines from each picture to the word that describes that person.

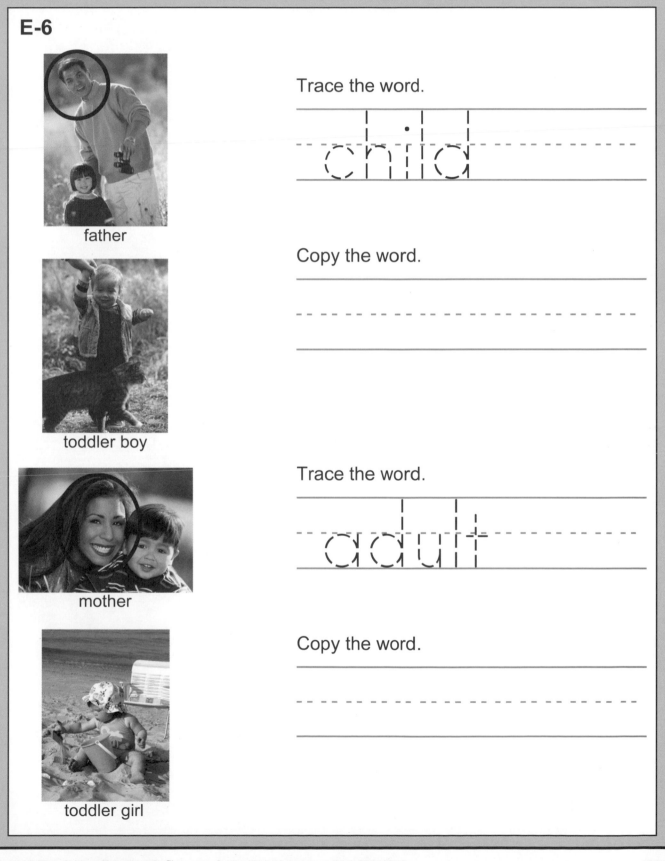

E-6

father

toddler boy

mother

toddler girl

Trace the word.

child

Copy the word.

Trace the word.

adult

Copy the word.

DESCRIBING FAMILY MEMBERS—EXPLAIN

DIRECTIONS: Describe this family member to your partner. Then trace and copy the names.

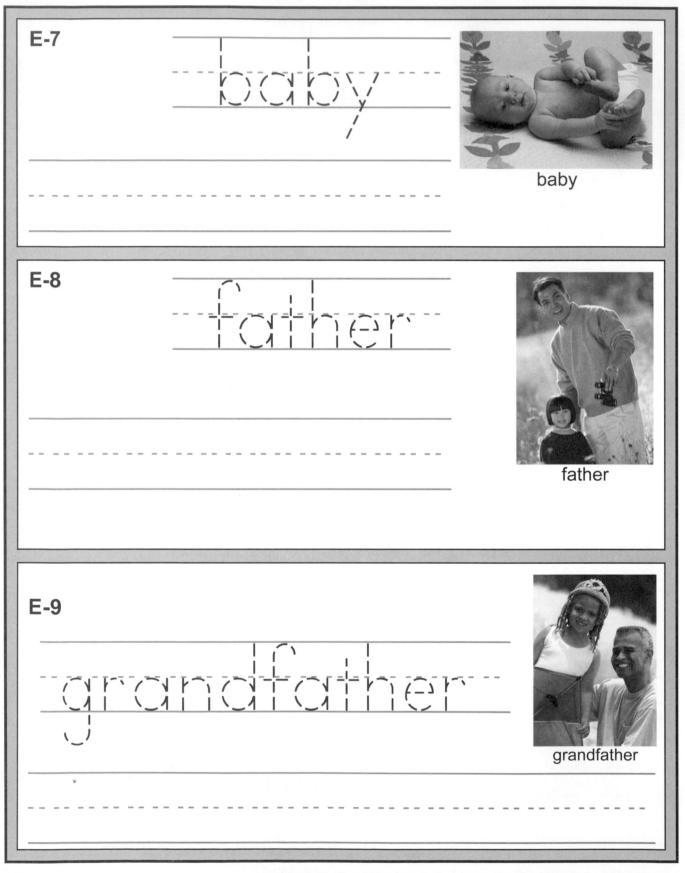

E-7

baby

baby

E-8

father

father

E-9

grandfather

grandfather

NAMING FAMILY MEMBERS—MATCHING

DIRECTIONS: Trace and copy the names of each family member. Then draw a line from each picture to the name of the family member.

E-10

EXAMPLE

father

grandfather

grandmother

mother

girl

NAMING FAMILY MEMBERS—WRITING

DIRECTIONS: Find the names of these family members in the WORD BOX. Then write the correct names in the four blanks.

E-11

WORD BOX
baby, boy, girl, mother, toddler

mother

NAMING FAMILY MEMBERS—WRITING

DIRECTIONS: Find the names of these family members in the WORD BOX. Then write the correct names in the four blanks.

E-12

WORD BOX
father, grandfather, grandmother, toddler

SIMILAR FAMILY MEMBERS—SELECT

DIRECTIONS: Circle the picture of the family member most like the one on the left. Then explain why you chose each picture.

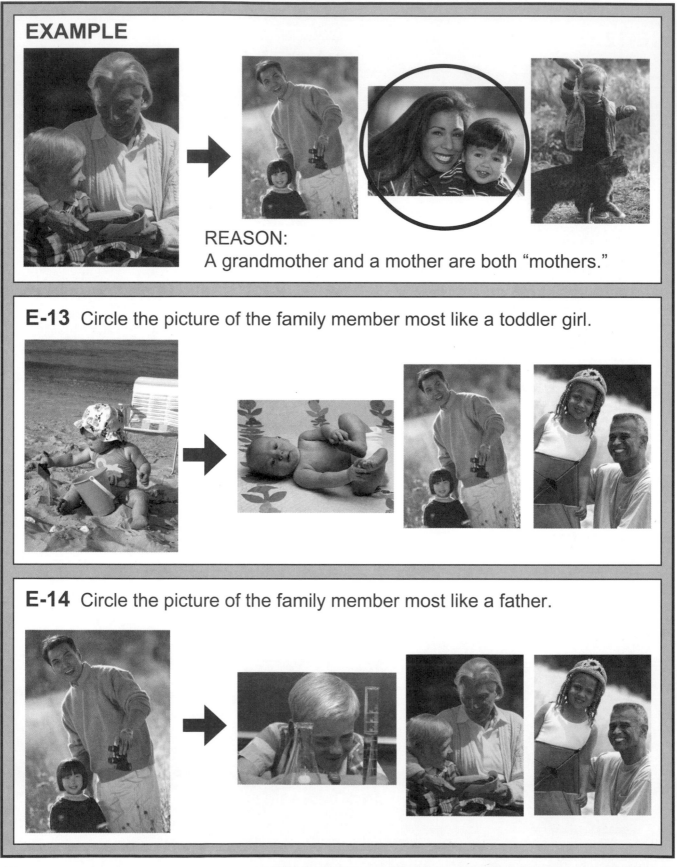

EXAMPLE

REASON:
A grandmother and a mother are both "mothers."

E-13 Circle the picture of the family member most like a toddler girl.

E-14 Circle the picture of the family member most like a father.

SIMILAR FAMILY MEMBERS—EXPLAIN

DIRECTIONS: Explain how each two family members are alike. Then trace and copy each word.

E-15

father　father

grandfather

E-16

toddler girl

girl

E-17

mother

grandmother

RANKING FAMILY MEMBERS

DIRECTIONS: Write the names of the family members from youngest to oldest.

E-18

boy

grandfather

father

baby

YOUNGEST

baby

OLDEST

RANKING FAMILY MEMBERS

DIRECTIONS: Write the names of the family members from youngest to oldest.

E-19

grandmother

girl

mother

baby

YOUNGEST

OLDEST

CHARACTERISTICS OF FAMILY MEMBERS

DIRECTIONS: Draw a line from each picture to the words that describe that family member. Then trace and copy each word.

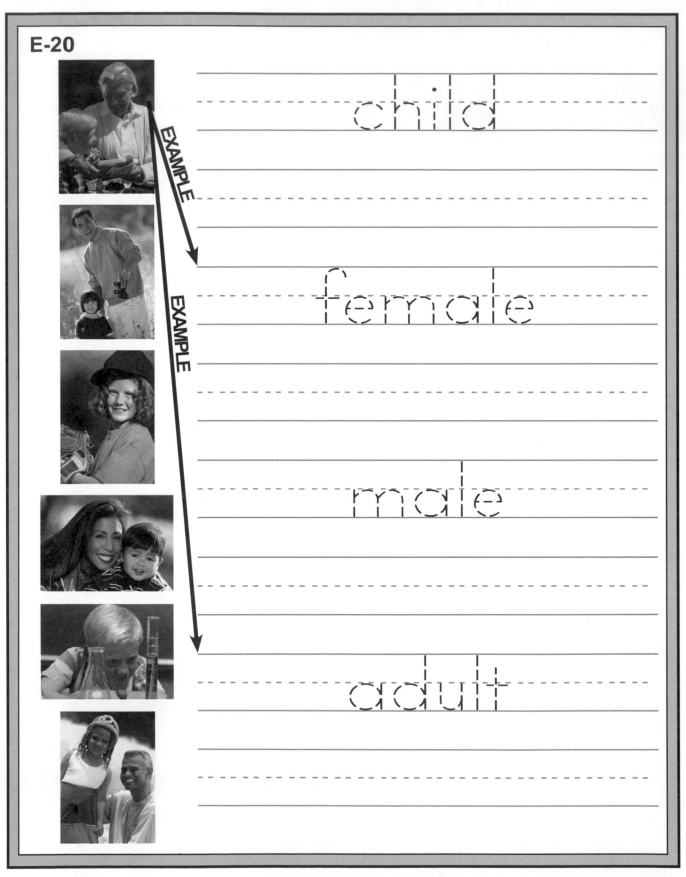

E-20

EXAMPLE

child

EXAMPLE

female

male

adult

NAME THE CLASS—FAMILY MEMBERS

DIRECTIONS: Write the class (group) on the top line. Then, using the words in the WORD BOX, write the names of the family members on the three lines.

E-21

WORD BOX
baby, children, toddler boy, toddler girl

CLASS _____

children

MEMBERS _____

_____

_____

E-22

WORD BOX
females, girl, grandmother, mother

CLASS _____

MEMBERS _____

_____

_____

EXPLAIN THE EXCEPTION—FAMILY MEMBERS

DIRECTIONS: Three family members belong to the same class. Using the words in the WORD BOX, trace the class and write the members on the lines. Then trace why one person is an exception.

E-23

WORD BOX

boy, children, father, girl, adult, toddler girl

CLASS

children

MEMBERS

EXCEPTION

father

EXPLAIN THE EXCEPTION

The father is an adult.

The others are children.

EXPLAIN THE EXCEPTION—FAMILY MEMBERS

DIRECTIONS: Three family members belong to the same class. Using the words in the WORD BOX, write the class and members on the lines. Then explain why one person is an exception.

E-24

WORD BOX
female, boy, grandfather, father, males, mother

CLASS

_____

MEMBERS

_____

_____

_____

_____

EXCEPTION

_____

EXPLAIN THE EXCEPTION

_____

_____

EXPLAIN THE EXCEPTION—FAMILY MEMBERS

DIRECTIONS: Three family members belong to the same class. Using the words in the WORD BOX, write the class and members on the lines. Then explain why one person is an exception.

E-25

WORD BOX
adult, child, boy, grandmother, father, mother

CLASS

MEMBERS

EXCEPTION

EXPLAIN THE EXCEPTION

Chapter Six
Thinking About Food

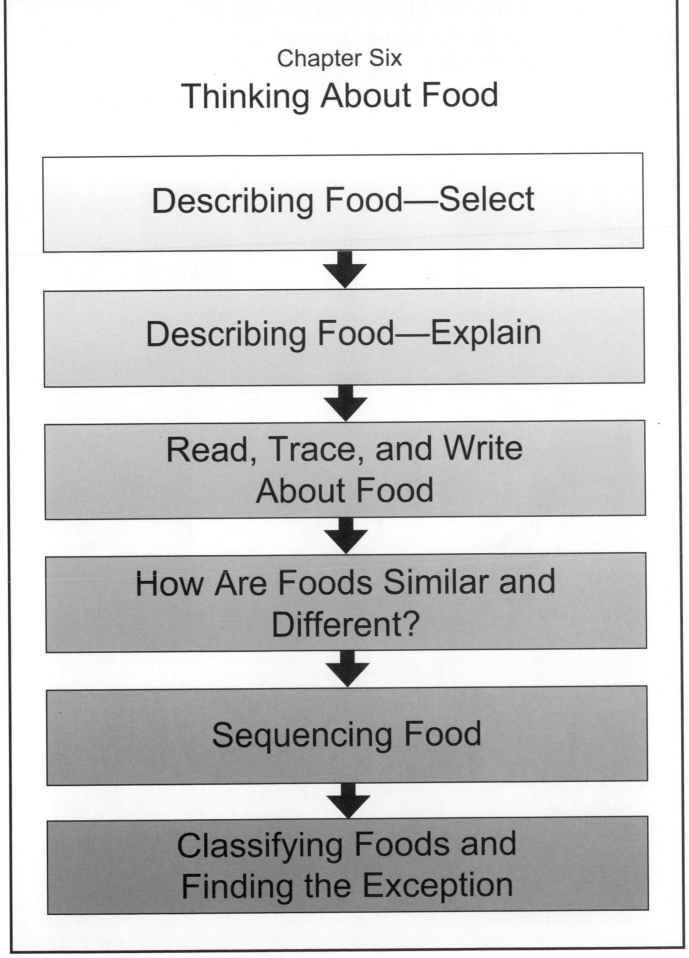

Describing Food—Select

Describing Food—Explain

Read, Trace, and Write About Food

How Are Foods Similar and Different?

Sequencing Food

Classifying Foods and Finding the Exception

DESCRIBING FOODS—SELECT

DIRECTIONS: Circle the picture of the food that your teacher describes.
(Teacher: see pages 262-263.)

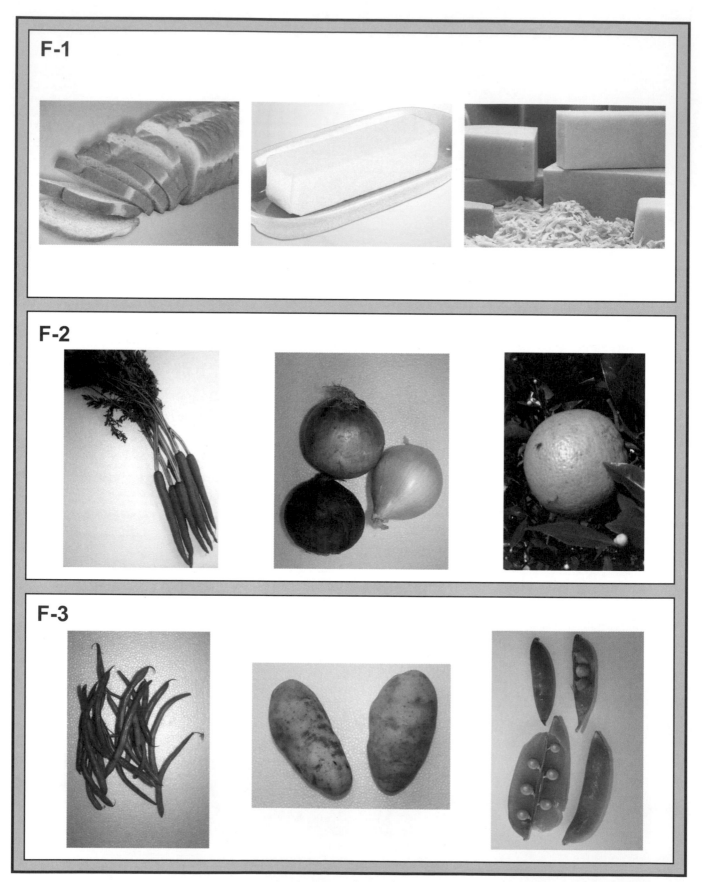

F-1

F-2

F-3

DESCRIBING FOODS—EXPLAIN

DIRECTIONS: Describe this food to your partner. Then trace and copy each word.

F-4

ham

F-5

grapes

F-6

celery

NAMING FOODS—MATCHING

DIRECTIONS: Trace and copy each food name. Then draw a line from each food to its name.

F-7

EXAMPLE

cabbage

celery

onions

peas

steak

NAMING FOODS—MATCHING

DIRECTIONS: Trace and copy each food name. Then draw a line from each food to its name.

F-8

bread

cheese

eggs

chicken

potatoes

NAMING FOODS—WRITING

DIRECTIONS: Using the words in the WORD BOX, write the name of each food.

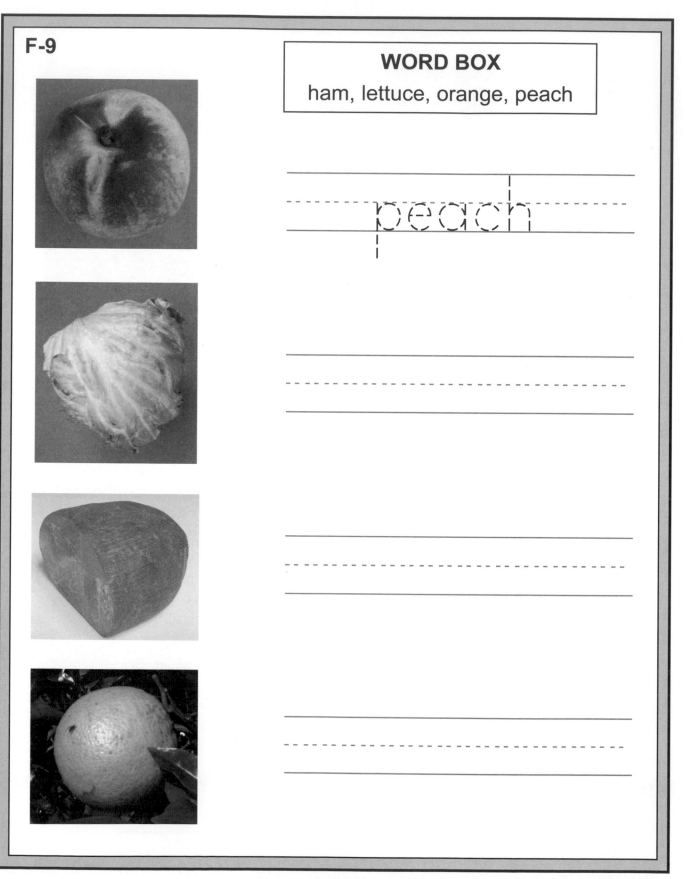

F-9

WORD BOX
ham, lettuce, orange, peach

peach

NAMING FOODS—WRITING

DIRECTIONS: Using the words in the WORD BOX, write the name of each food.

F-10

WORD BOX
butter, grapes, milk, peas

DESCRIBING FOODS

DIRECTIONS: Draw a line from each picture to the word that describes that food. Then trace and copy the words.

F-11

EXAMPLE → dairy

grain

DESCRIBING FOODS

DIRECTIONS: Draw a line from each picture to the word that describes that food. Then trace and copy the words.

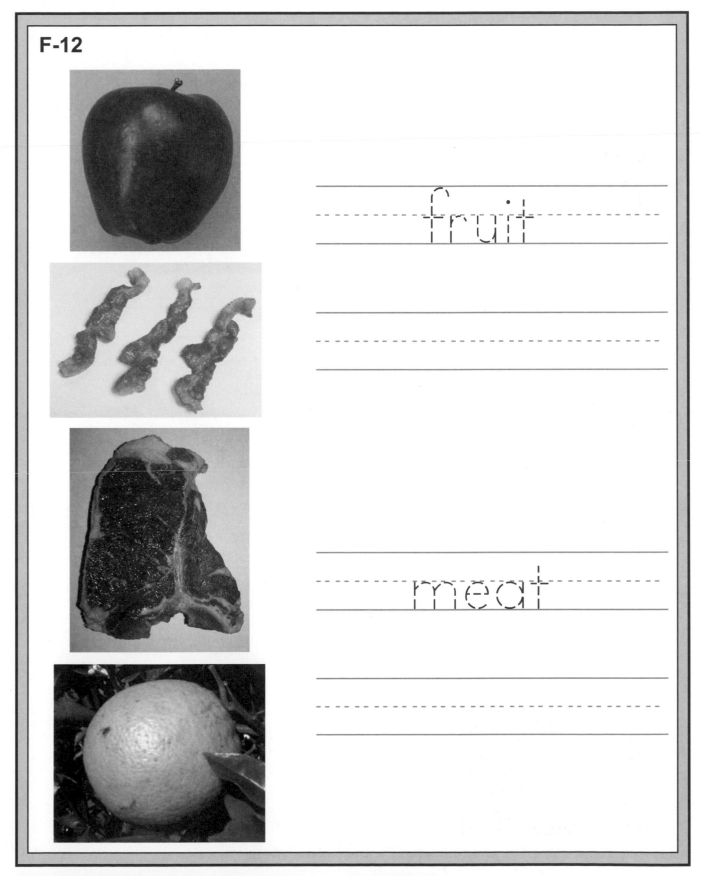

F-12

fruit

meat

DESCRIBING FOODS

DIRECTIONS: Draw lines from each picture to the words that describe the part of the plant we eat. Then trace and copy the words.

F-13

fruit

leaf

root

grain

stem

SIMILAR FOODS—SELECT

DIRECTIONS: Circle the picture of the food most like the one on the left.

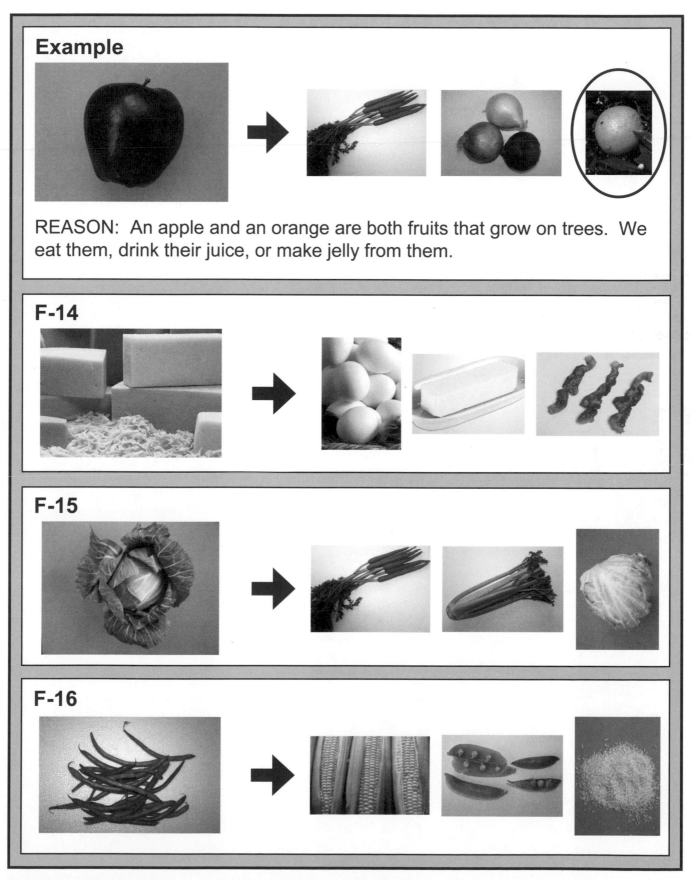

Example

REASON: An apple and an orange are both fruits that grow on trees. We eat them, drink their juice, or make jelly from them.

F-14

F-15

F-16

SIMILAR FOODS—EXPLAIN

DIRECTIONS: Tell your partner or teacher how these foods are alike. Then trace and copy each word.

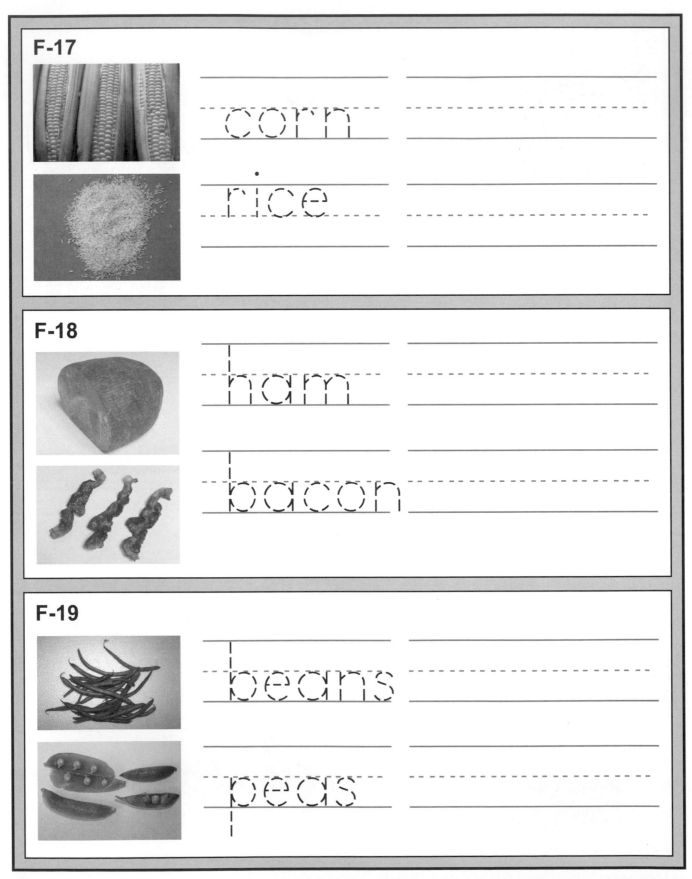

F-17

corn

rice

F-18

ham

bacon

F-19

beans

peas

SIMILARITIES AND DIFFERENCES—FOOD

DIRECTIONS: Trace and copy the words. Then explain how these foods are ALIKE and explain how these foods are DIFFERENT.

F-20

apple

tomatoes

F-21

lettuce

cabbage

SIMILARITIES AND DIFFERENCES—FOOD

DIRECTIONS: Trace and copy the words. Then explain how these foods are ALIKE and explain how these foods are DIFFERENT.

F-22

milk

butter

F-23

steak

ham

RANKING FOODS

DIRECTIONS: In the top box, write in the names of the foods from smallest to largest. In the bottom box, arrange the foods by how often you eat them.

F-24

| cabbage | rice | tomatoes |

SMALLEST

rice

LARGEST

F-25

| bread | celery | potatoes |

SELDOM

OFTEN

MATCH FOODS TO THEIR CLASSES

DIRECTIONS: Trace and copy each of the food classes (groups). Then draw a line from each picture to the word describing its class.

F-26

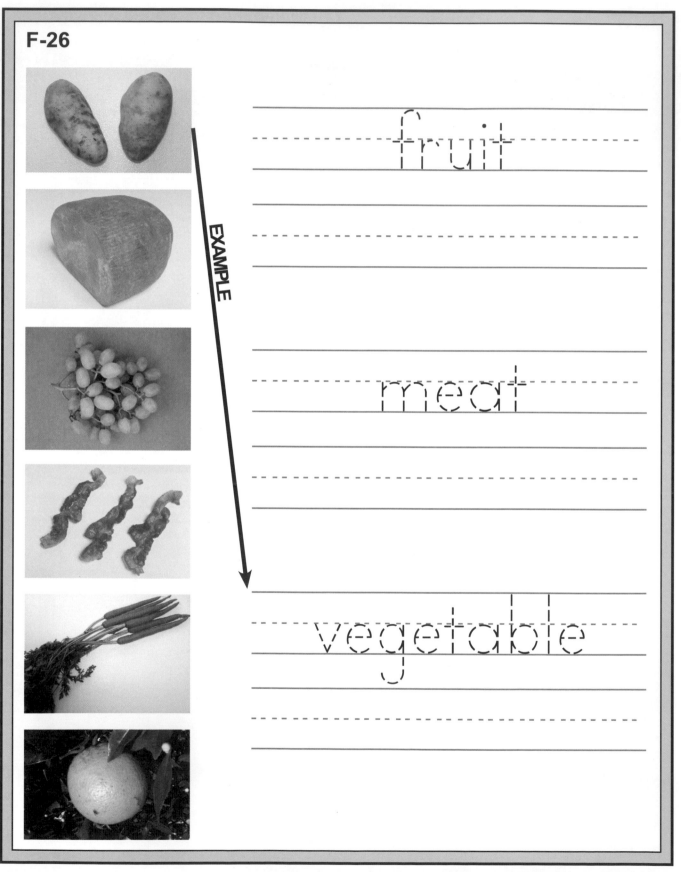

EXAMPLE

fruit

meat

vegetable

MATCH FOODS TO THEIR CLASSES

DIRECTIONS: Trace and copy each of the food classes (groups). Then draw lines from each picture to its class.

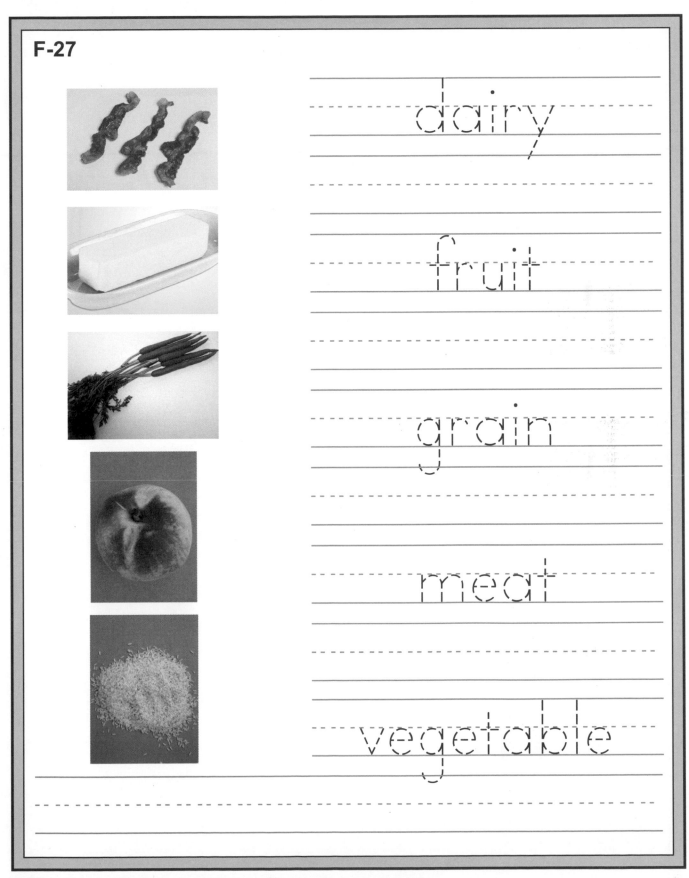

F-27

dairy

fruit

grain

meat

vegetable

MATCH FOODS TO THEIR CLASSES

DIRECTIONS: Trace and copy each of the food classes (groups). Then draw lines from each picture to its class.

F-28

dairy

fruit

grain

meat

vegetable

WRITE THE FOOD CLASS

DIRECTIONS: Using the words in the WORD BOX, write the class beside each food.

F-29

WORD BOX
dairy, fruit, meat, vegetable

vegetable

CHARACTERISTICS OF FOODS

DIRECTIONS: Some foods grow above ground and some grow below ground. Trace and copy each word. Then draw a line from each picture to the word that describes where that food grows.

F-30

EXAMPLE

above

below

CHARACTERISTICS OF FOODS

DIRECTIONS: Some foods grow above the ground on plants that are tall. Some foods grow on plants that are short. Draw a line from each picture to the word that describes the kind of plant on which that food grows.

F-31

low plant

tall plant

tree

vine

NAME THE CLASS—FOOD

DIRECTIONS: Using the words in the WORD BOX, write the class (group) on the top line. Then write the names of the foods on the three lines.

F-32

WORD BOX
apple, peach, fruit, orange

CLASS ___fruit___

MEMBERS _____

_____

_____

F-33

WORD BOX
celery, green vegetables, lettuce, peas

CLASS _____

MEMBERS _____

_____

_____

EXPLAIN THE EXCEPTION—FOOD

DIRECTIONS: Three foods in the WORD BOX belong to the same class. Write the class and members on the lines. Then trace why one food is an exception.

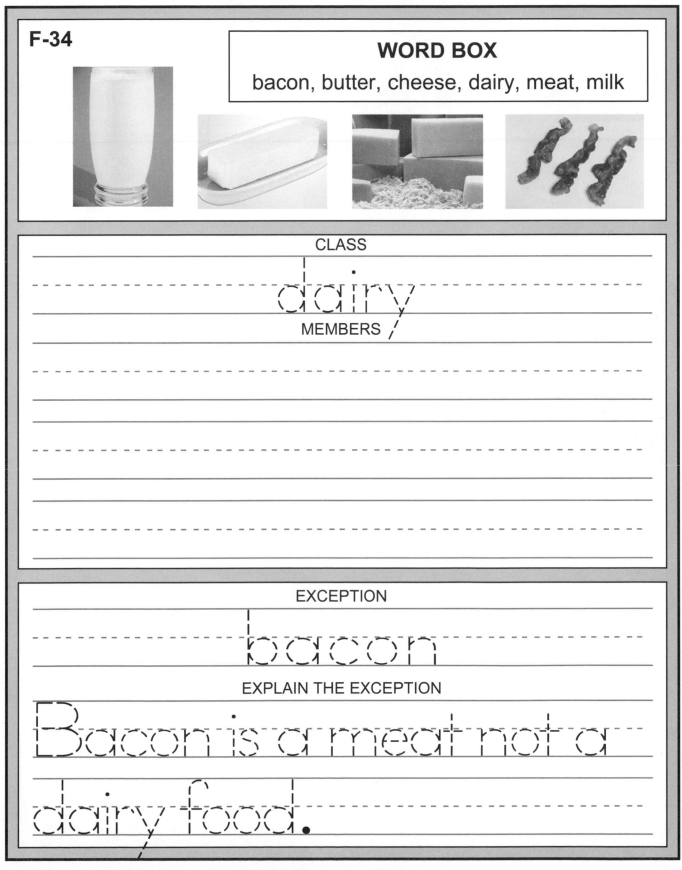

F-34

WORD BOX
bacon, butter, cheese, dairy, meat, milk

CLASS

dairy

MEMBERS

EXCEPTION

bacon

EXPLAIN THE EXCEPTION

Bacon is a meat not a dairy food.

EXPLAIN THE EXCEPTION—FOOD

DIRECTIONS: Three foods in the WORD BOX belong to the same class. Write the class and members on the lines. Then explain why one member is an exception.

F-35

WORD BOX
cabbage, carrot, celery,
green vegetables, lettuce, root

CLASS
_____

MEMBERS
_____

_____

_____

_____

EXCEPTION
_____

EXPLAIN THE EXCEPTION
_____

_____

SORTING INTO CLASSES—FOOD

DIRECTIONS: On the diagram on the next page, write each of these foods in the class to which it belongs.

F-36

apple

bacon

carrots

celery

chicken

grapes

beans

ham

orange

peach

potatoes

steak

FOOD

vegetable

MEMBERS

carrots

fruit

MEMBERS

apple

meat

MEMBERS

bacon

Chapter Seven
Thinking About Animals

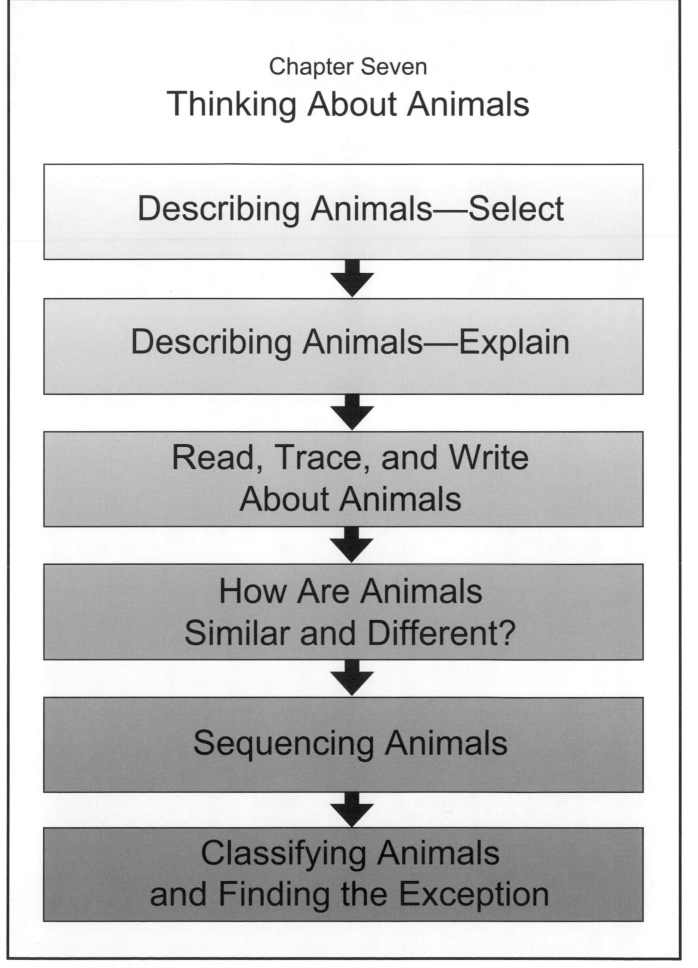

Describing Animals—Select

Describing Animals—Explain

Read, Trace, and Write
About Animals

How Are Animals
Similar and Different?

Sequencing Animals

Classifying Animals
and Finding the Exception

DESCRIBING ANIMALS—SELECT

DIRECTIONS: Circle the picture of the animal that your teacher describes. (Teacher: see page 263.)

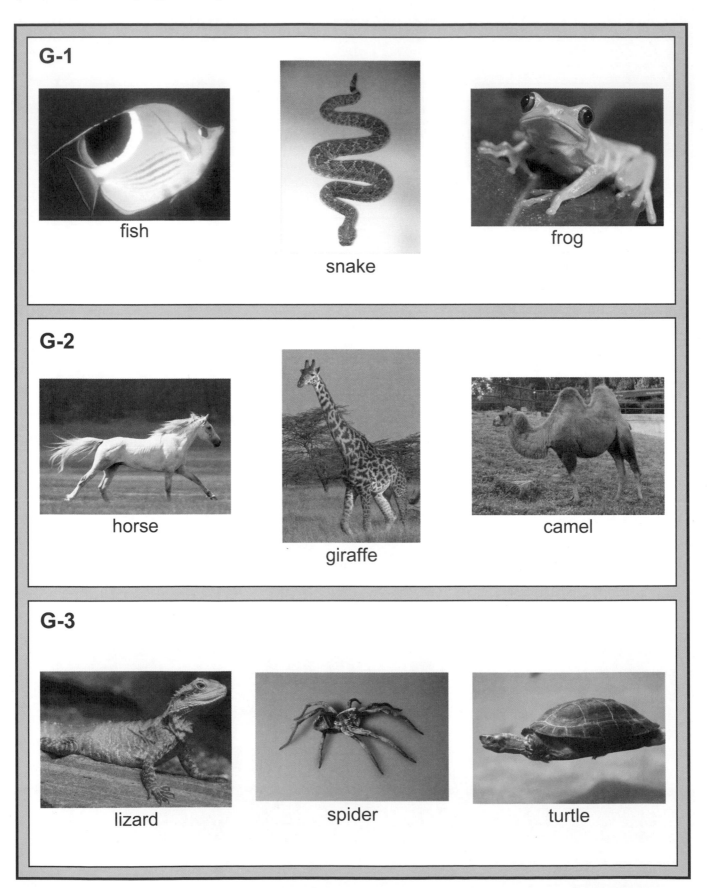

G-1

fish

snake

frog

G-2

horse

giraffe

camel

G-3

lizard

spider

turtle

DESCRIBING ANIMALS—EXPLAIN

DIRECTIONS: Describe this animal to your partner. Then trace and copy the animal names.

G-4

ostrich

G-5

turkey

G-6

zebra

NAMING ANIMALS—MATCHING

DIRECTIONS: Draw a line from each picture to the name of the animal shown in the picture. Then trace and copy each word.

G-7

EXAMPLE

camel

lizard

ostrich

snake

zebra

NAMING ANIMALS—MATCHING

DIRECTIONS: Trace and copy each animal name. Then draw a line from each animal to its name.

G-8

frog

giraffe

owl

shark

turtle

NAMING ANIMALS—WRITING

DIRECTIONS: Using the words in the WORD BOX, write the name of each animal.

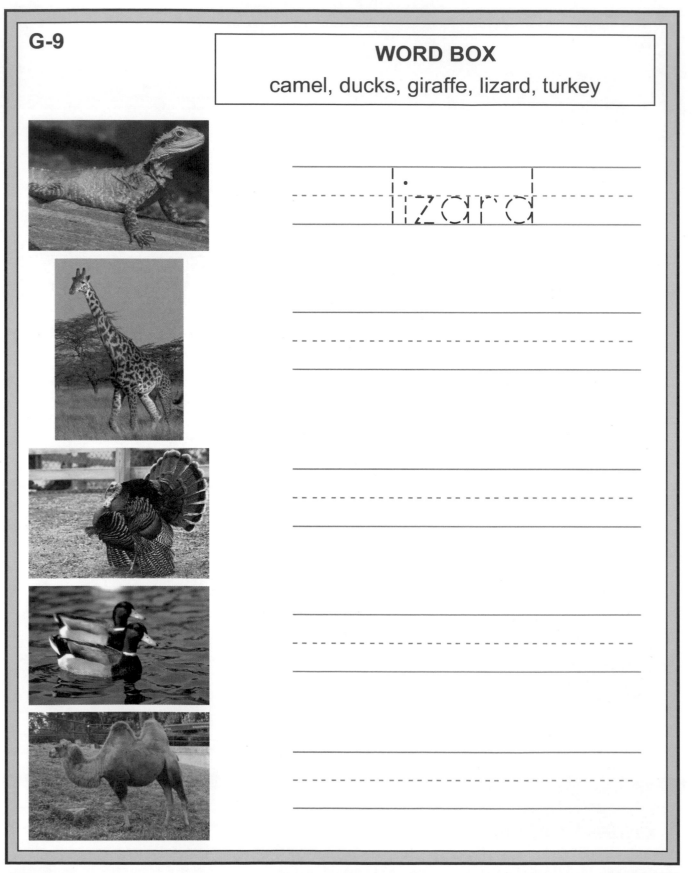

G-9

WORD BOX
camel, ducks, giraffe, lizard, turkey

lizard

NAMING ANIMALS—WRITING

DIRECTIONS: Using the words in the WORD BOX, write the name of each animal.

G-10

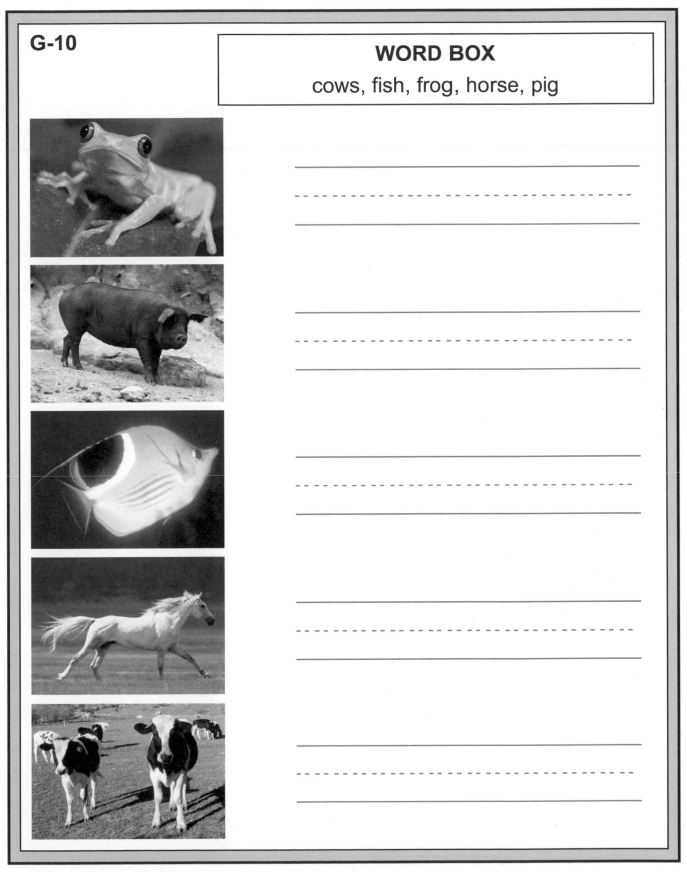

WORD BOX
cows, fish, frog, horse, pig

_____

- - - - - - - - - - - - - - - - - - - -

_____

_____

- - - - - - - - - - - - - - - - - - - -

_____

_____

- - - - - - - - - - - - - - - - - - - -

_____

_____

- - - - - - - - - - - - - - - - - - - -

_____

_____

- - - - - - - - - - - - - - - - - - - -

_____

CHARACTERISTICS OF ANIMALS

DIRECTIONS: Some animals produce foods that we eat. Draw a line from each picture to the name of the animal and the food it produces. Then trace and copy each word.

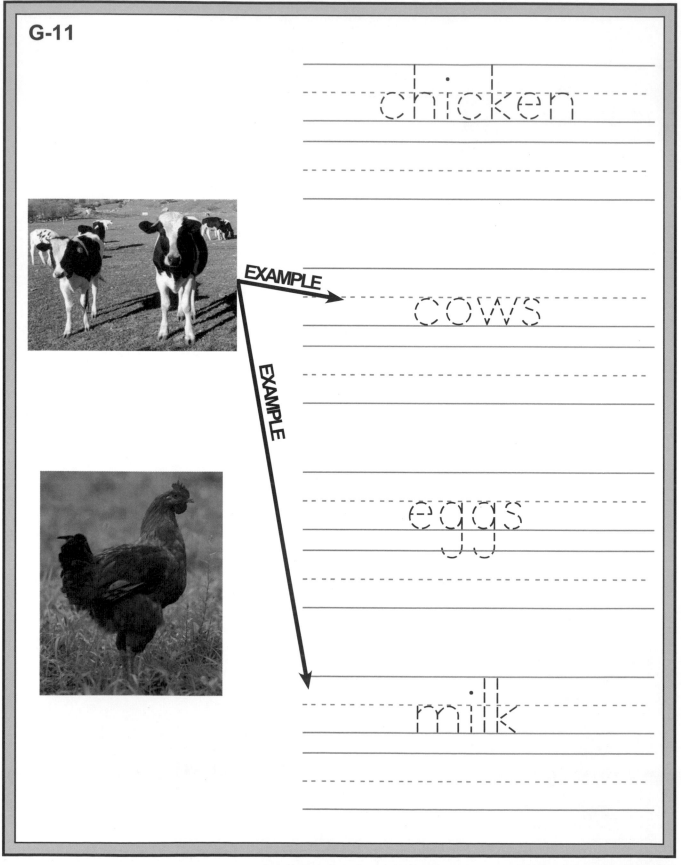

G-11

chicken

EXAMPLE

cows

EXAMPLE

eggs

milk

CHARACTERISTICS OF ANIMALS

DIRECTIONS: Some animals move fast and others move slowly. Some are tall and others are short. Trace and copy each word. Then draw a line from each picture to the words that describe that animal.

G-12

fast

slow

short

tall

CHARACTERISTICS OF ANIMALS

DIRECTIONS: Birds lay eggs and mammal mothers carry their young inside their bodies. Trace and copy each word. Then draw a line from each picture to the word that describes it.

G-13

bird

mammal

CHARACTERISTICS OF ANIMALS

DIRECTIONS: Fish must live in water. Reptiles breathe air and live on land. Trace and copy each word. Then draw a line from each picture to the word that describes it.

G-14

fish

reptile

SIMILAR ANIMALS—SELECT

DIRECTIONS: Circle the picture of the animal most like the one on the left.

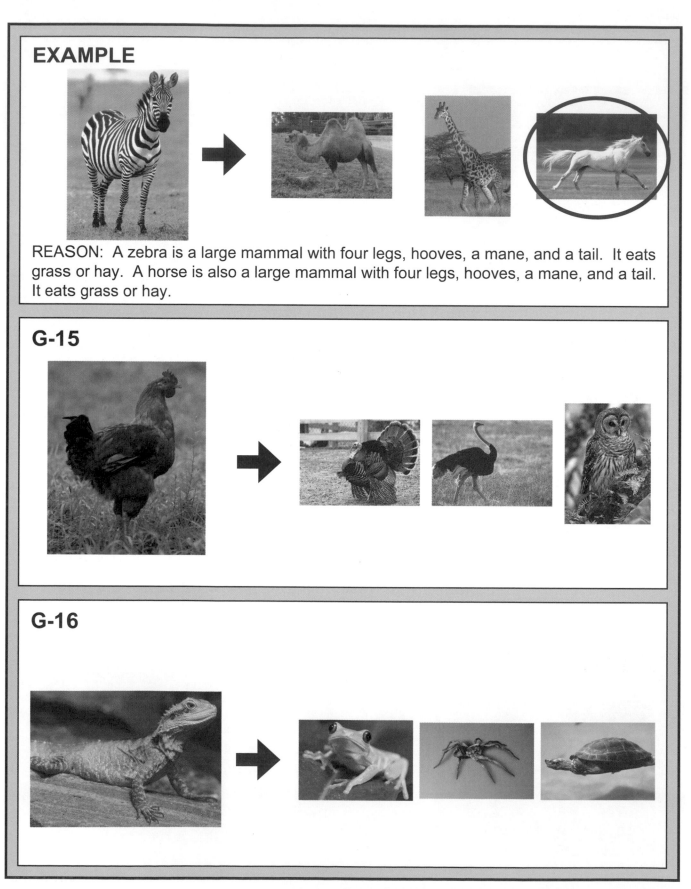

EXAMPLE

REASON: A zebra is a large mammal with four legs, hooves, a mane, and a tail. It eats grass or hay. A horse is also a large mammal with four legs, hooves, a mane, and a tail. It eats grass or hay.

G-15

G-16

SIMILAR ANIMALS—EXPLAIN

DIRECTIONS: Tell your partner or teacher how these animals are alike. Then trace and copy each word.

G-17

lizard

snake

G-18

ostrich

turkey

G-19

camel

horse

SIMILARITIES AND DIFFERENCES—ANIMALS

DIRECTIONS: Trace and copy the words. Then explain how these animals are ALIKE and how these animals are DIFFERENT.

G-20

chicken

ducks

G-21

spider

lizard

RANKING ANIMALS

DIRECTIONS: Write the names of the animals on the blanks arranged in order from smallest to largest.

G-22

pig   giraffe   chicken

SMALLEST

chicken

LARGEST

G-23

ducks   ostrich   turkey

SMALLEST

LARGEST

MATCH ANIMALS TO THEIR CLASSES

DIRECTIONS: Trace and copy each of the animal classes (groups). Then draw a line from each picture to the word describing its class.

G-24

EXAMPLE

mammal

bird

amphibian

reptile

MATCH ANIMALS TO THEIR CLASSES

DIRECTIONS: Trace and copy each of the animal classes (groups). Then draw a line from each picture to the word describing its class.

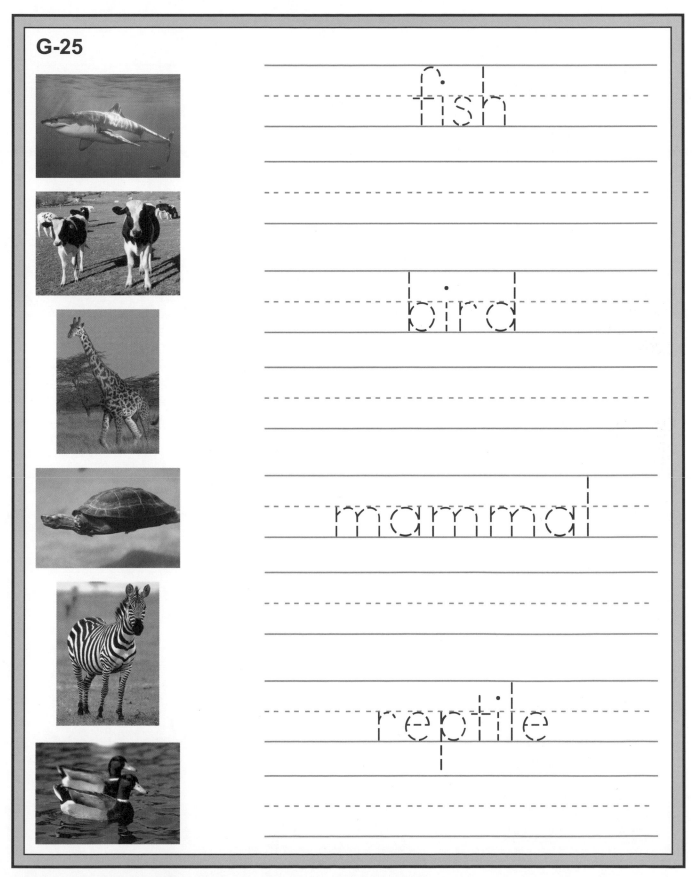

G-25

fish

bird

mammal

reptile

MATCH ANIMALS TO THEIR CLASSES

DIRECTIONS: Trace and copy each each of the animal classes (groups). Then draw a line from each picture to the word describing its class.

G-26

fish

bird

mammal

reptile

MATCH ANIMALS TO THEIR CLASSES

DIRECTIONS: Trace and copy each of the animal classes (groups). Then draw a line from each picture to the word describing its class.

G-25

fish

bird

mammal

reptile

MATCH ANIMALS TO THEIR CLASSES

DIRECTIONS: Trace and copy each each of the animal classes (groups). Then draw a line from each picture to the word describing its class.

G-26

fish

bird

mammal

reptile

NAME THE CLASS—ANIMALS

DIRECTIONS: Using the words in the WORD BOX, write the class (group) on the top line. Then write the names of the animals on the three lines.

G-27

WORD BOX

camel, hoofed mammals, giraffe, horse

CLASS   hoofed mammals

MEMBERS

G-28

WORD BOX

lizard, reptiles, snake, turtle

CLASS

MEMBERS

EXPLAIN THE EXCEPTION—ANIMALS

DIRECTIONS: Three animals belong to the same class (group). Using the words in the WORD BOX, write the class and members on the lines. Then trace why one animal is an exception.

G-29

WORD BOX
birds, chicken, ducks, mammal, pig, turkey

CLASS

birds

MEMBERS

EXCEPTION

pig

EXPLAIN THE EXCEPTION

The pig is a mammal.
The others are birds.

EXPLAIN THE EXCEPTION—ANIMALS

DIRECTIONS: Three animals belong to the same class (group). Using the words in the WORD BOX, write the class and members on the lines. Then explain why one member is an exception.

G-30

WORD BOX
bird, cows, horse, mammals, owl, zebra

CLASS

_____

MEMBERS

_____

_____

_____

EXCEPTION

_____

EXPLAIN THE EXCEPTION

_____

_____

EXPLAIN THE EXCEPTION—ANIMALS

DIRECTIONS: Three animals belong to the same class (group). Using the words in the WORD BOX, write the class and members on the lines. Then explain why one member is an exception.

G-31

WORD BOX
amphibian, frog, lizard, reptiles, snake, turtle

CLASS

_____

- -

_____

MEMBERS

_____

- -

_____

_____

- -

_____

_____

- -

_____

EXCEPTION

- -

_____

EXPLAIN THE EXCEPTION

_____

- -

_____

_____

- -

SORTING INTO CLASSES—ANIMALS

DIRECTIONS: On the diagram on the next page, write each of the animals in the class (group) in which it belongs.

G-32

lizard

owl

horse

pig

ostrich

snake

turkey

turtle

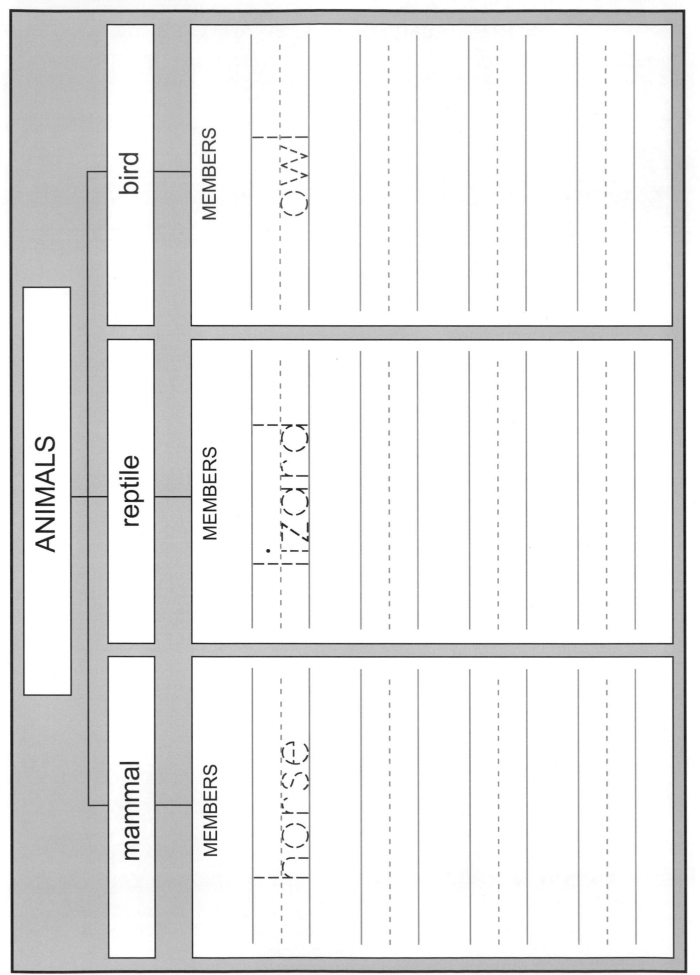

ANIMALS

bird

MEMBERS

owl

reptile

MEMBERS

lizard

mammal

MEMBERS

horse

Chapter Eight
Thinking About Occupations

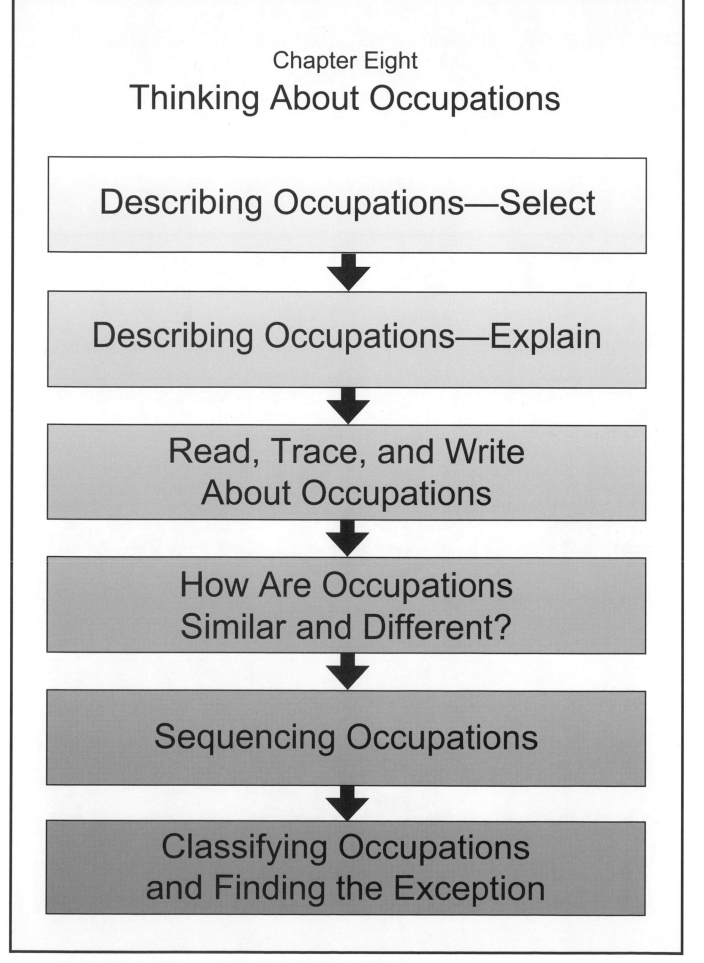

Describing Occupations—Select

Describing Occupations—Explain

Read, Trace, and Write
About Occupations

How Are Occupations
Similar and Different?

Sequencing Occupations

Classifying Occupations
and Finding the Exception

DESCRIBING JOBS—SELECT

DIRECTIONS: Circle the picture of the job that your teacher describes. (Teacher: see pages 263-264.)

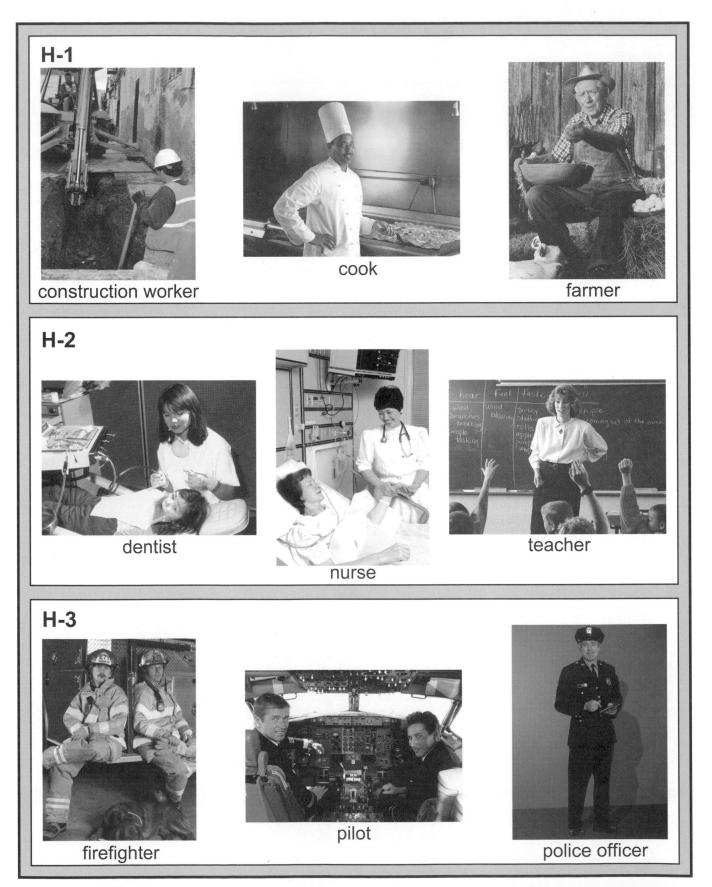

H-1

construction worker

cook

farmer

H-2

dentist

nurse

teacher

H-3

firefighter

pilot

police officer

DESCRIBING JOBS—EXPLAIN

DIRECTIONS: Describe this person's job to your partner or teacher. Then trace and copy the job names.

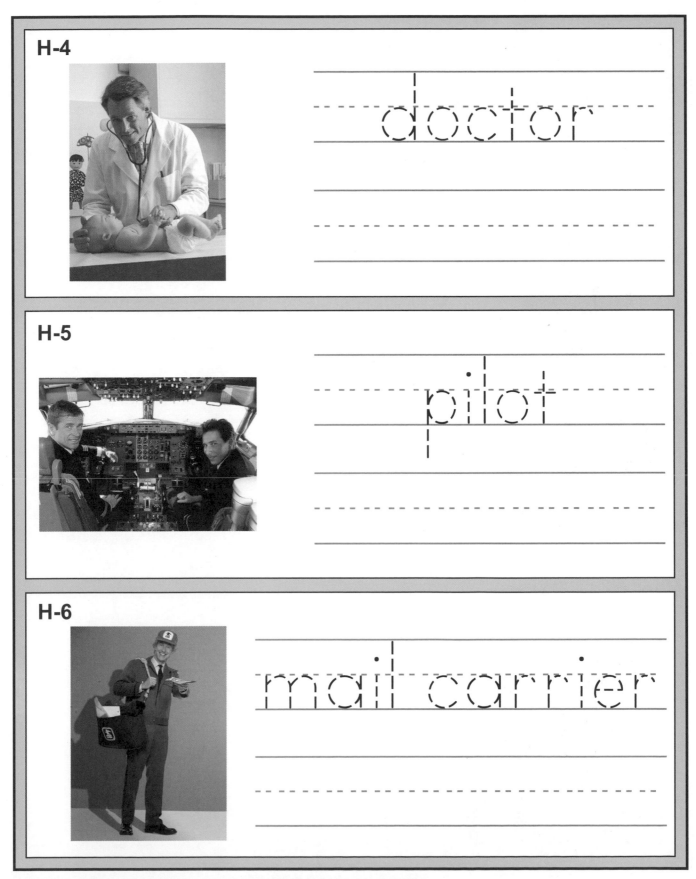

H-4

doctor

H-5

pilot

H-6

mail carrier

NAMING JOBS—MATCHING

DIRECTIONS: Draw a line from each picture to the name of that person's job. Then trace and copy each word.

H-7

EXAMPLE

artist

dentist

doctor

nurse

NAMING JOBS—MATCHING

DIRECTIONS: Trace and copy each of the job names. Then draw a line from each picture to the name of the job shown in the picture.

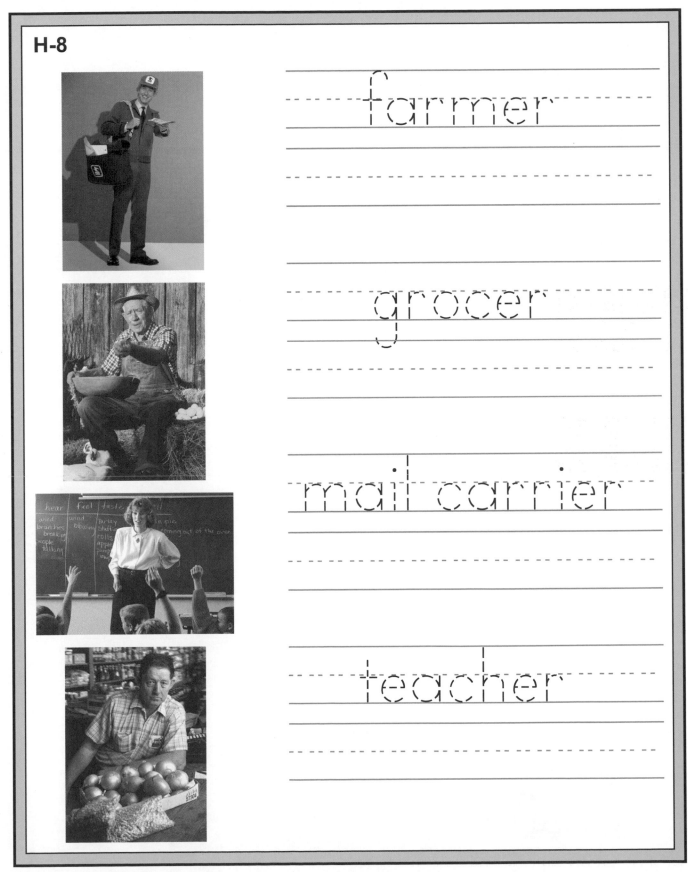

H-8

farmer

grocer

mail carrier

teacher

NAMING JOBS—WRITING

DIRECTIONS: Using the words in the WORD BOX, write the name of each job.

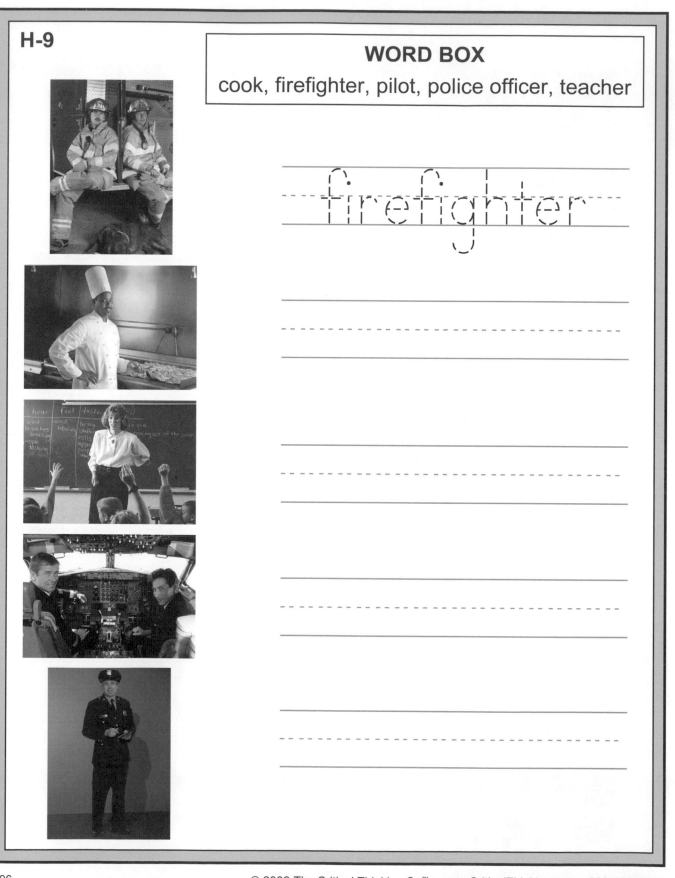

H-9

WORD BOX
cook, firefighter, pilot, police officer, teacher

firefighter

NAMING JOBS—WRITING

DIRECTIONS: Using the words in the WORD BOX, write the name of each job.

H-10

WORD BOX
barber, doctor, farmer, nurse

SIMILAR JOBS—SELECT

DIRECTIONS: Circle the picture of the job most like the one on the left.

EXAMPLE

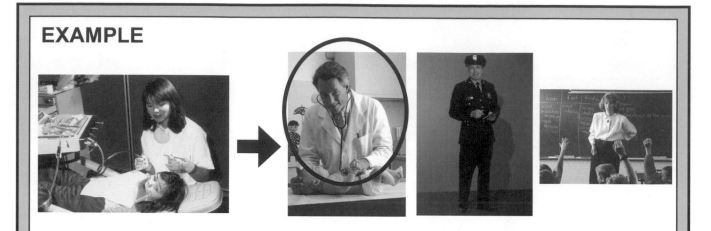

REASON: Both have special training in health care and use special instruments.

H-11

H-12

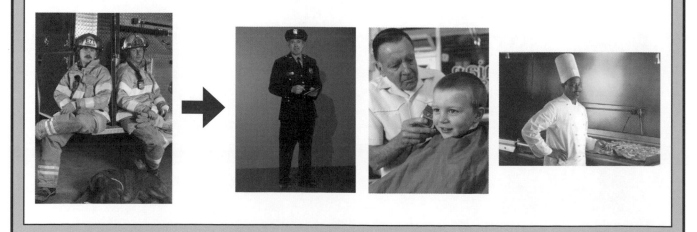

SIMILAR JOBS—EXPLAIN

DIRECTIONS: Tell your partner or teacher how these jobs are alike. Then trace and copy each job name.

H-13

doctor

nurse

H-14

mail carrier

police officer

H-15

grocer

cook

SIMILARITIES AND DIFFERENCES—JOBS

DIRECTIONS: Trace and copy the words. Then explain how these jobs are ALIKE and how these jobs are DIFFERENT.

H-16

barber

dentist

H-17

artist

worker

RANKING JOBS

DIRECTIONS: Write these jobs in the order in which they help us get food or in the order you or your family need the services of each worker.

H-18

cook

farmer

grocer

FIRST

farmer

LAST

H-19

teacher

firefighter

doctor

SELDOM

OFTEN

MATCH THE CLASS—JOBS

DIRECTIONS: Some people make things. They produce goods. Other people help, serve, or protect people. They have "service" jobs. Draw a line from each job to the word that describes it. Then trace and copy each word.

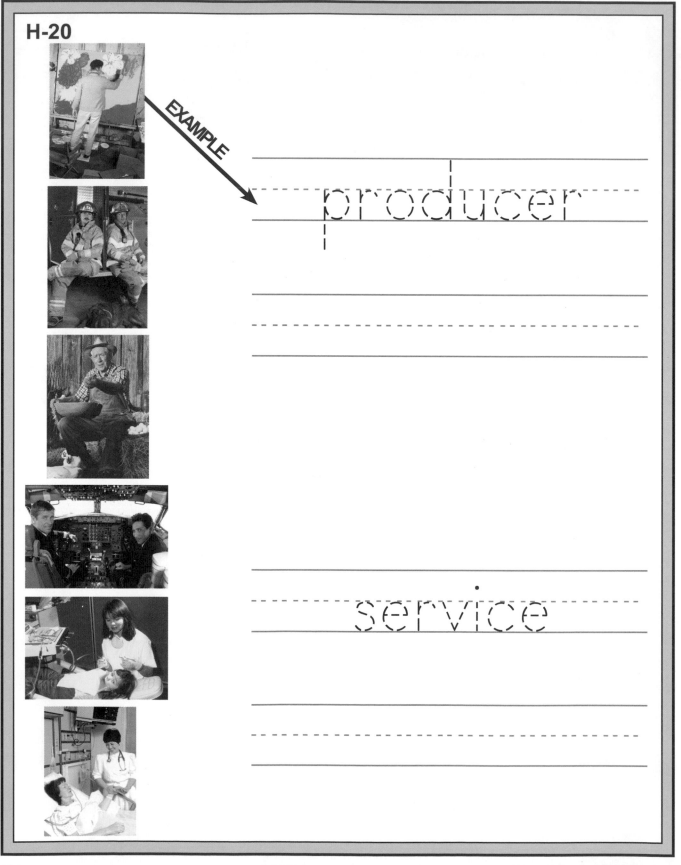

H-20

EXAMPLE

producer

service

NAME THE CLASS—JOBS

DIRECTIONS: Using the words in the WORD BOX, write the class (group) on the top line. Then write the names of the jobs on the three lines.

H-21

WORD BOX
artist, construction worker, farmer, producers

CLASS

producers

MEMBERS

H-22

WORD BOX
dentist, doctor, health workers, nurse

CLASS

MEMBERS

EXPLAIN THE EXCEPTION—JOBS

DIRECTIONS: Three jobs belong to the same class (group). Using the words in the WORD BOX, write the class and members on the lines. Then trace why one job is an exception.

H-23

WORD BOX
artist, barber, producer, service providers, teacher

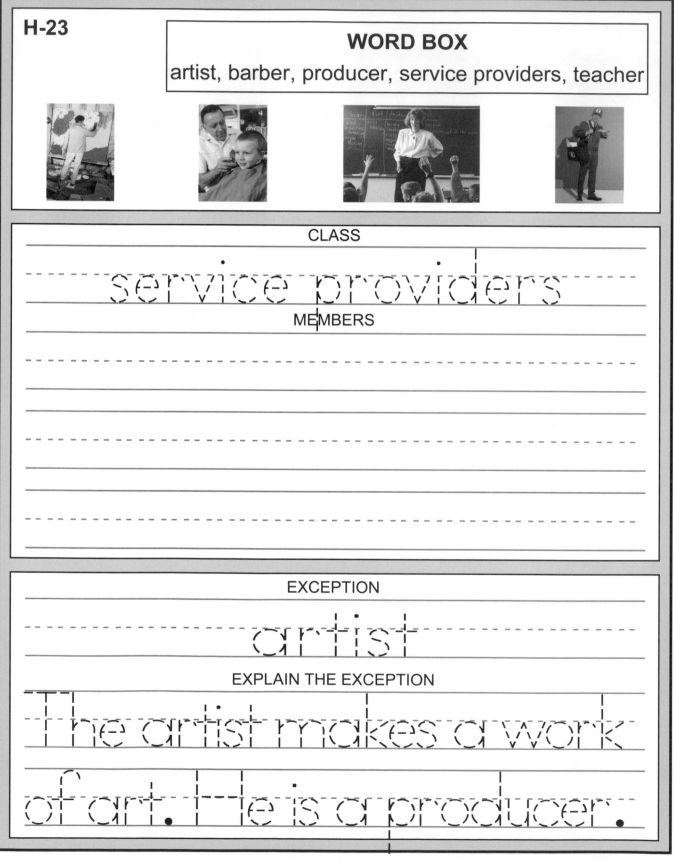

CLASS

service providers

MEMBERS

EXCEPTION

artist

EXPLAIN THE EXCEPTION

The artist makes a work of art. He is a producer.

EXPLAIN THE EXCEPTION—JOBS

DIRECTIONS: Three jobs belong to the same class (group). Using the words in the WORD BOX, write the class and members on the lines. Then explain why one job is an exception.

H-24

WORD BOX

artist, cook, farmer, food worker, grocer, producer

CLASS

MEMBERS

EXCEPTION

EXPLAIN THE EXCEPTION

SORTING INTO CLASSES—JOBS

DIRECTIONS: Write each of these jobs in the class (group) that it belongs (jobs that produce goods and jobs that provide services).

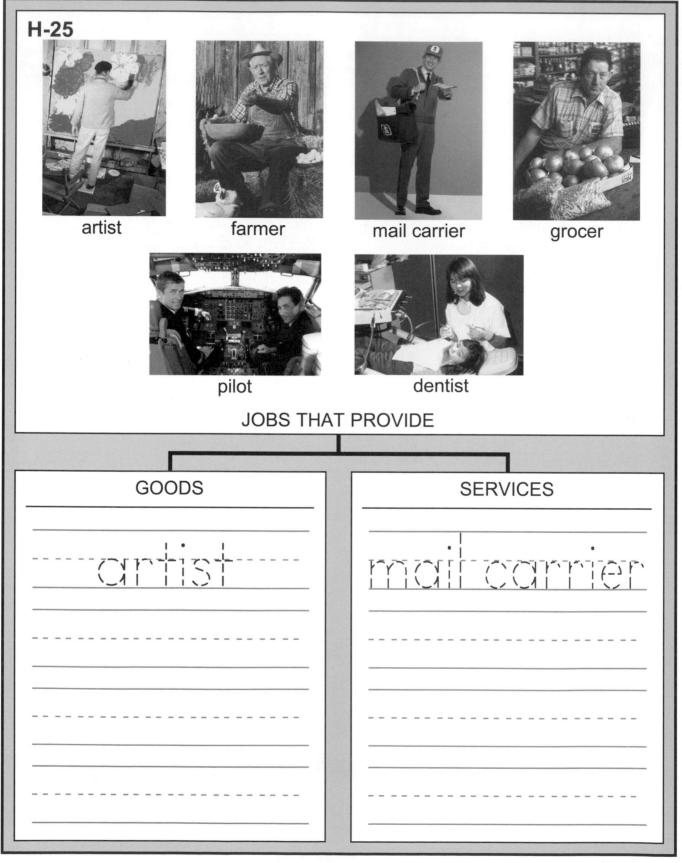

H-25

artist   farmer   mail carrier   grocer

pilot   dentist

JOBS THAT PROVIDE

GOODS	SERVICES
artist	mail carrier

Chapter Nine
Thinking About Vehicles

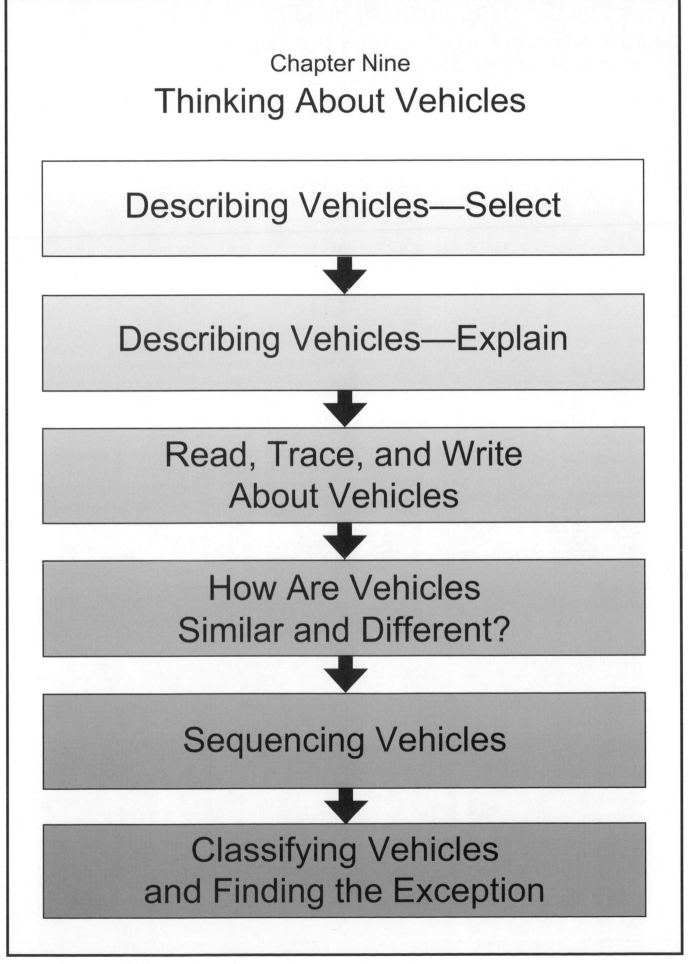

Describing Vehicles—Select

Describing Vehicles—Explain

Read, Trace, and Write
About Vehicles

How Are Vehicles
Similar and Different?

Sequencing Vehicles

Classifying Vehicles
and Finding the Exception

DESCRIBING VEHICLES—SELECT

DIRECTIONS: Circle the picture of the vehicle that your teacher describes.
(Teacher: see pages 264-265.)

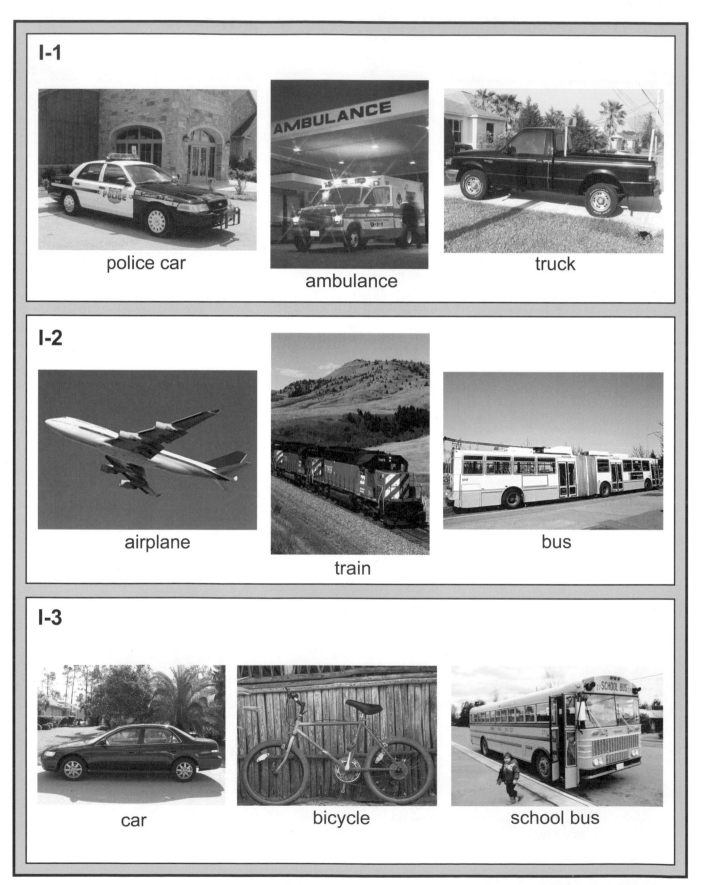

I-1

police car

ambulance

truck

I-2

airplane

train

bus

I-3

car

bicycle

school bus

DESCRIBING VEHICLES—EXPLAIN

DIRECTIONS: Describe this vehicle to your partner or teacher. Then trace and copy the vehicle names.

I-4

helicopter

I-5

train

I-6

ship

NAMING VEHICLES—MATCHING

DIRECTIONS: Draw a line from each picture to the name of the vehicle. Then trace and copy each word.

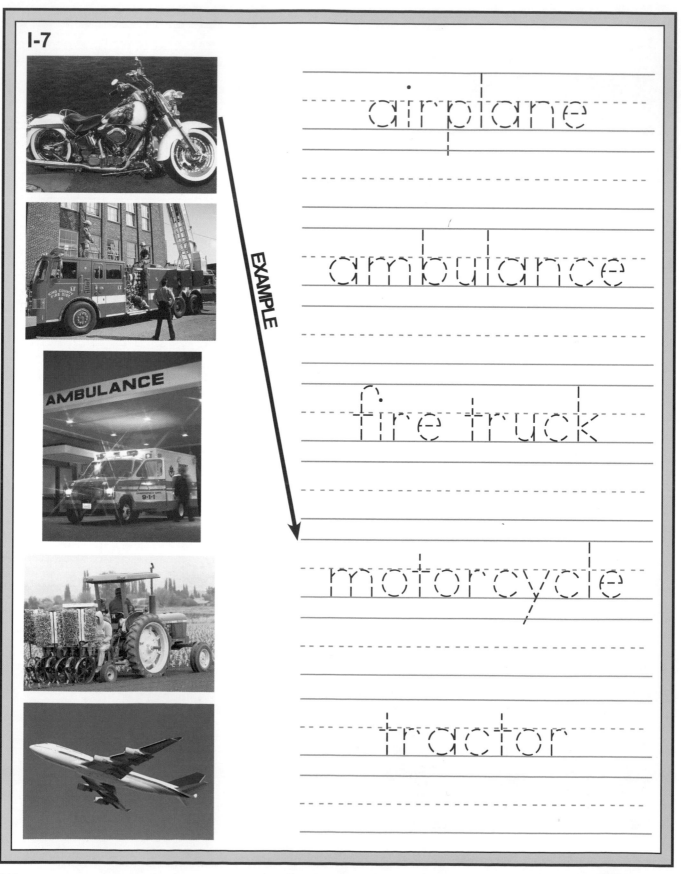

I-7

EXAMPLE

airplane

ambulance

fire truck

motorcycle

tractor

NAMING VEHICLES—MATCHING

DIRECTIONS: Draw a line from each picture to the vehicle shown in the picture. Then trace and copy each of the vehicle names.

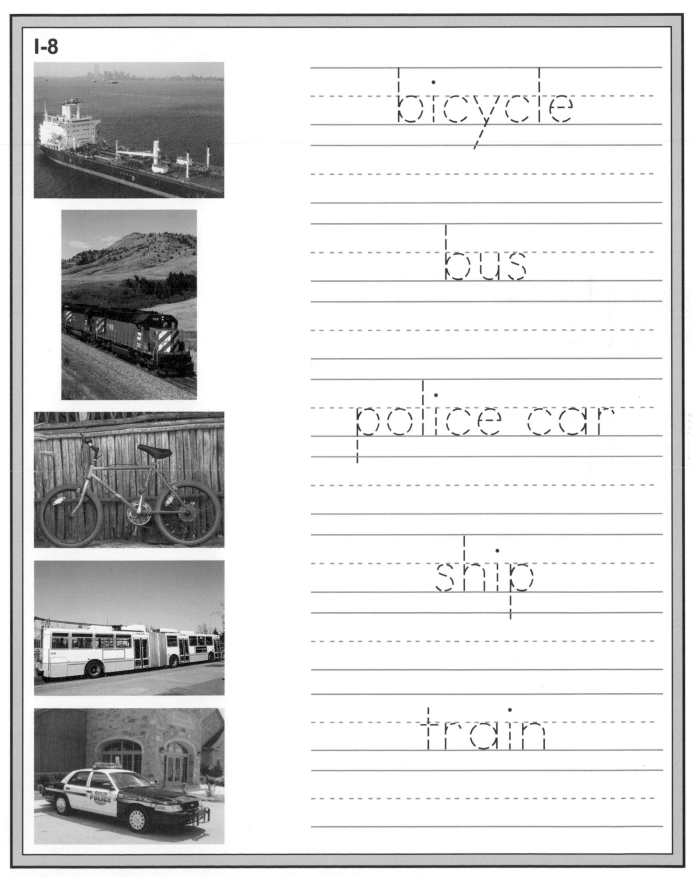

I-8

bicycle

bus

police car

ship

train

NAMING VEHICLES—WRITING

DIRECTIONS: Using the words in the WORD BOX, write the name of each vehicle.

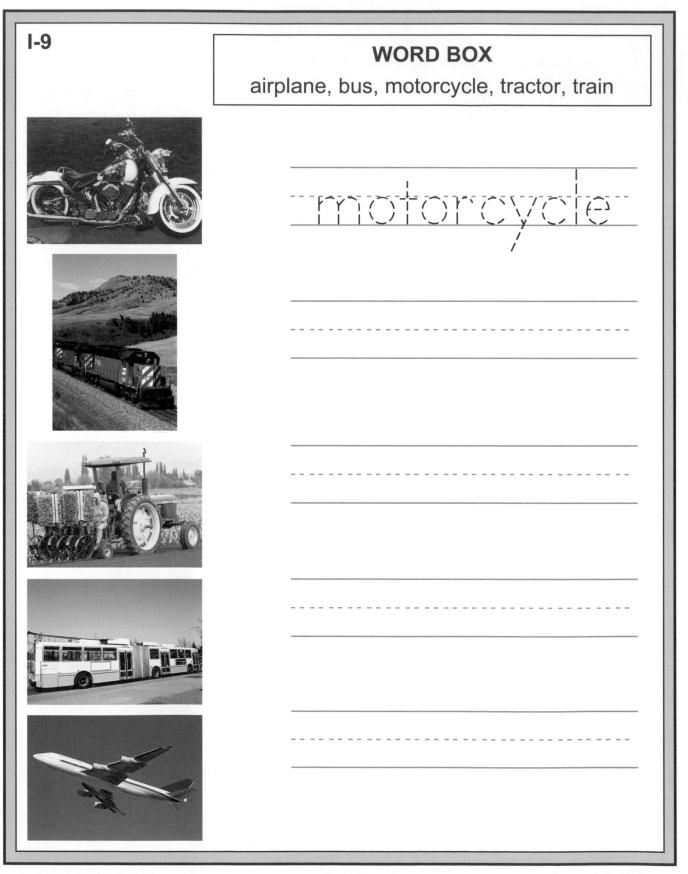

I-9

WORD BOX
airplane, bus, motorcycle, tractor, train

motorcycle

NAMING VEHICLES—WRITING

DIRECTIONS: Using the words in the WORD BOX, write the name of each vehicle.

I-10

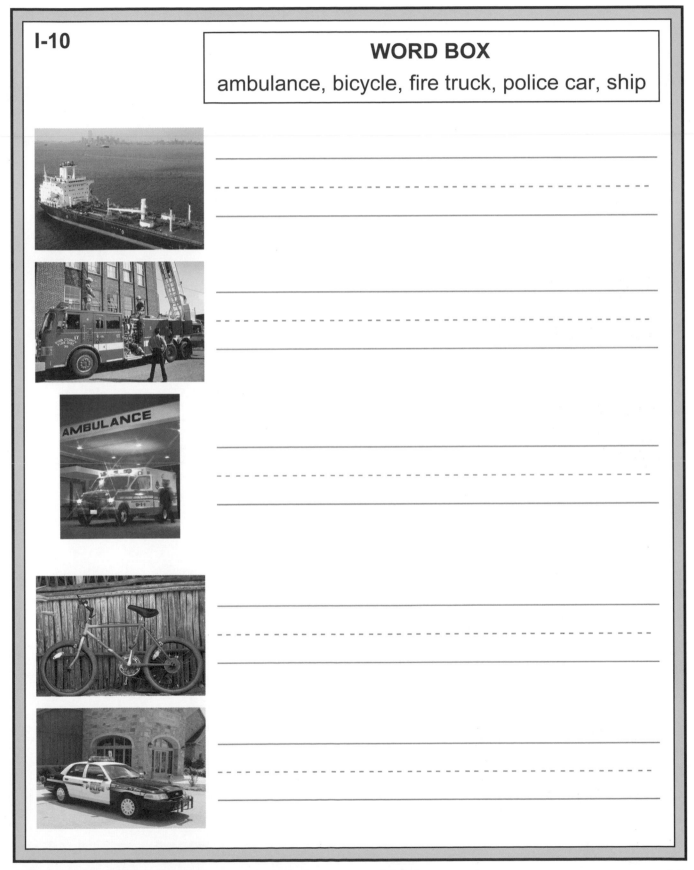

WORD BOX
ambulance, bicycle, fire truck, police car, ship

CHARACTERISTICS OF VEHICLES

DIRECTIONS: Some vehicles move fast and some move slow. Draw lines from each picture to the words that describe that vehicle. Then trace and copy each word.

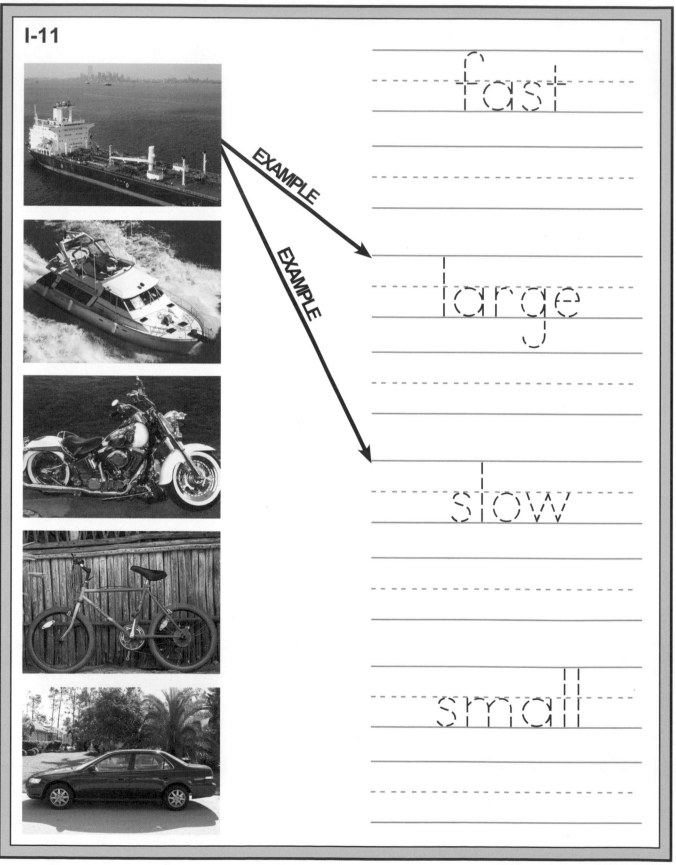

I-11

EXAMPLE

EXAMPLE

fast

large

slow

small

SIMILAR VEHICLES—SELECT

DIRECTIONS: Circle the picture of the vehicle most like the one on the left.

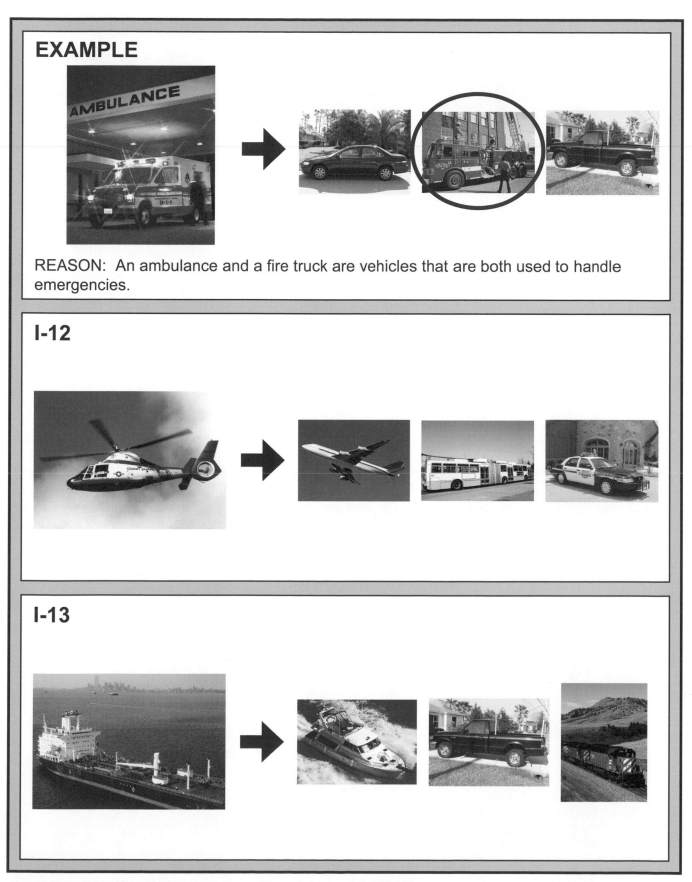

EXAMPLE

REASON: An ambulance and a fire truck are vehicles that are both used to handle emergencies.

I-12

I-13

SIMILAR VEHICLES—EXPLAIN

DIRECTIONS: Tell your partner or teacher how these vehicles are alike. Then trace and copy each word.

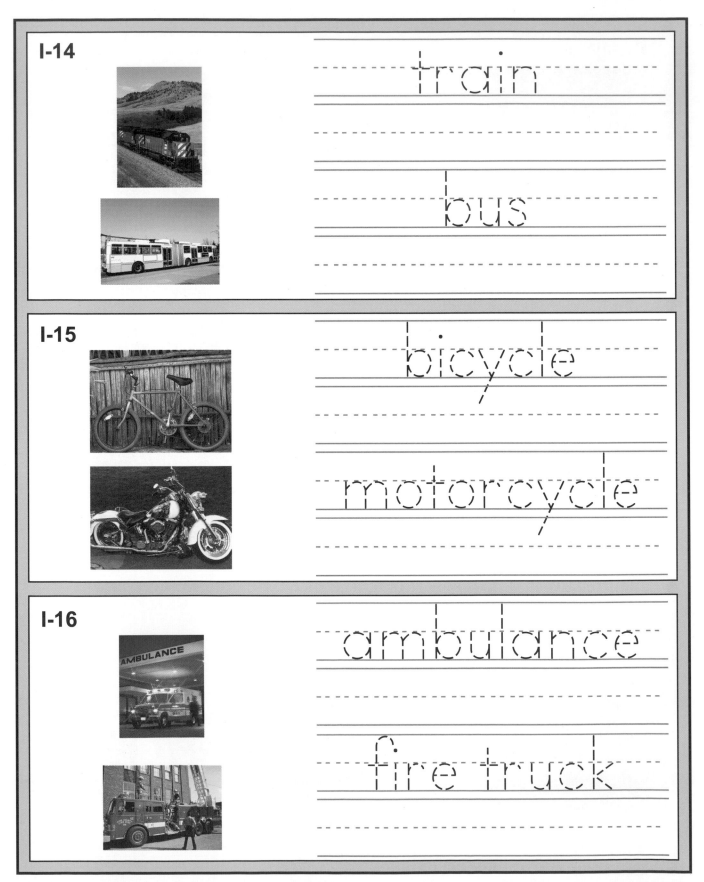

I-14

train

bus

I-15

bicycle

motorcycle

I-16

ambulance

fire truck

SIMILARITIES AND DIFFERENCES—VEHICLES

DIRECTIONS: Trace and copy the words. Then explain how these vehicles are ALIKE and how these vehicles are DIFFERENT.

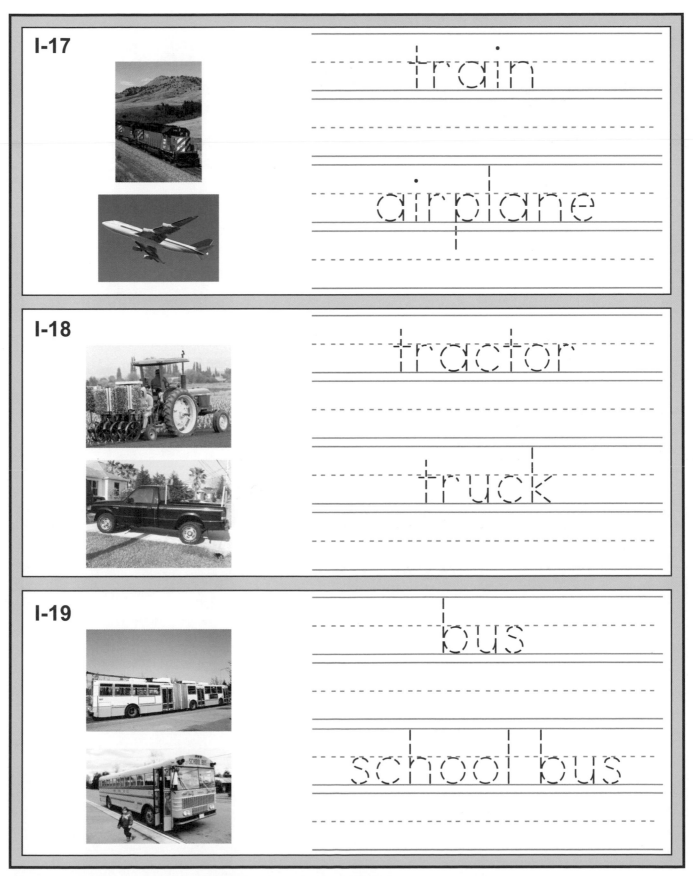

I-17

train

airplane

I-18

tractor

truck

I-19

bus

school bus

RANKING VEHICLES

DIRECTIONS: Write the names of the vehicles in order of how many passengers they carry and how often you ride on them.

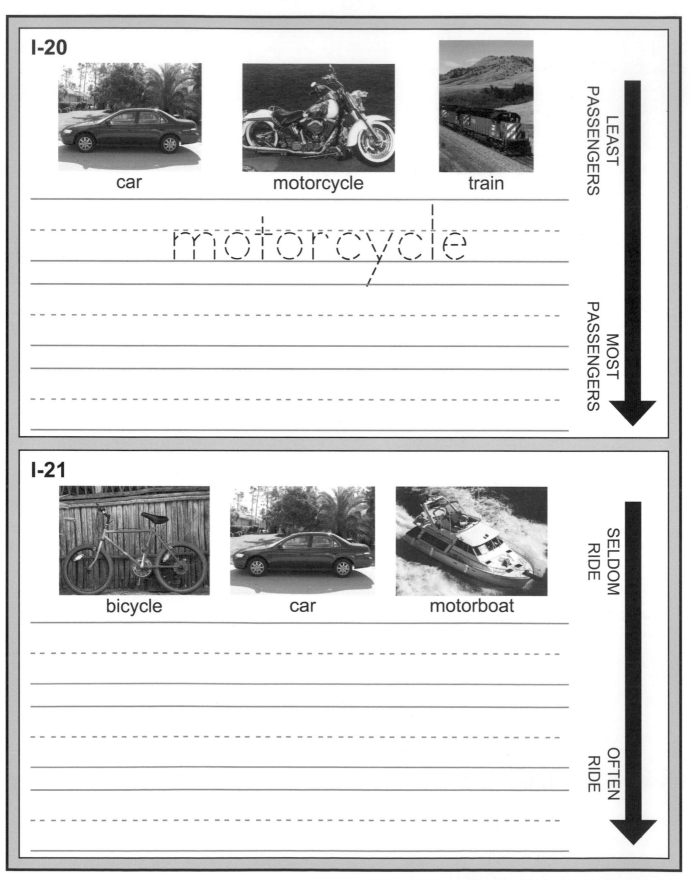

I-20

car   motorcycle   train

LEAST PASSENGERS

motorcycle

MOST PASSENGERS

I-21

bicycle   car   motorboat

SELDOM RIDE

OFTEN RIDE

NAMING CLASSES—MATCHING

DIRECTIONS: Trace and copy each of the vehicle classes (groups). Then draw a line from each picture to its class (group).

I-22

emergency
vehicle

public
transportation

recreation
vehicle

NAME THE CLASS—VEHICLES

DIRECTIONS: Using the words in the WORD BOX, write the class (group) on the top line. Then write the names of the vehicles on the three lines.

I-23

WORD BOX

ambulance, emergency vehicles, fire truck, police car

CLASS

emergency vehicles

MEMBERS

I-24

WORD BOX

bicycle, motorboat, motorcycle, recreation vehicles

CLASS

MEMBERS

NAME THE CLASS—VEHICLES

DIRECTIONS: Using the words in the WORD BOX, write the class (group) on the top line. Then write the names of the vehicles on the three lines.

I-25

WORD BOX
airplane, bus, train, public transportation

CLASS _____

MEMBERS _____

_____

_____

I-26

WORD BOX
cargo vehicles, pickup truck, ship, train

CLASS _____

MEMBERS _____

_____

_____

EXPLAIN THE EXCEPTION—VEHICLES

DIRECTIONS: Three vehicles belong to the same class (group). Using the words in the WORD BOX, write the class and members on the lines. Then trace why one vehicle is an exception.

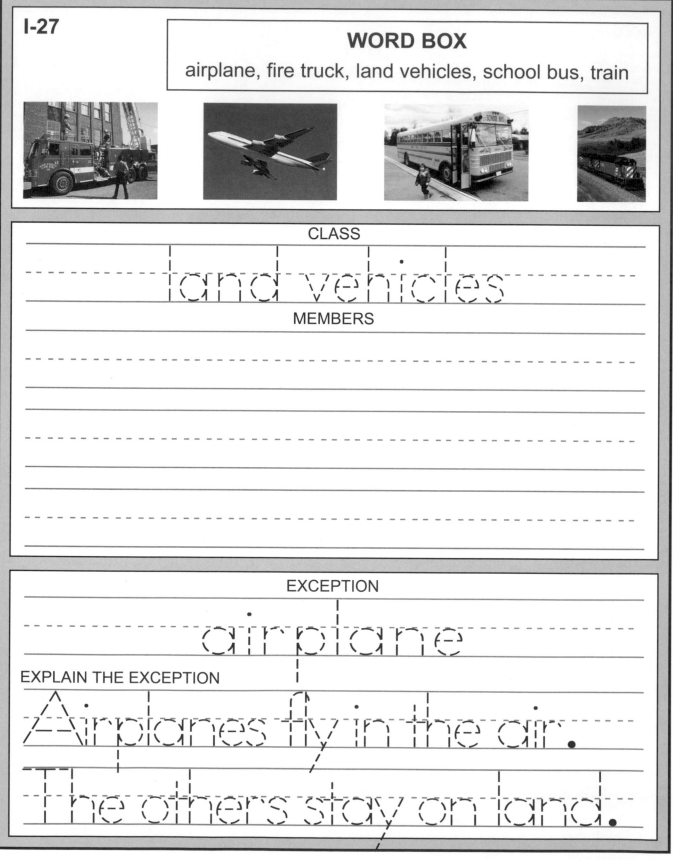

I-27

WORD BOX

airplane, fire truck, land vehicles, school bus, train

CLASS

land vehicles

MEMBERS

EXCEPTION

airplane

EXPLAIN THE EXCEPTION

Airplanes fly in the air.
The others stay on land.

EXPLAIN THE EXCEPTION—VEHICLES

DIRECTIONS: Three vehicles belong to the same class (group). Using the words in the WORD BOX, write the class and members on the lines. Then explain why one vehicle is an exception.

I-28

WORD BOX
bicycle, motorboat, motorcycle, recreation vehicles, tractor, work

CLASS

MEMBERS

EXCEPTION

EXPLAIN THE EXCEPTION

MATCH DRIVERS TO THEIR VEHICLES

DIRECTIONS: Draw a line from each driver to their vehicle.

I-29

DRIVERS

VEHICLES

EXAMPLE

SORTING INTO CLASSES—VEHICLES

DIRECTIONS: Write the vehicle names in the three class boxes.

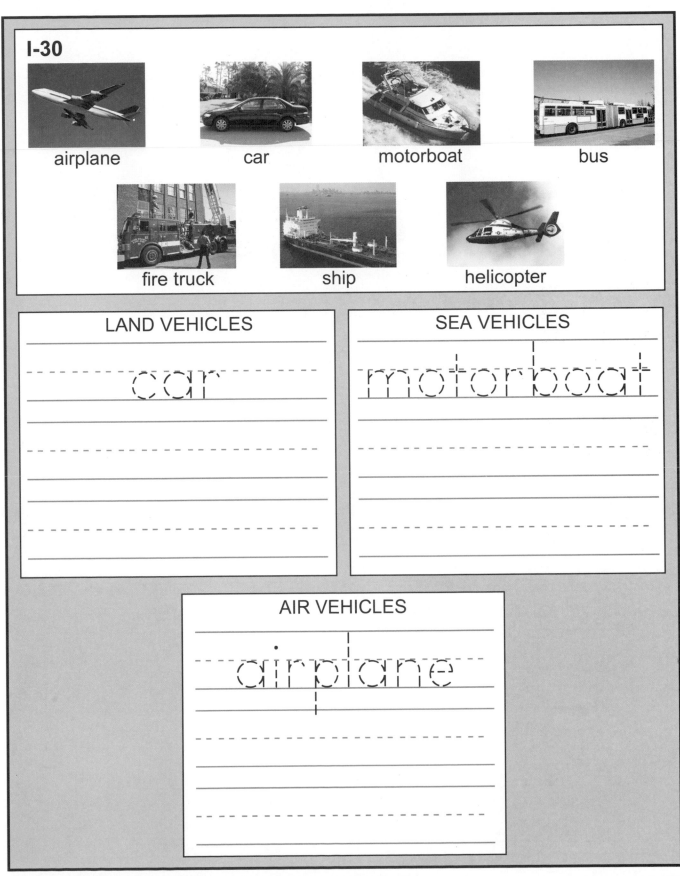

I-30

airplane   car   motorboat   bus

fire truck   ship   helicopter

LAND VEHICLES

car

SEA VEHICLES

motorboat

AIR VEHICLES

airplane

SORTING INTO CLASSES—VEHICLES

DIRECTIONS: Write the vehicle names in the four class boxes.

I-31

airplane

motorcycle

ambulance

motorboat

fire truck

ship

train

police car

PASSENGER VEHICLES

RECREATION VEHICLES

EMERGENCY VEHICLES

CARGO VEHICLES

Chapter Ten
Thinking About Buildings

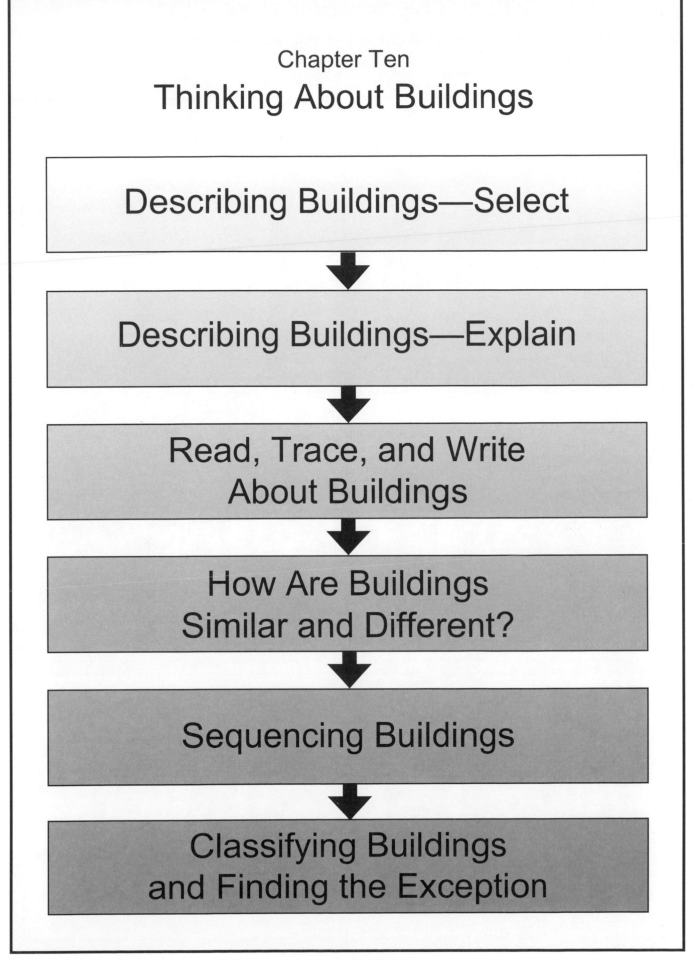

Describing Buildings—Select

Describing Buildings—Explain

Read, Trace, and Write
About Buildings

How Are Buildings
Similar and Different?

Sequencing Buildings

Classifying Buildings
and Finding the Exception

DESCRIBING BUILDINGS—SELECT

DIRECTIONS: Circle the picture of the building that your teacher describes.
(Teacher: see page 265.)

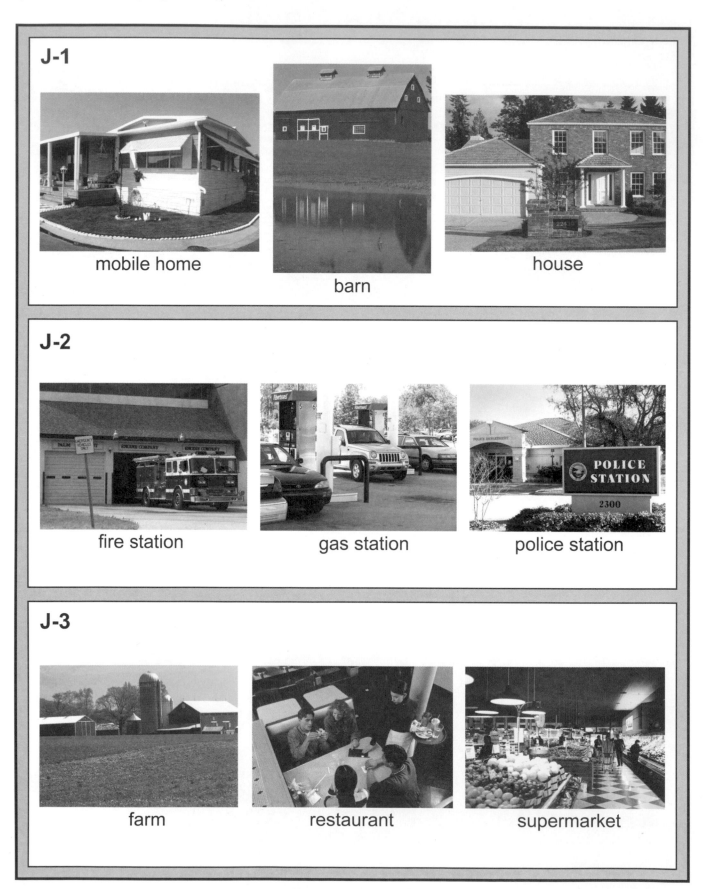

J-1

mobile home

barn

house

J-2

fire station

gas station

police station

J-3

farm

restaurant

supermarket

DESCRIBING BUILDINGS—EXPLAIN

DIRECTIONS: Describe this building to your partner or teacher. Then trace and copy the building names.

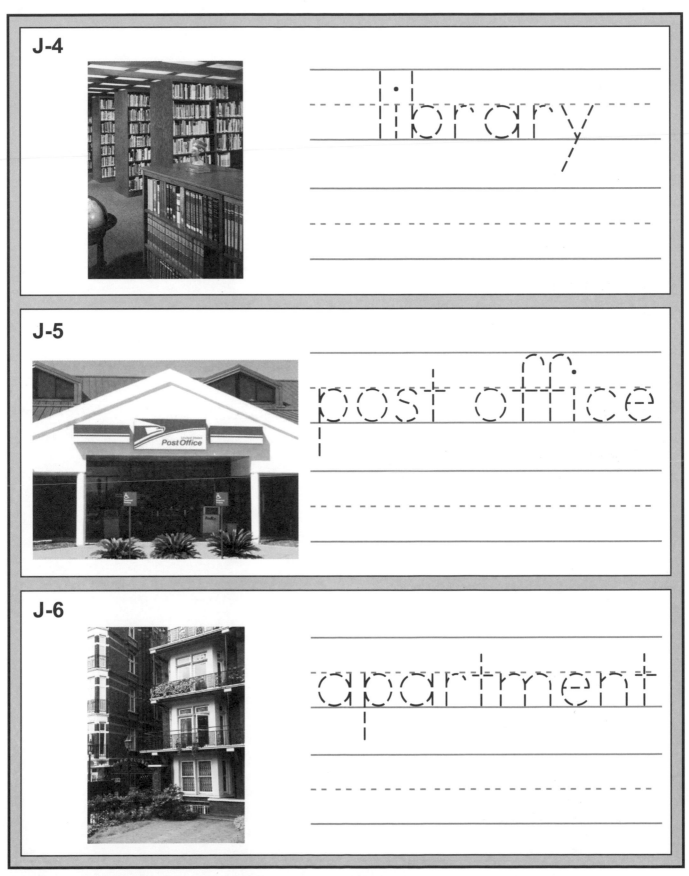

J-4

library

J-5

post office

J-6

apartment

NAMING BUILDINGS—MATCHING

DIRECTIONS: Draw a line from each picture to the name of the building. Then trace and copy each word.

J-7

EXAMPLE

apartment

barber shop

fire station

mobile home

school

NAMING BUILDINGS—MATCHING

DIRECTIONS: Draw a line from each picture to the name of the building shown in the picture. Then trace and copy each of the building names.

J-8

gas station

house

police station

restaurant

supermarket

POLICE
STATION

2300

NAMING BUILDINGS—WRITING

DIRECTIONS: Using the words in the WORD BOX, write the names of the buildings.

J-9

WORD BOX
barn, hospital, library, playground, post office

library

NAMING BUILDINGS—WRITING

DIRECTIONS: Using the words in the WORD BOX, write the name of each building.

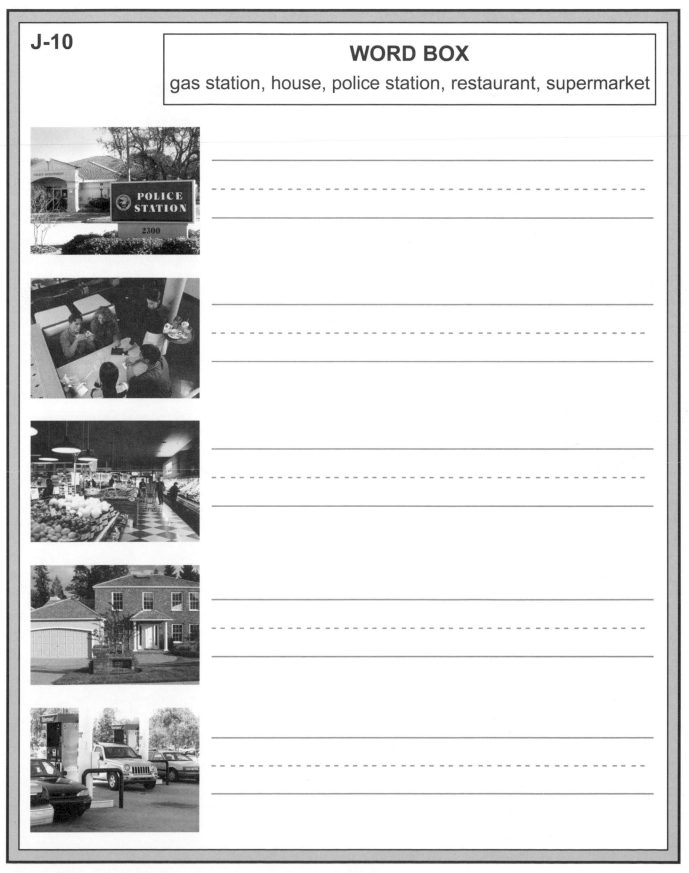

J-10

WORD BOX
gas station, house, police station, restaurant, supermarket

SIMILAR BUILDINGS—SELECT

DIRECTIONS: Circle the picture of the building most like the one on the left.

EXAMPLE

REASON: Both are places where families sleep, prepare their food, store belongings, and stay safe and warm.

J-11

J-12

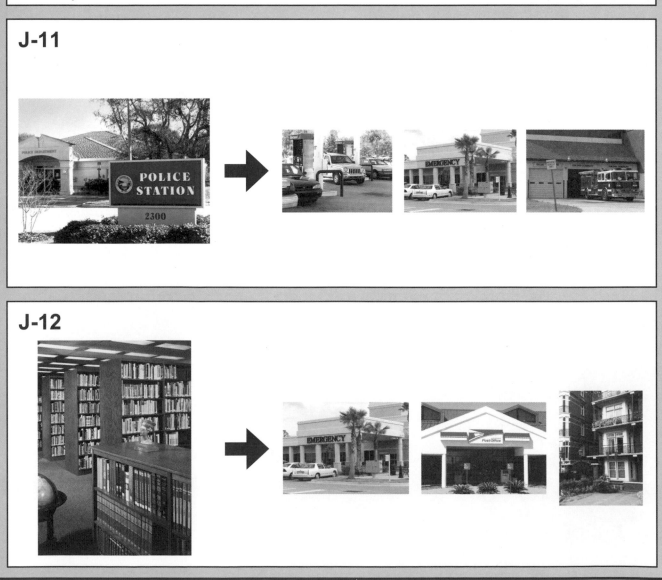

SIMILAR BUILDINGS—EXPLAIN

DIRECTIONS: Tell your partner or teacher how these buildings are alike. Then trace and copy each word.

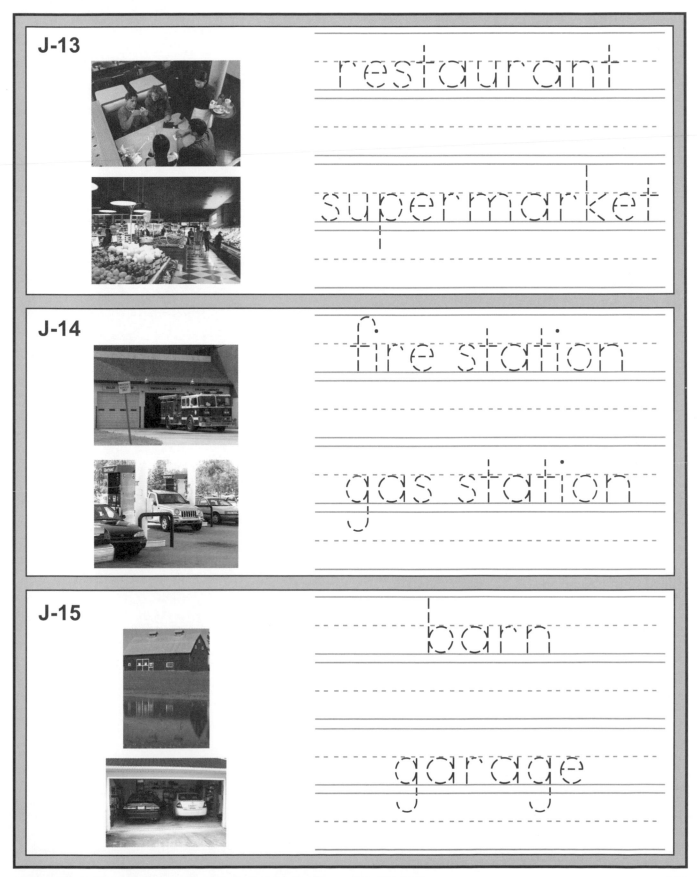

J-13

restaurant

supermarket

J-14

fire station

gas station

J-15

barn

garage

SIMILARITIES AND DIFFERENCES—BUILDINGS

DIRECTIONS: Trace and copy the words. Then explain how these buildings are ALIKE and how these buildings are DIFFERENT.

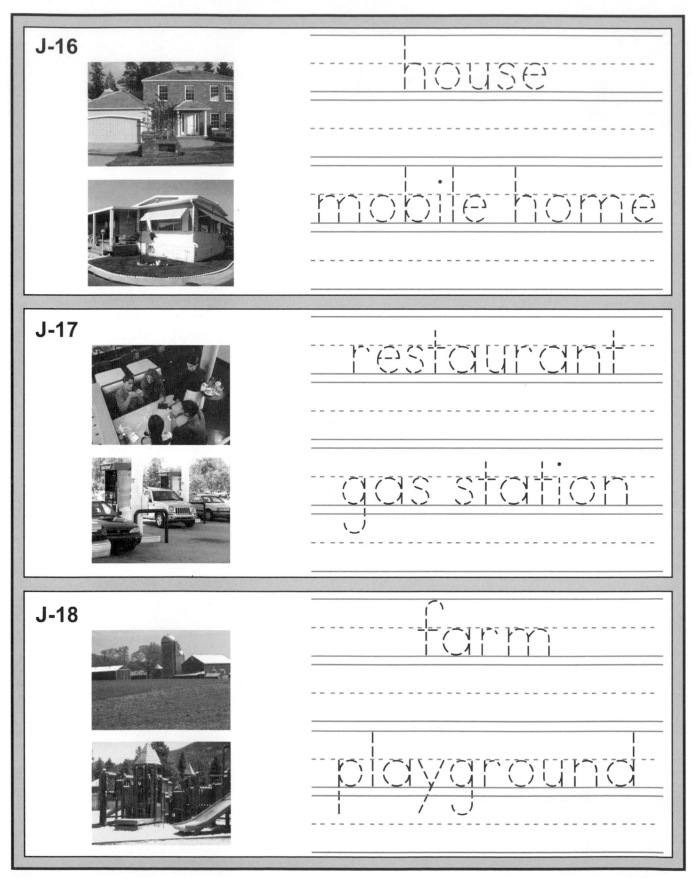

J-16

house

mobile home

J-17

restaurant

gas station

J-18

farm

playground

RANKING BUILDINGS

DIRECTIONS: Write the names of the buildings in order of size and how often you go into them.

J-19

house

apartment building

mobile home

SMALL

mobile home

LARGE

J-20

house

library

school

SELDOM
GO IN

OFTEN
GO IN

WRITE THE CLASS—BUILDINGS

DIRECTIONS: Find the class (group) of each building in the WORD BOX. Then write the class beside each picture.

J-21

WORD BOX
business, government, residence, storage

government

RANKING BUILDINGS

DIRECTIONS: Write the names of the buildings in order of size and how often you go into them.

J-19

house

apartment building

mobile home

mobile home

SMALL

LARGE

J-20

house

library

school

SELDOM
GO IN

OFTEN
GO IN

WRITE THE CLASS—BUILDINGS

DIRECTIONS: Find the class (group) of each building in the WORD BOX. Then write the class beside each picture.

J-21

WORD BOX
business, government, residence, storage

government

WRITE THE CLASS—BUILDINGS

DIRECTIONS: Find the class (group) of each building in the WORD BOX. Then write the class beside each picture.

J-22

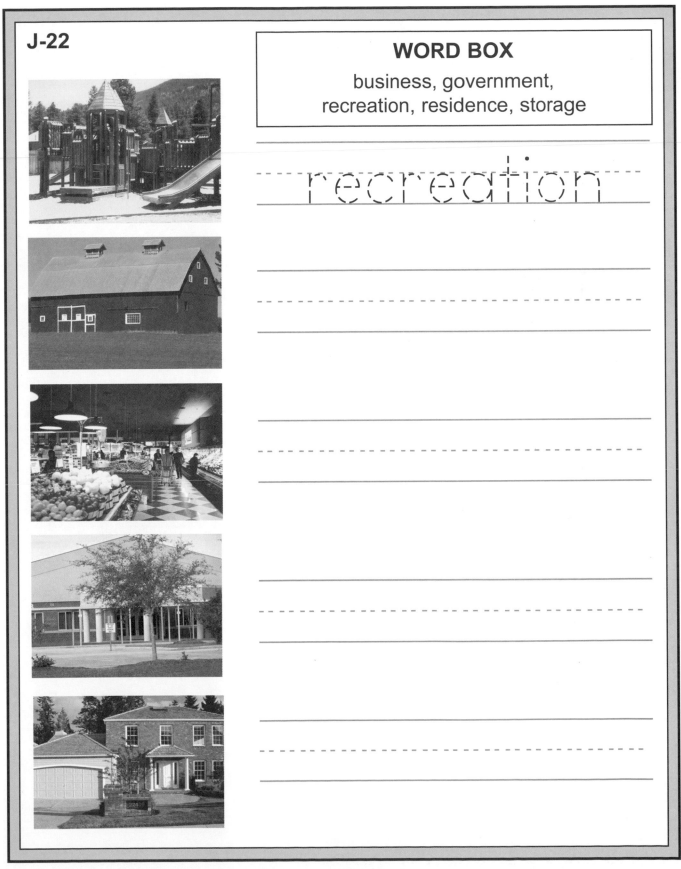

WORD BOX
business, government,
recreation, residence, storage

recreation

NAME THE CLASS—BUILDINGS

DIRECTIONS: Using the words in the WORD BOX, write the class (group) of each building on the top line. Then write the names of the buildings on the three lines.

J-23

WORD BOX
fire station, government buildings, police station, school

CLASS _government buildings_

MEMBERS _____

_____

_____

J-24

WORD BOX
barn, fire station, garage, storage buildings

CLASS _____

MEMBERS _____

_____

_____

EXPLAIN THE EXCEPTION—BUILDINGS

DIRECTIONS: Three buildings belong to the same class (group). Write the class and members on the lines. Then trace why one building is an exception.

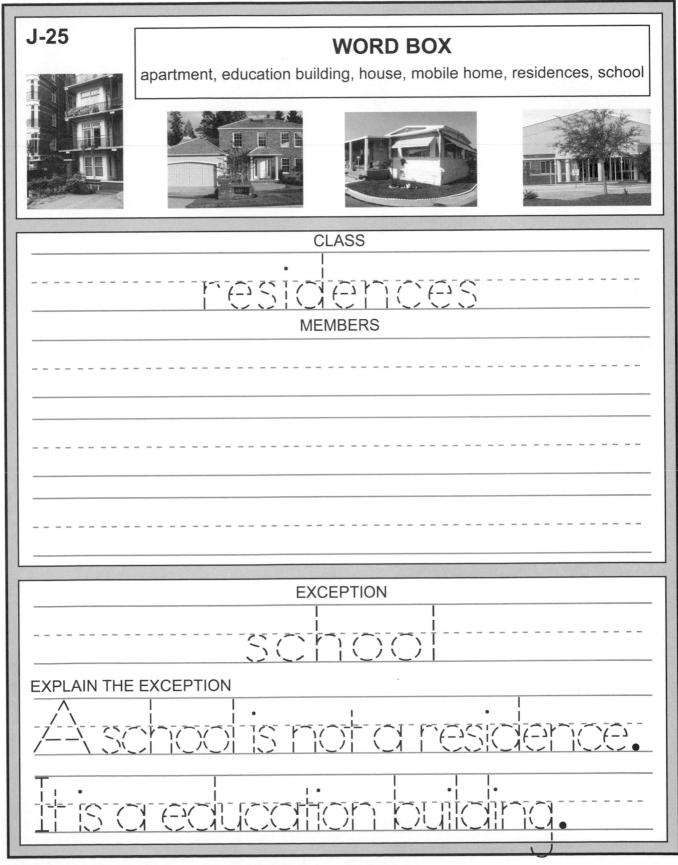

J-25

WORD BOX
apartment, education building, house, mobile home, residences, school

CLASS

residences

MEMBERS

EXCEPTION

school

EXPLAIN THE EXCEPTION

A school is not a residence.

It is a education building.

EXPLAIN THE EXCEPTION—BUILDINGS

DIRECTIONS: Three buildings belong to the same class (group). Write the class and members on the lines. Then explain why one building is an exception.

J-26

WORD BOX
barber shop, business buildings, government building, library, restaurant, supermarket

CLASS

_____

_____

MEMBERS

_____

_____

_____

_____

EXCEPTION

_____

EXPLAIN THE EXCEPTION

_____

_____

_____

SORTING INTO CLASSES—BUILDINGS

DIRECTIONS: Write the building names in the three class boxes.

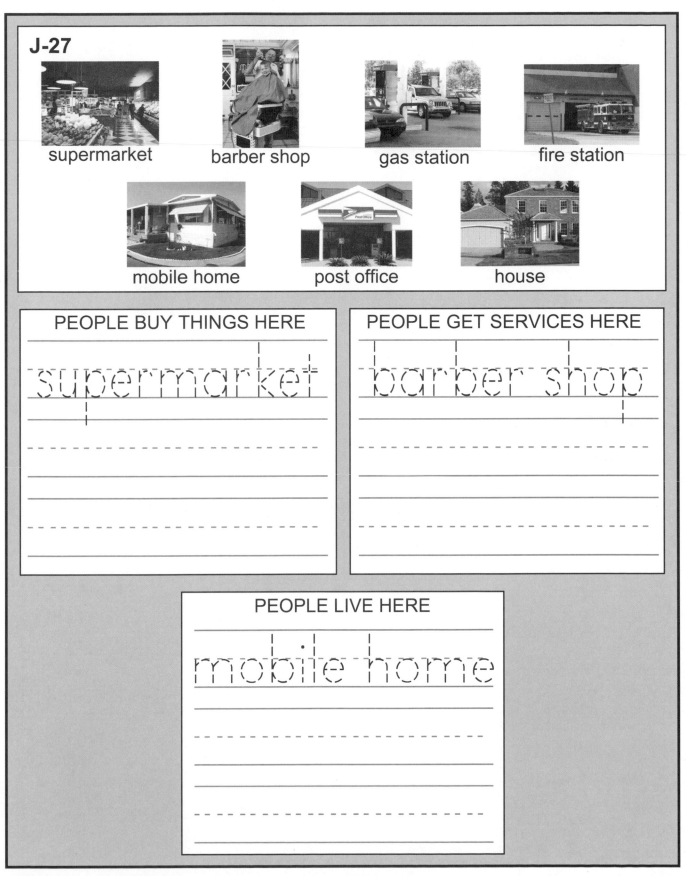

J-27

supermarket   barber shop   gas station   fire station

mobile home   post office   house

PEOPLE BUY THINGS HERE	PEOPLE GET SERVICES HERE
supermarket	barber shop

PEOPLE LIVE HERE

mobile home

Chapter Eleven
Thinking About Analogies

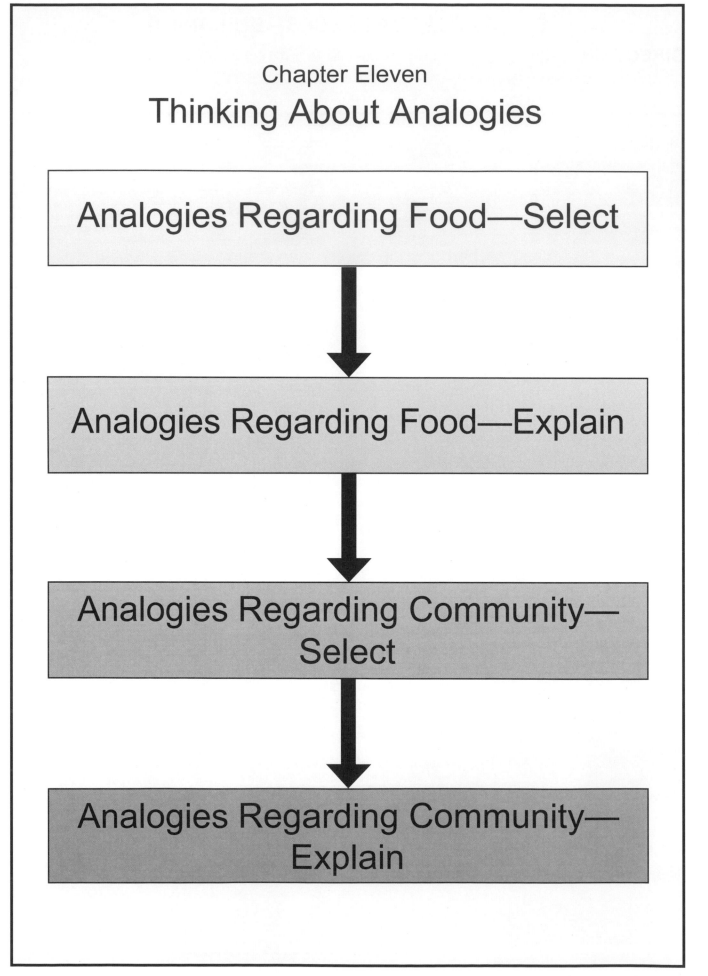

Analogies Regarding Food—Select

Analogies Regarding Food—Explain

Analogies Regarding Community—Select

Analogies Regarding Community—Explain

NAMING CLASSES—MATCHING

DIRECTIONS: This page helps you review what you learned about putting people and things into classes. Trace and copy each word. Then draw a line from each picture to its class.

K-1

EXAMPLE

building

family member

food

job

vehicle

NAMING CLASSES—MATCHING

DIRECTIONS: This page helps you review what you learned about putting people and things into classes. Trace and copy each word. Then draw a line from each picture to its class.

K-2

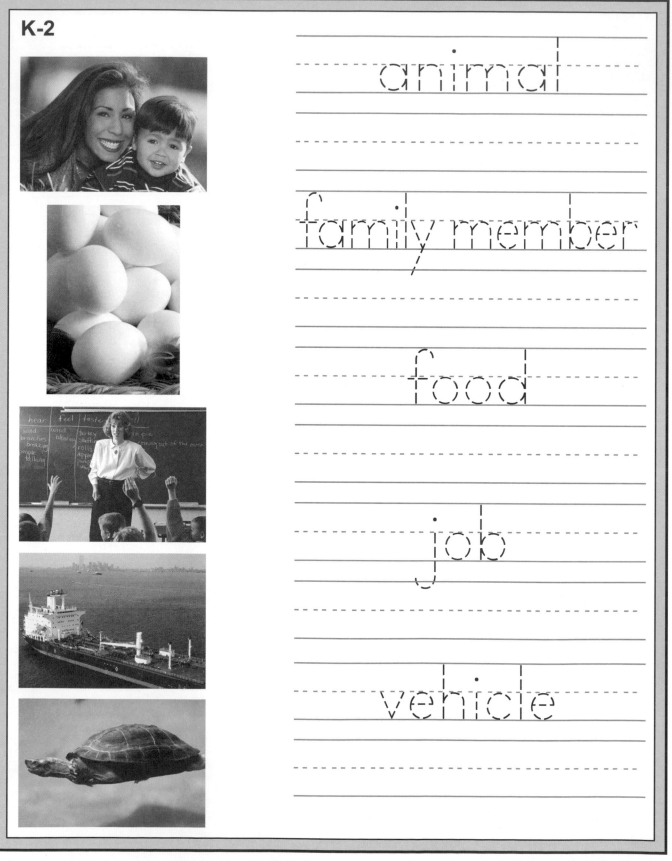

animal

family member

food

job

vehicle

MATCH A JOB TO A BUILDING

DIRECTIONS: This page helps you review what you learned about putting people and things into classes. Draw a line from each job to the building where the person goes to work.

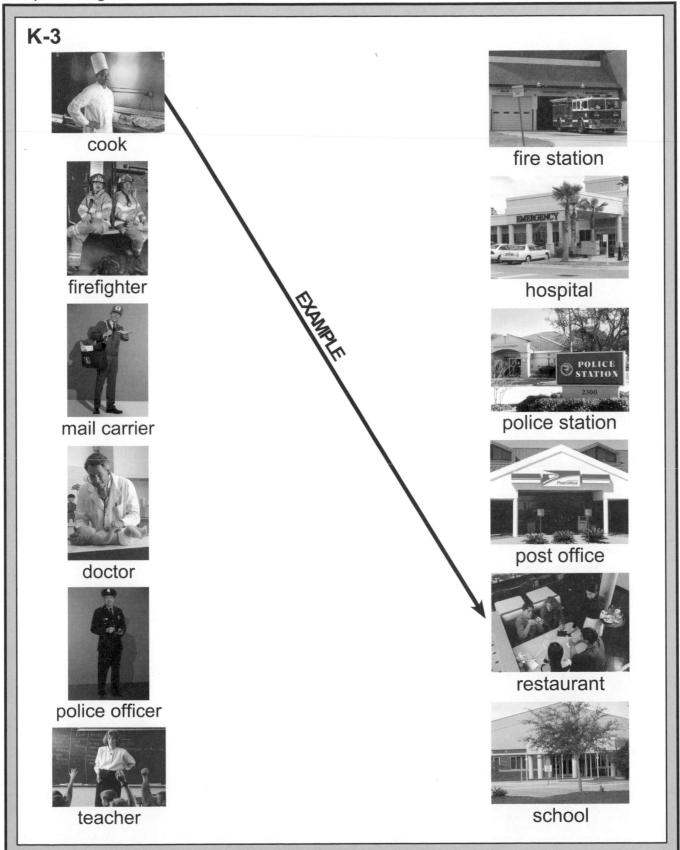

K-3

cook

firefighter

mail carrier

doctor

police officer

teacher

EXAMPLE

fire station

hospital

police station

post office

restaurant

school

WRITE THE CLASS

DIRECTIONS: This page helps you review what you learned about putting people and things into classes. Find the class of each person or object in the WORD BOX. Then write the class beside each picture.

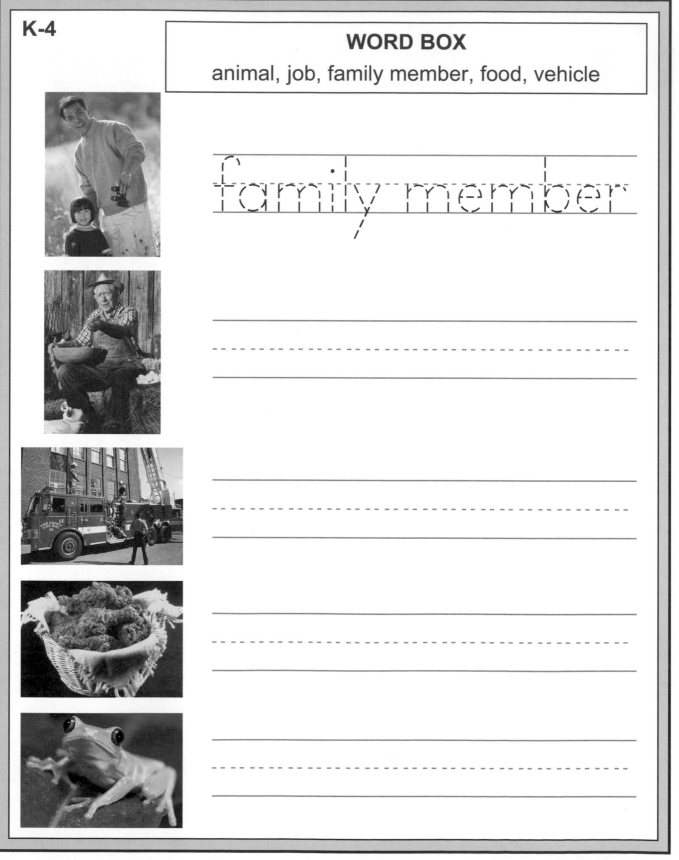

K-4

WORD BOX
animal, job, family member, food, vehicle

family member

WRITE THE CLASS

DIRECTIONS: This page helps you review what you learned about putting people and things into classes. Find the class of each person or object in the WORD BOX. Then write the class beside each picture.

K-5

WORD BOX
animal, building, family member, food, vehicle

ANALOGIES REGARDING FOOD—SELECT

DIRECTIONS: When pairs of things are connected in the same way, that connection is called an *analogy*. Circle the picture that completes the analogy.

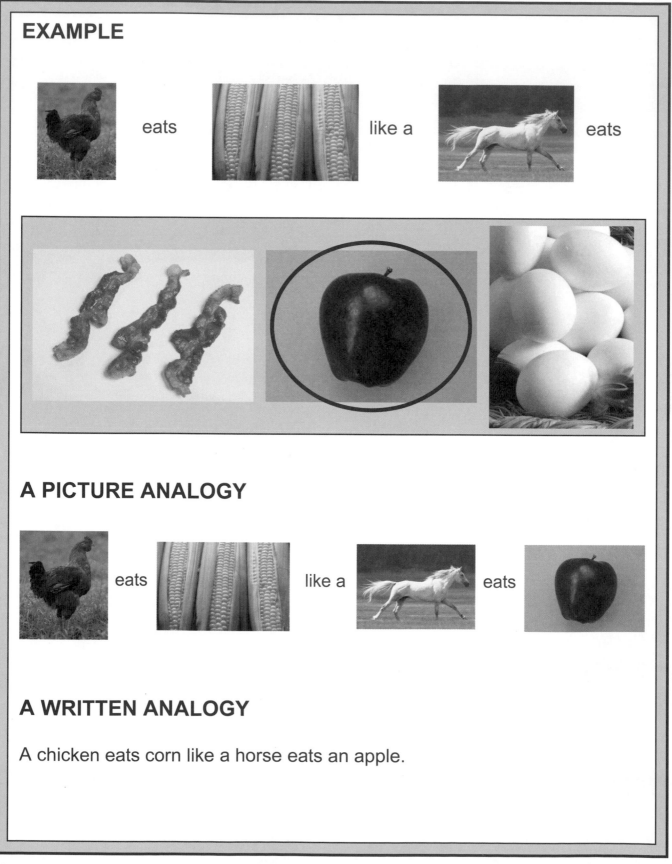

EXAMPLE

eats   like a   eats

A PICTURE ANALOGY

eats   like a   eats

A WRITTEN ANALOGY

A chicken eats corn like a horse eats an apple.

ANALOGIES REGARDING FOOD—SELECT

DIRECTIONS: Circle the picture that completes each analogy.

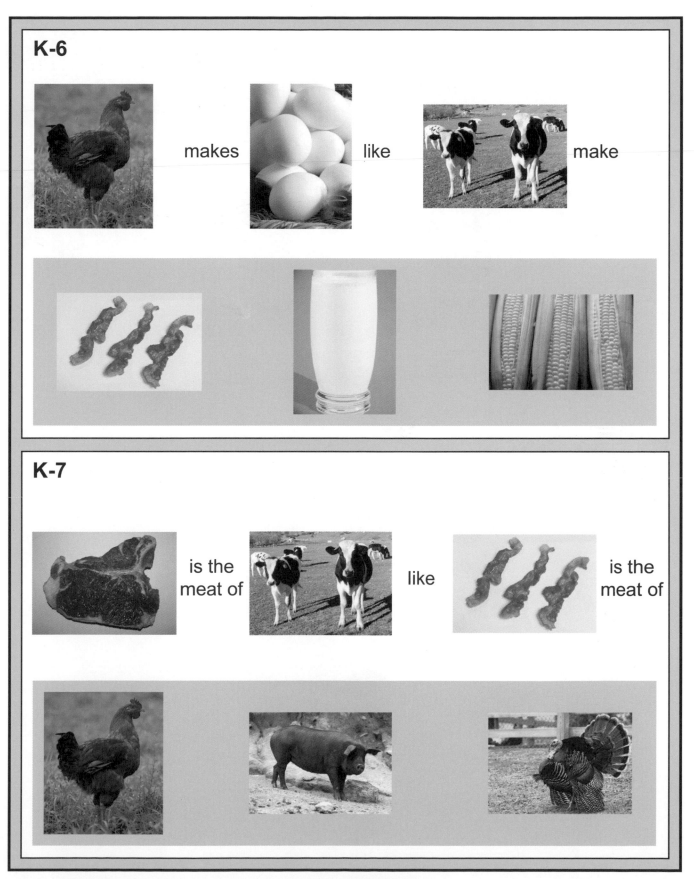

K-6

makes   like   make

K-7

is the
meat of   like   is the
meat of

ANALOGIES REGARDING FOOD—EXPLAIN

DIRECTIONS: Using the words in the WORD BOX, complete the sentences.

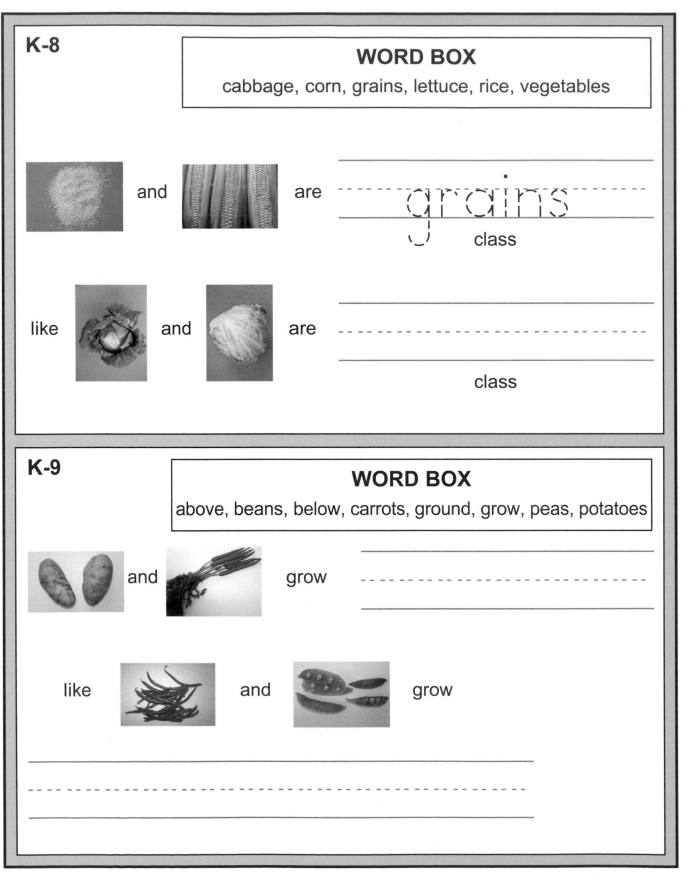

K-8

WORD BOX
cabbage, corn, grains, lettuce, rice, vegetables

rice and corn are ___grains___

class

like and are _____

class

K-9

WORD BOX
above, beans, below, carrots, ground, grow, peas, potatoes

and grow _____

like and grow _____

_____

WRITE THE CLASS

DIRECTIONS: This page helps you review what you learned about putting people and things into classes. Find the class of each person or object in the WORD BOX. Then write the class beside each picture.

K-5

WORD BOX
animal, building, family member, food, vehicle

ANALOGIES REGARDING FOOD—SELECT

DIRECTIONS: When pairs of things are connected in the same way, that connection is called an *analogy*. Circle the picture that completes the analogy.

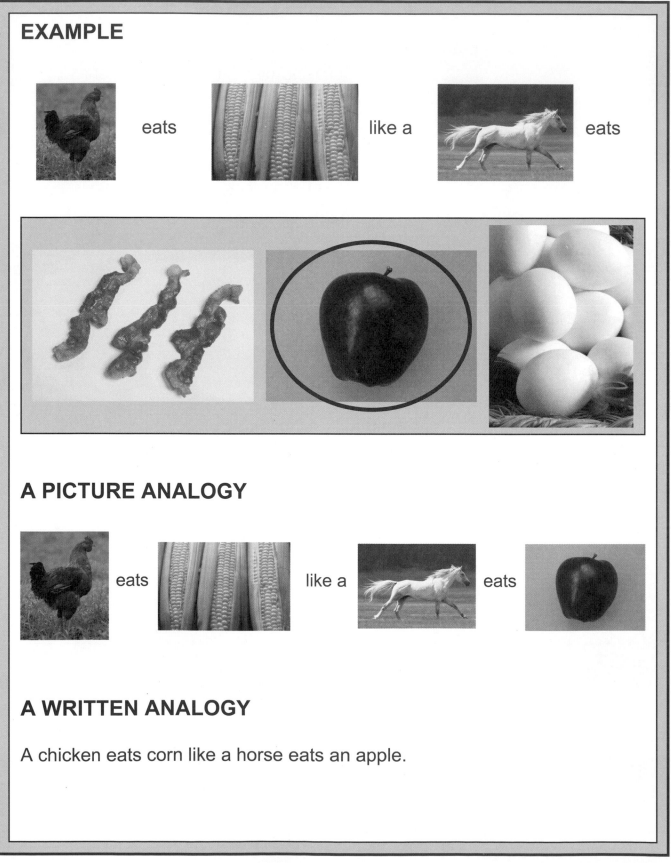

EXAMPLE

eats   like a   eats

A PICTURE ANALOGY

eats   like a   eats

A WRITTEN ANALOGY

A chicken eats corn like a horse eats an apple.

ANALOGIES REGARDING FOOD—SELECT

DIRECTIONS: Circle the picture that completes each analogy.

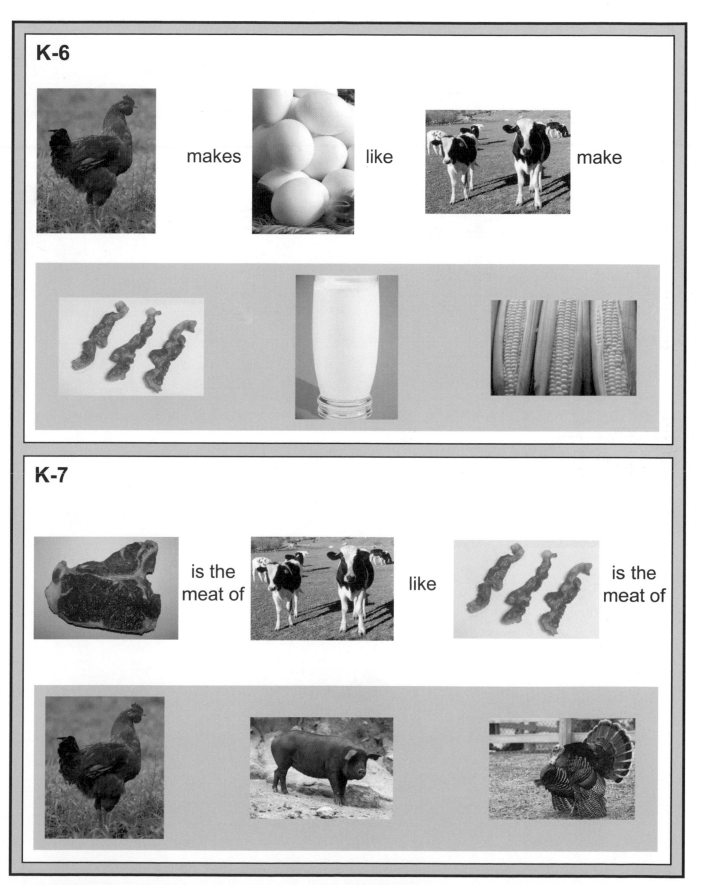

K-6

makes ☐ like ☐ make

K-7

☐ is the meat of ☐ like ☐ is the meat of

ANALOGIES REGARDING FOOD—EXPLAIN

DIRECTIONS: Using the words in the WORD BOX, complete the sentences.

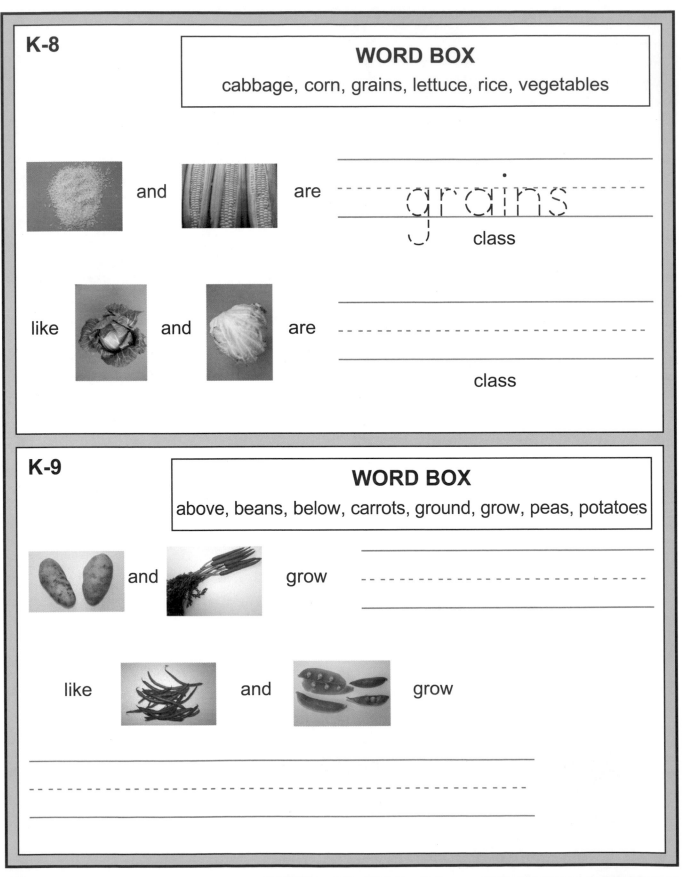

K-8

WORD BOX
cabbage, corn, grains, lettuce, rice, vegetables

[image] and [image] are _____ grains _____

class

like [image] and [image] are _____

class

K-9

WORD BOX
above, beans, below, carrots, ground, grow, peas, potatoes

[image] and [image] grow _____

like [image] and [image] grow

_____

ANALOGIES REGARDING FOOD—SELECT

DIRECTIONS: Circle the picture that completes each analogy.

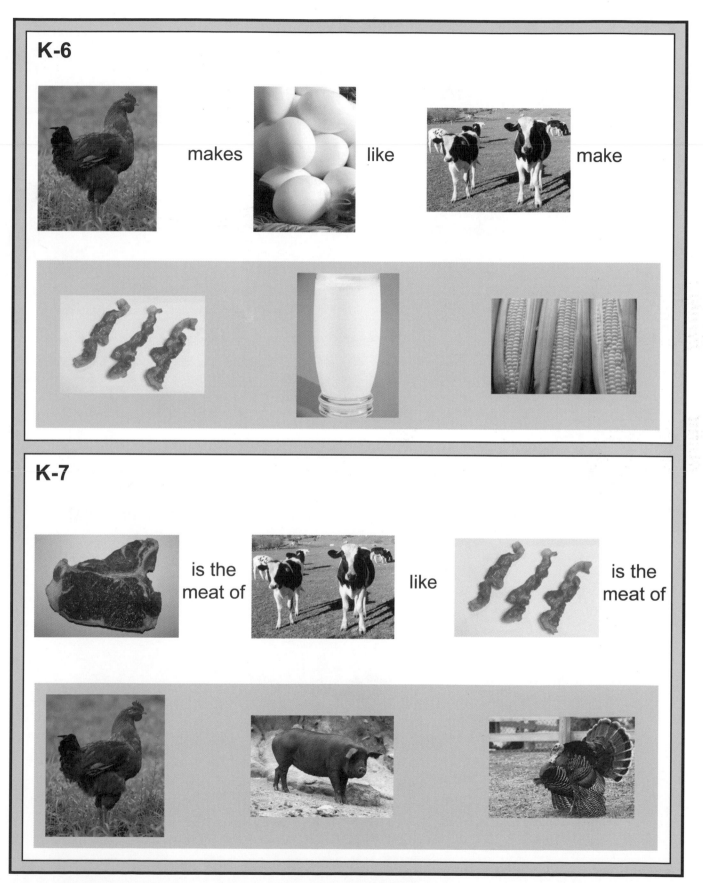

ANALOGIES REGARDING FOOD—EXPLAIN

DIRECTIONS: Using the words in the WORD BOX, complete the sentences.

K-8

WORD BOX
cabbage, corn, grains, lettuce, rice, vegetables

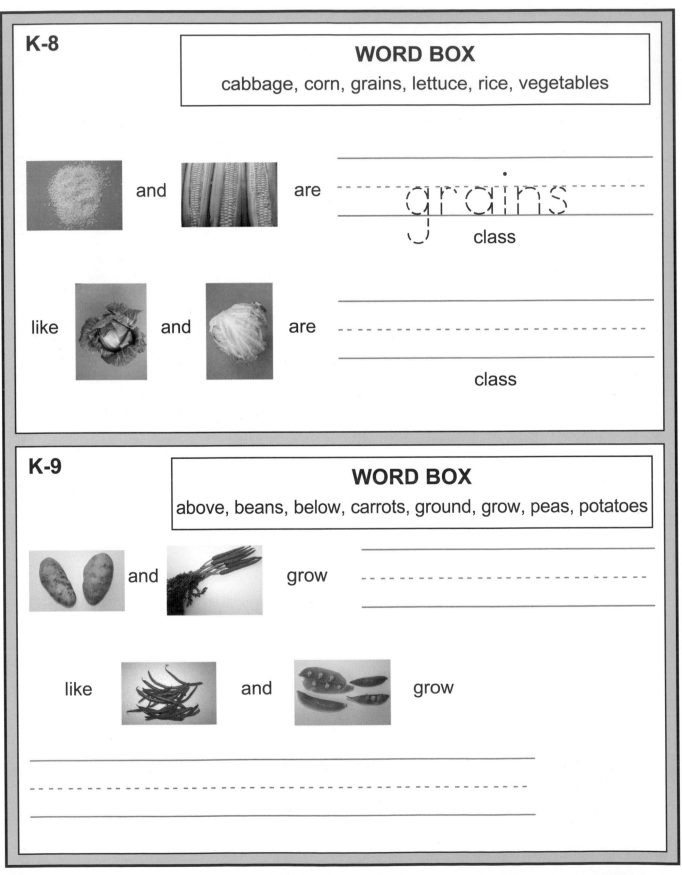

and ___ are _grains_

class

like ___ and ___ are _____

class

K-9

WORD BOX
above, beans, below, carrots, ground, grow, peas, potatoes

___ and ___ grow _____

like ___ and ___ grow

_____

ANALOGIES REGARDING FOOD—WRITE

DIRECTIONS: Trace the answers, which uses the words in the WORD BOX to explain this analogy.

K-10

WORD BOX
apple, corn, fruit, grains, orange, rice

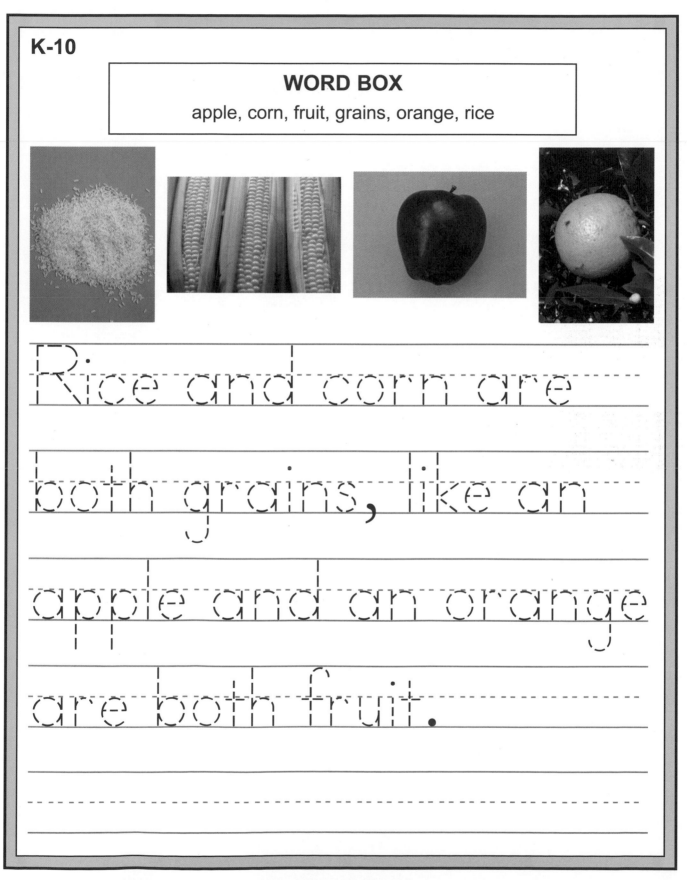

Rice and corn are both grains, like an apple and an orange are both fruit.

ANALOGIES REGARDING FOOD—WRITE

DIRECTIONS: Using the words in the WORD BOX, write this analogy.

K-11

WORD BOX

bacon, cheese, dairy, meat, milk, steak

ANALOGIES REGARDING COMMUNITY—SELECT

DIRECTIONS: Circle the picture that completes each analogy.

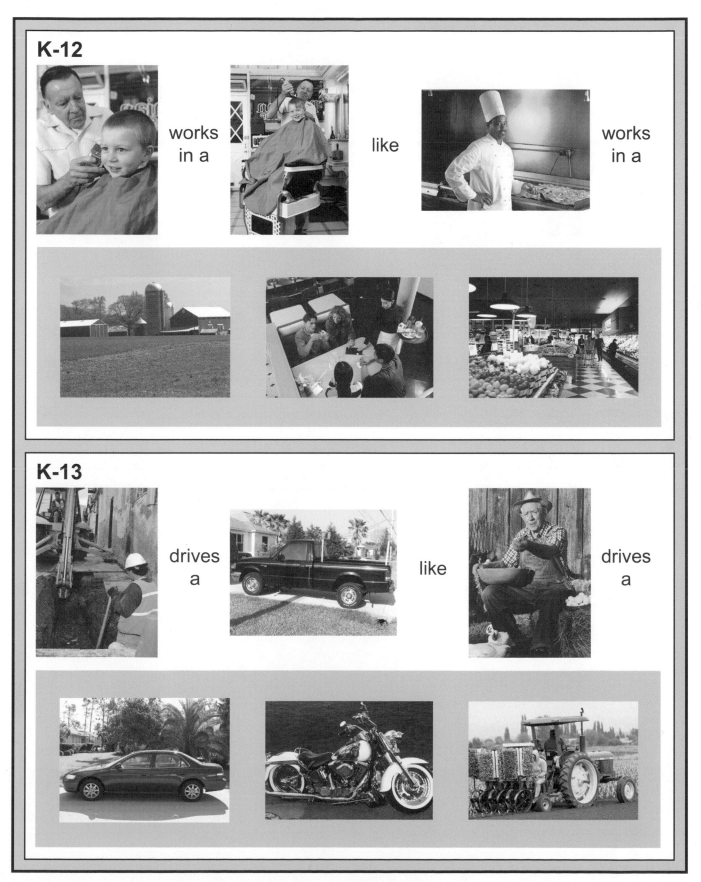

ANALOGIES REGARDING COMMUNITY—EXPLAIN

DIRECTIONS: Using the words in the WORD BOX, complete the sentences.

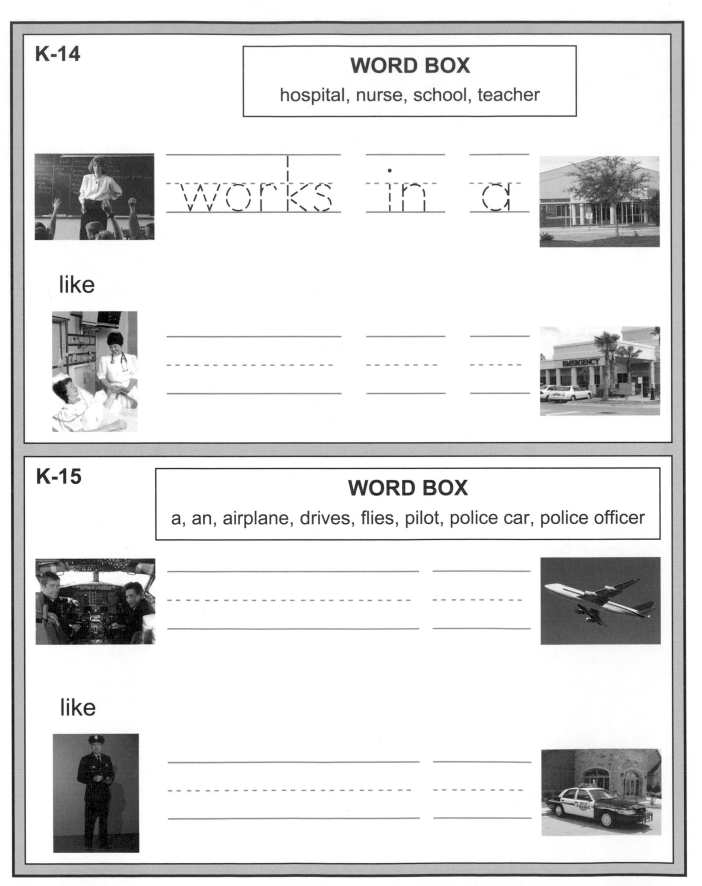

K-14

WORD BOX

hospital, nurse, school, teacher

works in a

like

K-15

WORD BOX

a, an, airplane, drives, flies, pilot, police car, police officer

like

ANALOGIES REGARDING COMMUNITY—WRITE

DIRECTIONS: Using the words in the WORD BOX, finish this analogy.

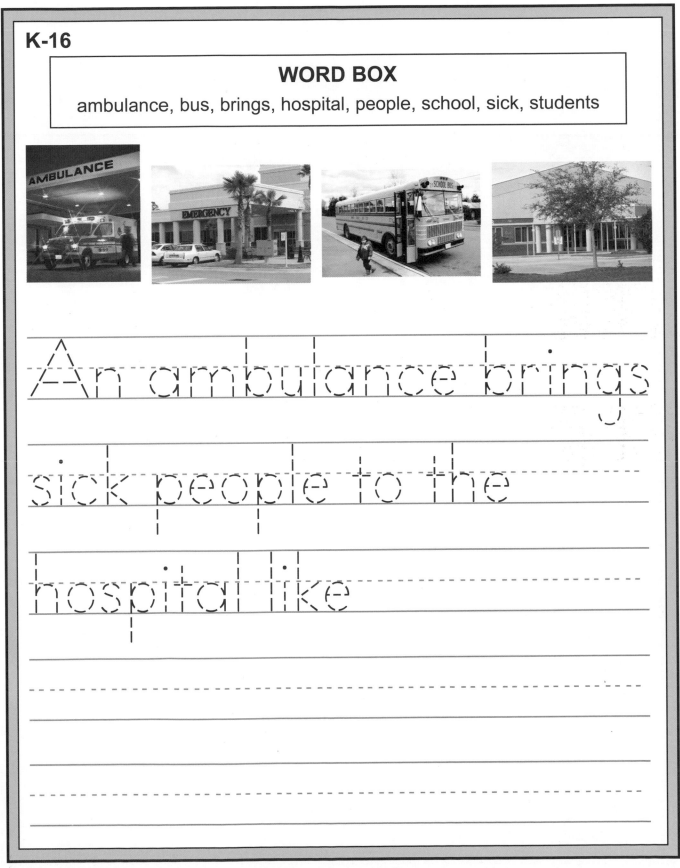

K-16

WORD BOX

ambulance, bus, brings, hospital, people, school, sick, students

An ambulance brings

sick people to the

hospital like

ANALOGIES REGARDING COMMUNITY—WRITE

DIRECTIONS: Using the words in the WORD BOX, write this analogy.

K-17

WORD BOX

farm, farmer, grocer, supermarket, works

GLOSSARY OF TERMS

adult - a person who is fully grown or of responsible age according to law

amphibian - an animal that can live on land or water; It is cold-blooded, lays eggs, and has a backbone

Examples: frog, toad, salamander

apartment - a room or group of rooms where a family or person lives

apartment building - a large building with many small residences

belongings - what a person owns

cargo - a load carried by a ship, train, or plane

consumer - a person who uses things

dairy product - milk or a food made from milk

Examples: butter, cheese, ice cream, yogurt

emergency - an unexpected situation when there is danger

emergency worker - a person who helps people or buildings that are in danger

female - an animal that belongs to the sex that gives birth or lays eggs

food worker - a person who grows, sells, prepares, or delivers food

Examples: cook, farmer, restaurant server, grocer

fruit - the parts of some trees and plants, consisting of the seeds and surrounding flesh that may be eaten

gender - a category of one of two possibilities, male or female

goods - things a person owns that can be moved

government - the organizations that run cities, states, and nations

government building - a building where the work of the government is done

Examples: court house, fire station, library, police station, post office, school

grain - the seed of certain plants, such as wheat and corn, which may be eaten

health - the condition of being free from sickness

health worker - a person who treats the sick or injured or helps keep a person from getting sick

Examples: doctor, dentist, firefighter, nurse

hoofed animal - a four-legged animal that has feet with a very hard covering

leaf - one of the green parts that grows from the stems on trees, plants, and bushes

mammal - animals whose babies are born live (without eggs) and the females of which carry their unborn young inside their bodies

male - an animal that belongs to the sex that fathers the young

parent - a father or mother

producer - a person who makes things

public - owned or used by all the people

    Example: public transportation, public schools, libraries

reptile - a cold-blooded animal that creeps or crawls

    Examples: lizard, snake, turtle

recreation - an activity that one does for fun or entertainment

    Examples: games, sports, movies, plays

residence - a place where a person lives

restaurant - a public place where meals are served for money

root - the part of the plant that holds it in the ground and takes food from the soil

seed - the part of a plant from which a new plant grows

services - things done by one person for another

    Examples of people who provide services: barber, repairman, doctor, dentist, police officer, firefighter

stalk - the main stem of a plant

stem - the part of a plant from which the leaves and flowers grow

storage building - a structure in which things are kept for use

toddler - a young child who walks unsteadily with short steps

transportation - carrying things or people from one place to another

vegetable - a plant that is grown for food

vehicle - anything upon which or in which a person or thing may ride or be carried

DESCRIPTIONS – to be used with DESCRIBING ... SELECT exercises

For a complete set of lessons plans, please go on-line to:
http://www.criticalthinking.com/teachingsupport/
You can also purchase *Building Thinking Skills® - Primary* Teacher's Manual
from The Critical Thinking Co™.

DESIGN OF THE LESSONS

Building Thinking Skills-Primary is designed for cooperative learning in which students share their responses with a student partner before discussing the exercise with the whole class. For home-schoolers or teachers working with a single student, the teacher is the partner and acts as a coach.

DESCRIBING FAMILY MEMBERS—SELECT

E-1: mother, <u>grandmother</u>, girl,

- Listen to this description and then name the family member I am describing.

- This family member remembers events and places that other family members don't know about. She lives nearby or far away. She is an older woman whose son or daughter is a mother or father. She helps her grandchildren know they are loved and special. She sometimes takes care of her grandchildren.

E-2: baby, <u>toddler boy</u>, boy

- Listen to this description and then name the family member I am describing.

- This family member is not as tall as a sink. His mother can lift him, but he is too heavy to carry very far. He is learning to talk and walk by himself. He has some teeth and can eat many cut-up foods by himself. He knows his family and where to find things in the house.

E-3: toddler girl, baby, <u>girl</u>

- Listen to this description and then name the family member I am describing.

- This family member has friends that she shares her things with. She may know how to swim, roller skate, or ride a bicycle. She is old enough to go to school. She can read books and solve some arithmetic problems.

DESCRIBING FOOD - SELECT

F-1: <u>bread</u>, butter, cheese

- Listen to this description and then name the food I am describing.

- This food is made by mixing flour, water, salt, and oil or butter. The dough seems light because yeast or baking powder makes tiny bubbles in the dough. This food is usually white or light brown and is not as sweet as desserts. The bakery often slices it so that we can use it for toast or sandwiches.

F-2: <u>carrots</u>, onion, orange

- Listen to this description and then name the food I am describing.

- This orange vegetable can be eaten cooked or served raw in a salad. It can be sliced, chopped, or eaten whole. The part that we eat is the root of the plant. It is pulled out of the ground by grabbing the green leaves that stick up above the surface. Rabbits and horses like to eat it.

F-3: beans, <u>potatoes</u>, peas

- Listen to this description and then name the food I am describing.

- We eat the root (tuber) of this plant. This root has a colored skin and is white inside. This is eaten boiled, mashed, pan fried, french fried, or baked.

DESCRIBING ANIMALS—SELECT

G-1: fish, <u>snake</u>, frog

- Listen to this description and then name the animal I am describing.

- This animal is long and thin, has a backbone, and is cold-blooded. Its babies hatch from eggs and look like the adult when they are born. It moves on its belly by moving many small muscles, making it seem to slide along the ground. It is covered with shiny scales. Some kinds are dangerous to people. Some can live near water; others can live in the desert. They eat small animals.

G-2: camel, <u>horse</u>, giraffe

- Listen to this description and then name the animal I am describing.

- This animal has a backbone and is warm-blooded. The babies look similar to their parents when they are born. It has a mane on its head and a long tail. It eats grass and hay. It lives on a farm.

G-3: lizard, <u>spider</u>, turtle

- Listen to this description and then name the animal I am describing.

- This animal has eight legs. It is cold-blooded. It doesn't have a backbone; instead, its body looks like several parts which are connected. Its babies hatch from tiny eggs and look like the adult. This animal makes webs out of a thin thread it makes from its body. The webs become its home and a trap for flies and other insects which it eats.

DESCRIBING OCCUPATIONS – SELECT

H-1: construction worker, cook, <u>farmer</u>

- Listen to this description and then name the occupation I am describing.

- This person grows fruits or vegetables or raises animals for us to eat. He cares for large fields with lots of trees or plants. He must be sure that his plants or animals have enough water and food to grow healthy and large. He checks his crops or his animals to prevent pests (weeds, insects, or disease). He uses large machines, such as tractors, plows, and sprayers to grow large amounts of food. He has learned about plants and animals from other farmers, by growing up on a farm, or by going to school for a long time. He must keep good records about how his crops or animals grow and how to sell them for a good price.

H-2: dentist, nurse, <u>teacher</u>

• Listen to this description and then name the occupation I am describing.

• This person helps boys and girls learn things they need to know: how to read, write, draw, play music, and get along with other people. She helps students learn to use numbers and shapes and to understand our city, our country, and nature. She works with the children from early morning to the middle of the afternoon. When the children leave, she checks their work and plans what they will do on the next day. She understands how children learn and how to explain things to them easily. She uses books, maps, computers, pictures, and a chalkboard to help children understand ideas. She went to school a long time to learn how to do this well.

H-3: firefighter, pilot, <u>police officer</u>

• Listen to this description and then name the occupation I am describing.

• This law enforcement officer protects people and property and helps prevent crime. He sometimes rides in a car or on a motorcycle, wears a uniform, and has a badge to let people know that he is an official. He studies laws and learns how to keep himself and other people safe.

DESCRIBING VEHICLES—SELECT

I-1: police car, <u>ambulance</u>, truck

• Listen to this description and then name the vehicle I am describing.

• This vehicle carries emergency equipment, gives treatment to people in need, and carries sick or injured people to the hospital. It contains medicine, tables for moving people, and bandages. Emergency workers use its machines to help doctors understand what the patient needs and to keep people safe on the trip to the hospital. It can go fast in traffic because flashing lights and sirens warn people to get out of the way. It doesn't stop for signs or lights on its trip to the hospital.

I-2: airplane, train, <u>bus</u>

• Listen to this description and then name the vehicle I am describing.

• This vehicle is much taller and longer than a car and carries lots of people. Some travel the same streets around the city many times each day. Some carry passengers from one city to another. People usually pay to ride on them. Some are used by anyone who pays the fare. Some are operated by companies for their employees or customers.

I-3: car, <u>bicycle</u>, school bus

- Listen to this description and then name the vehicle I am describing.

- This vehicle has two wheels and handle bars. The driver pedals it to make it go. It is usually ridden by only one person. Children sometimes ride to school on one.

DESCRIBING BUILDINGS—SELECT

J-1: <u>mobile home</u>, barn, house

- Listen to this description and then name the building I am describing.

- This building can be moved on wheels, so that it can be pulled by a car or truck. Some can be as big as a small house. Some people use this building as their permanent home. Other people live in one while traveling or on vacation. This building may be used as an office or as a classroom for a school that runs out of space.

J-2: <u>fire station</u>, gas station, police station

- Listen to this description and then name the building I am describing.

- Firefighters and their equipment are located in this large building with a large open area that looks like a garage and is used to store the fire truck. Firefighters usually spend the night in this building while they are on duty. Firefighters spend time there getting their equipment ready, exercising, and practicing rescue skills.

J-3: farm, <u>restaurant</u>, supermarket

- Listen to this description and then name the building I am describing.

- This business is a place where people sometimes go to eat. Customers may sit at a table or a counter. Someone usually takes an order of what you would like to eat, gets food from the cooks, and brings it to you. You must pay for the food before you leave.